LIVING VATICAN II
The 21st Council for the 21st Century

GERALD O'COLLINS

Paulist Press
New York/Mahwah, N.J.

Cover design by Cindy Dunne
Book design by Lynn Else

Library of Congress Cataloging-in-Publication Data

O'Collins, Gerald.
   Living Vatican II : the 21st council for the 21st century / Gerald O'Collins.
     p.   cm.
   Includes bibliographical references and index.
   ISBN 0-8091-4290-2 (alk. paper)
   1. Vatican Council (2nd : 1962–1965) I. Title.
BX8301962 .O36 2006
262′.52—dc22

2005035833

Published by Paulist Press
997 Macarthur Boulevard
Mahwah, New Jersey 07430

www.paulistpress.com

Printed and bound in the
United States of America

CONTENTS

INTRODUCTION

The crucial process of reception, that all-important part of any church council...can take several generations. It continues today.
Cardinal Franz König, *The Tablet*, Christmas 2002

Called by Pope John XXIII of blessed memory on January 29, 1959, Vatican II was the most significant religious event in the twentieth century. Trusting utterly in the Holy Spirit, Pope John hoped that this meeting of all the Catholic bishops would bring about a new Pentecost. He wanted to update and renew spiritually the Catholic Church, heal division within Christendom, and alter the church's reactionary attitude to the world. The Roman Catholic Church will never be the same again.

When he set this huge project in motion, John had been pope for only ninety days. He lived long enough to open the first session in October 1962, but died in June 1963 before the council met again the following October. Pope Paul VI presided over the second, third, and fourth sessions, and formally closed the proceedings on December 8, 1965. With courage and gentleness, he then faced the awesome task of leading the implementation of Vatican II's general policies and particular decisions—right through to his death in August 1978. When he was elected pope on October 16, 1978, John Paul II at once pledged himself to continue the work of putting the council's teaching into effect. Benedict XVI did the same when he became pope on April 19, 2005.

Vatican II was the first council in the story of Catholic Christianity to deserve being labeled intercontinental and intercultural. What has been its impact? How should one describe and evaluate its reception by Catholics and its wider follow-up among others? Catholics recognize it as the twenty-first ecumenical or general council in the history of the church. How should this twenty-first council be heard, received, and lived as we move further ahead into the twenty-first century? What perspectives does it offer for the future to those who seek to assimilate it creatively?

The council produced sixteen documents, shaped or reshaped a number of institutions in Rome and around the world, and altered the lives of millions of Catholics and others. The documents amount to 30 percent of the written texts coming from all twenty-one general councils of Catholic Christianity. The first to be promulgated, the Constitution on the Liturgy *(Sacrosanctum Concilium)*, set the scene for the inner renewal of the church. The last and longest, the Pastoral Constitution on the Church in the Modern World *(Gaudium et Spes)*, spelled out the church's desire to live in solidarity with men and women everywhere, sharing their joys, hopes, and sufferings. Without having planned this outcome in advance, the 2,500 bishops assembled for Vatican II moved from approving in 1963 a constitution aimed at revitalizing the worship of Catholics to approving at the very end of the council in 1965 a constitution directed at promoting the dignity and ultimate well-being of the whole human community.

The sixteen documents approved from 1963 to 1965 were to give rise to subsequent documents through which popes, world synods, episcopal conferences, and other bodies aimed to implement the teaching and decrees of Vatican II. I will speak later of many of these documents: for instance, various liturgical texts, the codes of canon law (promulgated in 1983 and 1990), and the *Catechism of the Catholic Church* (1992).

This book begins by sketching the ways in which I was personally affected by the council (chapter 1). Subsequent chapters explore the work of some institutions in implementing the teaching and decisions of Vatican II (chapter 2), the guidelines provided by a fourth-century example of creative fidelity in receiving conciliar teaching (chapter 3), the liturgical renewal after Vatican II (chapter 4), the reception of the council's moral teaching (chapter 5), postconciliar relations with "others" (chapter 6), the impact of

Vatican II on theology (chapter 7), and the future life of the church (chapter 8). My concluding evaluations (chapter 9) are followed by a bibliography and four texts that illuminate the way in which the teaching and decisions of Vatican II have been interpreted, implemented, and frustrated.

At the center of my inquiry are several questions. To what extent and in what ways has the Catholic Church around the world harnessed the power of the Second Vatican Council? How far have key institutions and individuals facilitated and developed the conciliar heritage, or else acted as "gatekeepers" concerned to screen the heritage and let only some things through? How might Catholics in the early years of the third millennium count their conciliar blessings and promote the legacy of Vatican II? Beyond question, much still needs to be done toward receiving and living what the council taught and stood for. As the late Cardinal Franz König, archbishop of Vienna, wrote in the London *Tablet* at Christmas 2002, "The crucial process of reception, that all-important part of any church council, can take several generations. It continues today."

I hope this book will prove informative and useful for students and teachers, theologians, historians, and ordinary readers. I wish to thank Chris Bellitto, Brian Johnstone, Lori King, Mark Langham, Maev O'Collins, Keith Pecklers, Norman Tanner, and others for various suggestions and corrections. I acknowledge with gratitude the permission granted by Darton, Longman & Todd to use in chapter 4 an extract from the Jerusalem Bible. With warm thanks and admiration this book is dedicated to John Wilkins, the best of friends, who trimmed and shaped much of what follows with great skill.

Gerald O'Collins, SJ
May 25, 2005

ABBREVIATIONS

DzH H. Denzinger and P. Hünermann, *Enchiridion symbolorum, definitionum et declarationum* (Freiburg im Breisgau: Herder, 17th ed., 1991).

NCE *New Catholic Encyclopedia*, 15 vols. (Washington, DC: Catholic University of America, 2nd ed., 2003).

ND J. Neuner and J. Dupuis, eds., *The Christian Faith* (Bangalore/New York: Theological Publications in India/Alba House, 7th ed., 2001).

1

HOW VATICAN II
CHANGED MY CHURCH

The Second Vatican Council was an extraordinary event
called by an extraordinary Pope, and it is one of the main
reasons why I personally am a Catholic today.
John Wilkins, *The Tablet*, October 12, 2002

Receiving and living the Second Vatican Council begins at home.
Hence, instead of writing at once about what others did or failed to
do, I want to tell first the personal story of my own reactions to the
council.

During the First and Second Sessions
of the Council

I followed the first two sessions of Vatican II (October–December
1962 and October–December 1963) from a great distance, since I
was completing my basic theological training at Canisius College,
a seminary in a northern suburb of Sydney, Australia. Twelve years
earlier I had entered the Society of Jesus and begun my long training with a view to being ordained a priest. Back in 1950 some lines
from "The Hound of Heaven" by Francis Thompson haunted me:
"I fled Him, down the nights and down the days; I fled Him, down
the arches of the years." The sense grew that I *had* to become a
priest; I would be running away from God and from myself if I
failed to do so. If I were to become a priest, that simply meant for
me joining the Jesuits. After five years at a high school and one year
at a university college run by them, I had come to admire deeply

what these dedicated priests achieved through their educational institutions. By late 1962, I had completed my novitiate, philosophical studies, a BA and an MA (by thesis) in classics at the University of Melbourne, and one year's teaching at a Jesuit high school in Western Australia, and was now more than halfway through my four years of theological studies.

Canisius College, called after St. Peter Canisius (1521–97), an early Jesuit who did much to meet the challenges of the Reformation in Austria, Bavaria, and other countries, stood on twenty acres of prime land that the Society of Jesus had bought thirty years earlier from an orchardist. About thirty-five seminarians (we called them "scholastics"), half a dozen priests, and three brothers made up the community. The liturgical ceremonies were still in Latin, a language I spoke well and read easily after many years of classical studies. The celebrant never preached a homily at Mass. In all the chapel services we had to follow the rubrics and prescribed texts meticulously. One newly ordained priest altered an invocation at benediction of the Blessed Sacrament by saying "St. Teresa of the *Child* Jesus," instead of "St. Teresa of the *Infant* Jesus." He was reprimanded for this and, without waiting for his normal term to come up again, had at once to give benediction again and say the prayer correctly. We often sang the office of compline and on some Sundays the office of vespers—always in Latin, of course. I belonged to the choir, did singing exercises regularly, and learned to sing a High Mass exactly.

We enjoyed first-rate scripture teachers in Bill Dalton and John Scullion. Both graduates of Melbourne University and the Biblical Institute in Rome, they were young, professionally competent, concerned to publish, and ecumenical in outlook. Thanks to them, I read some mainstream non-Catholic authors such as William Albright, C. H. Dodd, and Vincent Taylor. In dogmatic theology we had no access to Barth, Calvin, Luther, Tillich, and other classical and modern figures of Protestant thought. Bill and John took me regularly to an interdenominational biblical fellowship that met at Sydney University. At those meetings I came into contact for the first time with rabbis (one of whom showed me around his synagogue), made some new Anglican friends, and learned to shed more of my prejudices, even if I provocatively chose James 5:14–15 as the topic for the one paper I read to the fellowship. (Catholics have traditionally used this passage to justify the sacrament of "extreme unction," as we then still called the anointing of the sick.) There was no departure from my own assured vision of the church. I saw no reason to query or qualify Pius XII's 1943 encyclical, *Mystici Corporis*, which taught that those who did not "profess the true faith" could not "be accounted really members of the Church" (DzH 3802; ND 849).

Unlike scripture, for which the lectures were in English (with, of course, many references to the original texts in Greek and Hebrew), dogmatic theology was taught in Latin. A tall, swarthy Australian in his mid-forties, Peter ("Pedro") Kenny, offered us courses in such areas as grace, original sin, and the Eucharist. From postgraduate studies in Europe he brought home the fresh theological ideas of Karl Rahner (who was to prove one of the major theological advisors at Vatican II), spread them among Australian Catholics, and gave me an enduring admiration for Rahner's thought.[1] Pedro read the Latin and Greek fathers with deep affection, appealed to the scriptures (sometimes in a startlingly uncritical fashion), linked theology with liturgy, and kept his own reflections in check by constant reference to the authoritative pronouncements of popes and church councils.

Although not yet in orders, I occasionally took the part of subdeacon at High Masses that he sang at a nearby convent. Pedro looked particularly fine in red vestments, as he sat there in the marble-floored sanctuary on a large cushion, letting the silk chasuble flow across his feet, and waiting for the choir to finish the Gloria and the Credo. The breakfasts of strawberries and chicken that followed were fit for oriental potentates.

At Canisius College we studied moral theology in Latin, using the two volumes of a 1953 edition of *Theologiae Moralis Institutiones*, a manual for training newly ordained priests to "hear confessions" that had originally been written in the nineteenth century by the Belgian Edouard Genicot (d. 1900) and that, despite several major revisions, remained substantially the same. We acquired a traditional Catholic system of morality, dominated by (a) the decisions of popes, councils, and synods, and (b) the opinions of authoritative moral theologians from the past and present. We respected dead authorities like St. Alphonsus Liguori (d. 1787) and Arthur Vermeersch (d. 1936) and such living authorities as the American Jesuits John Ford and Gerald Kelly. On the good side, that study trained us to reach moral decisions on the basis of reasoned principles and not to exaggerate the extent of moral obligations.[2] On the bad side, Genicot represented a legalism that effectively divided human actions into sinful and nonsinful, bypassed the scriptures, and at times entertained us with trivial questions.

In December 1962 I was out at Sydney airport to greet a group of tired and unshaven Australian bishops on their return from the first session of Vatican II. Most of them were anxious not to disturb seminarians (and rank-and-file Catholics) by admitting that the council had already initiated a radical renewal of Catholic life and teaching. That was true of my uncle, Bishop James O'Collins, who happily agreed to ordain me a month later in his cathedral at Ballarat, a town about sixty miles from Melbourne. The approach of priesthood filled me with awe. I had prepared myself conscientiously to preach, hear confessions, and administer the other sacraments. But it was the Mass that mattered. Long before in a small country church I had learned to share the parish priest's intense devotion for the eucharistic presence. With his back to the congregation, he stooped over the altar and whispered the words of consecration so softly that only the small boys serving the Mass could hear them. With slow reverence he then lifted the host high above his head, and for some seconds held it there framed by his fingers. Ordination was to initiate me into that sacred function of standing at the altar to say: *"Hoc est enim corpus meum"* (This is my body) and *"Hic est enim calix sanguinis mei"* (This is the chalice of my blood). The awesome holiness of the Mass has never left me, but it now touches me also in other ways. It seems mysteriously wonderful to address God the Father on behalf of all the faithful gathered in worship. Who am I to raise my voice in praise to the ultimate Source of all reality and life and pray that the Holy Spirit descend on the elements and on the people assembled for the Eucharist?

During the Third Session

Eighteen months after my ordination, I left Australia to spend a year of "tertianship," or final spiritual formation, with twenty-four other Jesuits (from eight countries) in Münster. So I followed the third session of the council in Germany (October–December 1964). By late 1964 liturgical changes stemming from the council's first document, *Sacrosanctum Concilium* (the 1963 Constitution on the Liturgy), were beginning to arrive in Germany. On weekends I often went to a British boarding school in Hamm that housed around five hundred boys, about one hundred of them Catholics and all of them sons of British soldiers serving with the army of the Rhine. My companion was a trim, forty-six-year-old ex-army major, Myles Lovell. Myles had joined the British army before World War II, took part in the 1940 retreat to Dunkirk, fought in North Africa and Italy, and somewhere along the way turned from agnosticism to embrace Catholicism and then enter the Society of Jesus. Myles blended a convert's dedication with immense cheerfulness and an officer's sense of orders. When we moved the altar around so that to my delight we could face the congregation when saying Mass, Myles muttered: "Don't like this, but we're supposed to do it."[3] Back home at the house for "tertians" in Münster, I found it a great relief when we finally began to have concelebrated Mass. Instead of each young priest being led out of the sacristy by a small German altar boy to say Mass in Latin, "privately" and in a "side" chapel, we could celebrate the Mass together in German[4] and express together in worship the community we actually were. The first such concelebration in my priestly life occurred on February 2, 1965, when I said Mass with a number of the tertians in the main chapel and was asked to preach.

During my time in Münster, some visitors provided personal contact with what was happening in Rome. Otto Semmelroth, an important *peritus* or theological consultor at the council, gave us a report on *Lumen Gentium*, the Dogmatic Constitution on the Church, promulgated in November 1964. Johannes Hirschmann, a famous spokesperson for the German bishops, talked to us for three and a half hours on the progress achieved at the council. The topic was fascinating, but Hirschmann's performance astonished me. I never imagined that someone could address me in a foreign language, continue for over three hours, and remain consistently eloquent and entertaining.

Another German Jesuit, Wilhelm Bertrams, a professor of canon law at the Gregorian University in Rome, came to defend the traditional Catholic ban on contraception, a ban supposedly based on rational principles and not directly on revealed truth. Along with nearly all the tertians, I found his dry legalism unpersuasive. The arguments he offered no longer seemed to command assent to the negative conclusions. Before he died, Pope John XXIII had withdrawn from the council's debate the question of birth control and entrusted it to a commission. The question continued to be widely discussed among Catholics. Many were to be disillusioned in 1968, when Pope Paul VI declined to follow the majority of the commission (who recommended change) and maintained the official rejection of contraception in his encyclical letter *Humanae Vitae* (Of Human Life).

The ecumenism promoted by Vatican II touched my life in Germany. In November 1964, during the third session of the council, the archbishop of Canterbury, Michael Ramsey, visited Windsor Girls School in Hamm. This counterpart to the boys school was about a mile away and had its own permanent Catholic chaplain. Myles Lovell and I were invited across to the reception for the archbishop. We sat behind him on the stage, facing an audience of five hundred girls plus most of the boys from our school. After speeches from the Anglican chaplain of the girls school, the headmistress and the headgirl (who happened to be a Catholic), the archbishop spoke and concluded by asking the boys and girls to repeat after him a prayer by St. Richard of Chichester (d. 1253).[5] Even though he did not explain his choice, Ramsey presumably selected this lovely prayer because it came from a saintly bishop in the undivided Christian church of medieval England. Over afternoon tea I chatted with him about the visit he was to make to Australia the following March. I mentioned to him the sorry theological and ecumenical state of the Anglican Archdiocese of Sydney. "Could you as a visitor do something about that?" I asked. He smiled behind his attractive, bushy eyebrows: "Yes, yes, I know all about that." In Sydney he gave a newspaper interview that called for big changes of attitude, but the local Anglicans shrugged it all off as "misreporting."

The year in Germany also involved pastoral work for Germans, including the six weeks of Lent I spent in a church on the marketplace in Trier, the oldest city in Germany and once a capital of the Roman Empire. For the first time I officiated at weddings and administered baptism—the ceremonies now being almost entirely in German.[6] I rejoiced in the fact that ordinary people could now follow much more easily what was being done *and said* by the minister. The situation would be further improved when, in the aftermath of Vatican II, the revised rituals for marriage (in March 1969), baptism (in May 1969), and the other sacraments appeared. These new rituals in the language of the people work most effectively as "sacred signs" that teach those gathered to celebrate the sacraments, especially when the ministers and people have joined in preparing carefully the ceremonies. The new texts meet even better the felt need for ritual at important moments in people's lives. The revised rituals offer a rich variety of choices in prayers, readings, and blessings, as well as providing for appropriate music, hymns, and actions to accompany the service. A little preparation goes a long way in allowing the sacraments to express what Jesus Christ, the invisible minister of all the sacraments, wants to do for us. It delights me how much happens when an engaged couple chooses the readings, prayers, and blessings for their marriage ceremony. The hours we spend together become the occasion for spiritual sharing and renewing their faith and insight into the powerful presence of Christ in their lives. Often they make the service very personal (in a way that had not been possible before Vatican II), not only by picking the scriptural readings but also by telling me what themes they wish to be expressed in my homily. The same kind of personal shaping of the sacramental ceremony happens when they come later and prepare the baptismal service for their newborn children. In my experience, laymen and laywomen have taken over the new rituals with ease and grace. But occasionally I hear priests who insist on "explaining" in their own words what the rituals mean and adding "their own" prayers. I find the new rituals are beautifully crafted and speak for themselves. Stage directions from the celebrant seem as strange as if one were to "improve" on Shakespeare's plays by announcing: "Next we will see Lady Macbeth enter and show us her mental state." I feel like crying out: "Just do it, please, and get on with the liturgical drama."

During the Fourth Session

A year in Germany (1964–65) nurtured in me a sense of the ecumenical and liturgical renewal of Vatican II. In the summer of 1965 I crossed to England to begin my doctoral studies at Cambridge University and experience from there the fourth and closing session of the council (October–December 1965). Like any good Jesuit visiting London for the first time, I stayed at Farm Street and met Martin D'Arcy, James Brodrick, Archbishop Tom Roberts, and other legendary Jesuits who lived in that West End residence. After lunch I explained over coffee that I was off to Cambridge to do research in theology. One of the priests asked in surprise: "Why do you want to go and study with those heretics?" Archbishop Roberts, to my delight, exploded with laughter. I should have taken the occasion to hear his stories from the first three sessions of the council and comments on the five documents that had already been promulgated. But I was thinking about the topic for my doctoral research, modern theologies of revelation. The conciliar document that was especially relevant, the Constitution on Divine Revelation (*Dei Verbum*, the Word of God), was in its last stages of revision and would be approved only in the coming November.

I spent three years at Pembroke College doing research and then writing a doctoral thesis on four modern approaches to God's self-revelation. Three of my chosen authors were Protestant and one Anglican. At the same time, from Christmas 1965 the council's newly promulgated Constitution on Divine Revelation was holding my attention and shaping my thought. In *The Month* for June 1966, I published an article on *Dei Verbum*, calling it "one of the most significant results" from the fourth and final session of the council, because it showed "a deeply biblical, serene and historical approach" to its three major themes: "revelation itself, its transmission, scripture and its inspiration, interpretation and place in the life of the Church." I was delighted with the way the document described revelation as being primarily the self-revelation of the tripersonal God that involves a call to the personal self-commitment of faith and to sharing in the divine life. Those and further valuable themes from *Dei Verbum* fed into a small book I wrote as number 2 in a new series *(Theology Today)* edited by Ted Yarnold: *Theology and Revelation.*[7] I showed, for instance, how deeply rooted in the theology of St. Paul and St. John was Vatican II's sense that revelation and salvation belong inseparably together: The very fact that God speaks to us is a transforming grace. Christ is simultaneously the Light of the world and the Life of the world. For good measure my book ended by including as an appendix the first chapter of *Dei Verbum*, the heart of the council's teaching on revelation.

Even before I presented my PhD in mid-1968 and left Cambridge to begin teaching in Boston and Melbourne, I was already exploring more deeply another Vatican II document: the Constitution on the Church in the Modern World, *Gaudium et Spes*. Two Germans pushed me in that direction: the Christian theologian Jürgen Moltmann, a Protestant who grew up in Hamburg, and the Marxist philosopher Ernst Bloch. When Moltmann's *Theology of Hope* was published in German (1964), it quickly became a best seller and was translated into English (1967) and many other languages. Over the Christmas break of 1965/66 I read the book with enthusiasm and made Moltmann's future-oriented view of revelation one of the key four chapters in my doctoral dissertation. When he moved in 1967 to teach at the University of Tübingen, I attended his lectures for two months (June and July) and struck up a lasting friendship with him. I also used that time to study the thought of Ernst Bloch. The Communist Party in East Germany had found his brand of Marxism unacceptably personal, and was happy to see him defect to the West. Once or twice I went for afternoon tea with Bloch and his wife. A thatch of white hair, the thick-lensed glasses, and a lined face gave Bloch the look of a latter-day prophet. He enjoyed his contacts with Moltmann and other Christian thinkers but feared that they were taming his views—"spreading hotel-sauce over everything," he called it. Those contacts prompted me to write two articles on Bloch's philosophy and Moltmann's theology of hope.[8]

But, more significantly, the contact with Moltmann and Bloch encouraged me to write *Man and His New Hopes*.[9] The title indicates that I had so far failed to take on board what *Gaudium et Spes* (nos. 29, 60) taught about the equality of women. But the book showed that I had made my own a key question that this constitution aimed to answer: Can Christians, with their hope for a heaven to come, prove to be true and committed citizens of this world? The book opened with a quotation from *Gaudium et Spes:* "The future of humanity rests in the hands of those who are capable of handing on to the coming generations reasons for living and hoping" (no. 31). The book engaged in dialogue with Marxist thought, both West (Ernst Bloch and Karl Marx) and East (Mao Tse-tung), but not in order to introduce false compromises by mixing "Christian-Marxist cocktails." It argued that Christ "our hope" offers not only "the final truth" about human existence, but also strong reasons for "the practice of a deeply hopeful life." I gladly recalled what Dietrich Bonhoeffer had said in 1932, on the eve of Hitler's seizing power in Germany: Christ "does not lead human beings into the twilight of a religious flight from the world, but returns them to earth as its true sons and daughters. Only those who love the earth and God together can believe in the kingdom of God." With *Gaudium et Spes* and Bonhoeffer, I shared the conviction that the promise of the kingdom to come should not lead to patient resignation in the face of contemporary evil but provides "both motive and direction" for courageous human conduct[10] (p. 128).

A few years later *Gaudium et Spes* once again found a strong echo in another book I wrote at the invitation of Ted Yarnold, the editor of the *Theology Today* series: *The Theology of Secularity.*[11] In answering the objection that "otherworldliness" forms a fatal flaw in Christian engagement with earthly tasks, I quoted[12] the constitution's clear response:

> Christians, on pilgrimage toward the heavenly city, should seek and savor the things which are above. But this in no way decreases, but rather increases, the weight of their obligation to work with all people in constructing a more human world. In fact, the mystery of the Christian faith furnishes them with excellent incentives and helps towards discharging this task with greater commitment. (*Gaudium et Spes*, 57)

In the 1980s and 1990s other themes of the constitution would catch my attention, especially after the collapse of Western communism in 1989 moved debate away from (a) any residual Marxist accusations about Christian and other religious faiths being an "opium" that dulled people's desire to build a better world, and toward (b) even more serious dialogue with other religions.

After the Council

Once I settled into my teaching career, for five years in Boston and Melbourne (1968–73) and then full time at the Gregorian University in Rome (from 1974), *Dei Verbum* became the Magna Carta of my academic life. In 1971 my *Foundations of Theology*[13] contained a whole chapter on "Theology of Revelation out of Vatican II," as well as introducing the teaching of *Dei Verbum* in other appropriate contexts. But the role of the constitution became even more decisive once I began teaching "fundamental" theology at the Gregorian in October 1974. Fundamental theology deals with basic or foundational themes, above all, God's self-revelation, its transmission through tradition and the inspired scriptures, and its credibility or power to command the assent of faith. *Dei Verbum* was the central document for courses in fundamental theology, since it expounded revelation and faith (chapter 1), tradition (chapter 2), and the scriptures (chapters 3–6).

My new publications reflected the centrality of this Vatican II document. René Latourelle (the French-Canadian who reshaped theological studies at the Gregorian University) and I managed to bring together a star team (which included Avery Dulles and David Tracy from the United States, Carlo Martini from Italy, and Karl Rahner from Germany) for *Problems and Perspectives of Fundamental Theology*.[14] Many of the nineteen chapters introduced and commented on various documents from the council. My own chapter proposed various criteria for interpreting and discerning the value of particular traditions in Christian life, worship, and teaching. Some traditions can be little more than superstitious practices and misrepresent the good news that is Jesus Christ himself. Such criteria as fidelity to the biblical testimony distinguish life-giving from

11

decadent traditions. My chapter drew heavily on *Dei Verbum*, without neglecting other documents from the council. In a revised form the same chapter was soon to appear also in my *Fundamental Theology*,[15] a book that discussed the believer's experience of revelation, tradition, and the inspired scriptures. That book received and expressed Vatican II teaching more fully by using *Gaudium et Spes*, *Lumen Gentium*, and *Nostra Aetate* (The Declaration on the Relation of the Church to Non-Christian Religions) to construct a whole chapter ("Christ and the Non-Christians"), which reflected on how the divine self-communication takes place beyond Christianity. When examining the response of faith to God's self-manifestation, the book also moved beyond *Dei Verbum* to elaborate the basic human questions that make men and women everywhere "searchers" for meaning, "hearers" of God's revealing word, and so potential believers in Christ. *Gaudium et Spes* had developed these human questions and search, but I preferred to quote the more concise version to be found at the start of *Nostra Aetate* (no. 1).

When I became dean of the theology faculty at the Gregorian (1985–91), I had no time to serve as coeditor with Latourelle on his next two major projects, which embodied a wide-ranging reception of the council's teaching: the three volumes of *Vatican II: Assessments and Perspectives*[16] that he edited alone, and the large, single-volume *Dictionary of Fundamental Theology* that he coedited with Rino Fisichella,[17] a young professor at the Gregorian who was soon to become a bishop and the rector of the Lateran University in Rome. But I could make at least some contributions: In the former work I published a chapter on "Revelation: Past and Present," and in the latter four entries ("Anonymous Christians," "Experience," "Love," and "The Paschal Mystery"). In a revised form I reproduced the chapter ("Revelation: Past and Present") in my *Retrieving Fundamental Theology*.[18] It tackled the question that emerged from *Dei Verbum*: How can we speak of the divine self-disclosure in the past, present, and future tense? On the one hand, with the life, death, and resurrection of Jesus (together with the coming of the Holy Spirit) the self-revelation of God was completed. Yet, on the other hand, revelation is a present event that here and now invites human faith and will reach its definitive fullness only in the future.

Rereading more than a decade later *Retrieving Fundamental Theology*, I see the deep concern to exploit the rich teaching of *Dei Verbum*. The book ended with a thirty-nine-page bibliography of editions and commentaries on that conciliar document; at the time it was easily the longest such bibliography in existence. But, along with this passion for *Dei Verbum*, the book also demonstrated how much I wanted to glean everything available from all the Vatican II documents for the inseparably linked topics of revelation and salvation. In particular, I dedicated a chapter to the saving revelation God offered and offers to those of all cultures and religions. Themes about the revealing and saving activity of Christ and the Holy Spirit in the whole world caught my attention. I stressed the way in which the council read the situation of non-Christians in the key of two "missions": the mission of the Son of God and that of the Holy Spirit. To conclude the chapter, I drew on *Gaudium et Spes* and its classic statement about all people being called to share in the life and light that comes from the crucified and risen Jesus: "Since Christ died for all and since the final vocation of human beings is in fact one and the same, a divine vocation, we should hold that the Holy Spirit offers to all the possibility of sharing, in a way known to God, in the paschal mystery" (*Gaudium et Spes*, 22).

Long before publishing *Retrieving Fundamental Theology*, I had urged a number of doctoral students to do research on topics emerging from the Vatican II documents. In 1977 an Indian Jesuit, Ravi Santosh Kamath, defended the dissertation that he wrote with me in an ecumenical area directly developed by Pope John XXIII, Pope Paul VI, and the council: the Anglican-Roman Catholic Commission's agreed statement on the Eucharist (1971). I was glad to find how much Anglicans and Catholics agreed in their eucharistic beliefs. William Henn, an American Capuchin who was soon to join our theology faculty at the Gregorian, wrote with me and then published in our *Analecta Gregoriana* series *The Hierarchy of Truths According to Yves Congar, O.P.* With many others, I had welcomed Vatican II's teaching that "there exists a hierarchy of truths of Catholic doctrine" (*Unitatis Redintegratio*, 11) as a promising development for the future of Christian ecumenism. All revealed truths should be believed, but some (for example, the existence of three divine persons) stand higher or are more central than others (for example, the nature of our future heavenly happiness). Henn explored the background to this principle in the work of the figure chiefly credited with introducing it into the council's teaching, the Dominican ecumenist Yves Congar, who was to become a cardinal in 1994 before dying a year later.

In 1997 I published with Daniel Kendall, an American Jesuit who was my first doctoral student, *The Bible for Theology*. The book enunciated and exemplified the use of ten principles for using biblical texts in systematic theology. It was a joint attempt to practice the dream of *Dei Verbum* about the study of the scriptures being "the soul" of theology (no. 24). Ormond Rush, an Australian priest and nephew of Archbishop Frank Rush, defended in 1996 and then published in 1997 a thesis on the reception of doctrine. He showed how ideas on reception in the area of literature developed by Hans Robert Jauss (1921–97) could also work fruitfully in theology. His doctoral work led Ormond to write a book, published by Paulist Press in 2004, *Still Interpreting Vatican II: Some Hermeneutical Principles*.

In the early 1990s, when writing *Christology*,[19] my interest was sparked by some luminous lines in Vatican II's Constitution on the Sacred Liturgy on the various modes of Christ's presence in worship (*Sacrosanctum Concilium*, 7), a passage that strikes me as a wonderful source of wisdom and understanding about Jesus Christ and his redemptive work. It has been relentlessly neglected by almost all Catholics writing on Christology after the council. The inspiration of that passage lay behind the synthesis in terms of Christ as the "enfleshed" divine presence in our midst with which I concluded *Christology*. It also lay behind the encouragement I gave to William Kelly, a Boston priest, who wrote with me and successfully defended his thesis in 1996, "Towards a Christology of Presence."[20]

In 2001 Francesco Brancato, a Sicilian priest, completed a thesis with me on the developments in Catholic thinking about eschatology, or our vision of "the last things." More than a mere branch of theology, eschatology concerns the future-orientation of our Christian existence as we wait in active hope for the coming of God's final kingdom. The teaching of Vatican II (for example, about the church on pilgrimage to its final, heavenly destiny) helped to reshape what Catholic thinkers in the following decades wrote about eschatology. But not in every case, as Brancato discovered. While he was still archbishop of Munich, Cardinal Joseph Ratzinger published for a German series of textbooks in systematic theology the volume on eschatology.[21] But, although it appeared twelve years after Vatican II ended, the book did not contain even one reference to the rich eschatological doctrine (for example, about Christ's future coming in glory and the final kingdom of God) to be found in *Lumen Gentium* and other documents of the council.

It was Cardinal Ratzinger, as prefect of the Congregation for the Doctrine of the Faith (CDF), who launched an investigation in 1998 into a book by my colleague at the Gregorian, Jacques Dupuis (1923–2004).[22] I was involved myself not only as the official consultor (or one advisor permitted by the CDF) for Dupuis but also because I had accompanied him in the writing of that book and his next one.[23] I found myself rereading very carefully what the council taught about the activity of the Trinity in bringing to all people light and life. In particular, the council retrieved the teaching of some church fathers about the "seeds of the Word," or the divine manifestation to all human beings that comes through the action of the eternal Son of God (*Ad Gentes*, 11; *Lumen Gentium*, 17). Naturally I returned again and again to a classic passage (*Gaudium et Spes*, 22) quoted above, about the Holy Spirit's mysterious and universal work in drawing all to share in the grace of Christ's death and resurrection. Finally, it seemed important to retrieve the affirmation attached to Hebrews 11:6 that in a variety of "ways" God brings to faith, without which it is "impossible to please God," those who through no fault of their own do not know the gospel (*Ad Gentes*, 7). This conviction about a universal call to faith should rule out persistent views about "other religions" and their merely human search for God that results simply in "belief" and not in "theological" faith.[24]

The memory of what I have done directly and through my students to spread the teaching of Vatican II around the world gives me life and hope. I am very grateful to have been part of that international team of ambassadors for Vatican II, which included other professors at the Gregorian University such as Angel Antón, Carmen Aparicio Valls, Jacques Dupuis, Rino Fisichella, Bill Henn,

René Latourelle, Frank Sullivan, and Jared Wicks, who deployed their scholarly talents in understanding, interpreting, and communicating the riches of the council to teachers and students of theology everywhere.

Personal Debts

But what did the council do for me personally—as a Catholic Christian and a Jesuit priest? It reinforced two passions that had been growing in my life: a love for the scriptures and a commitment to fostering relations with other Christians and members of other faiths. The deep reverence for the scriptures that pervaded the whole of the council's work and in particular *Dei Verbum* strengthened my desire to live an existence that draws its light and life from the Bible. Right from my childhood, my parents had encouraged contacts with those of other churches and faiths. As I shall tell later, that "social" ecumenism developed under the influence of Vatican II into a deeper ecumenism "of the heart."

The council also nourished three new personal developments. First, the Decree on the Up-to-date Renewal of Religious Life *(Perfectae Caritatis)* prompted me and many other Jesuits to recover our roots in the teaching and life of our founder, St. Ignatius Loyola (1491–1556). That decree wanted members of religious institutes to retrieve, in the changed conditions of our times, "the spirit and aims" of their founders or foundresses (no. 2). Over the centuries various Jesuit practices had somewhat obscured what Ignatius taught and stood for, above all through his precious guide for times of intense prayer, *The Spiritual Exercises,* a devotional practice that has enriched the lives not only of Catholic priests, religious, and laypeople but also of many non-Catholics. In my novitiate in Australia (1950) and then again in my tertianship in Germany (1964), I had spent a month in prayer and silence, making the thirty-day "retreat." But on both occasions the director of the retreat followed a custom that had grown up after the time of Ignatius and preached instructions at us three or four times a day. To recover my Ignatian roots I decided to follow the example of many other Jesuits in the post-Vatican II years and seek personal renewal by making the thirty-day retreat a third time. I did so in the summer of 1977, and on a one-to-one basis under a director with whom I met only once a day. That silent month spent in a house of prayer in Los Angeles endorsed and encouraged my life as a Jesuit priest more than anything else I experienced in the aftermath of the council.[25]

A second wonderful development in my personal life that I owe to the council was the discovery of the public worship of the church. I had grown up as a rigidly precise altar boy who observed all the rubrics when serving Mass. That total attention to a set of prescribed words and actions, while admirable in some ways, often reduced one's attention to what the liturgy or the community's reverent veneration of the tripersonal God entails. At the heart of the liturgy is the celebration of the death and resurrection of Jesus.

The name of the Lord brings me to my third and greatest debt to Vatican II—the decision to center my theological work on Jesus in an unqualified way. I have always delighted in the providential fact that the council's first document, *Sacrosanctum Concilium* (promulgated in December 1963), dealt with the church's liturgy, while the last (and longest) document dealt with the church in the modern world, *Gaudium et Spes* (promulgated in December 1965). As we will see in chapter 3, *liturgy* originally referred to both Christian worship and the service of the world in need. In a remarkable but still neglected passage, *Sacrosanctum Concilium* links the priestly work of Christ with the entire world: "Jesus Christ, the High Priest of the New and Eternal Covenant, by assuming a human nature, has introduced into this earthly exile that hymn which is sung throughout all ages in the halls of heaven. He attaches to himself the entire human community and has them join him in singing this divine song of praise" (no. 83). The vital link between Christ and the world in all its joys, sufferings, and hopes was to be spelled out at length by *Gaudium et Spes*, along with the church's deep desire to help all human beings to know, love, and follow him. What I treasured in *Gaudium et Spes* was its capacity to hold together various themes about Jesus: his role as both creator and redeemer (no. 45), his life, death, and resurrection (no. 22), his inseparable relationship with the Father and the Holy Spirit (nos. 22, 92–93), and his vital link with every human being (no. 22).

17

By the time *Sacrosanctum Concilium* was promulgated, Paul VI had been elected pope (June 21, 1963) and right from the speech with which he opened the second session of the council the following September, he showed how he centered his life and ministry on Christ. He kept coming back to the two questions: "Who is Christ in himself? Who is Christ for us?"[26] That centering on Christ guided Paul VI in his not entirely successful efforts to implement the council.

When John Paul I became pope in 1978, I was in Rome for his election and the whole of his tragically short pontificate. One of his many remarks that I have cherished was: "It is only Jesus Christ we must present to the world." After a papacy lasting only thirty-three days, John Paul I died and was succeeded by the first non-Italian for more four and a half centuries, the Polish cardinal who took the name of John Paul II. Naturally I rejoiced when he dedicated his first encyclical, *Redemptor Hominis* (The Redeemer of Man) of March 1979 to Jesus Christ, "the center of the universe and of history" (no. 1). Paul VI, John Paul I, and John Paul II all strengthened my conviction that any efforts to renew the church through the teaching of Vatican II would remain spiritually empty, emotionally hollow, and doctrinally unsound unless they drew inspiration and life from the founder of Christianity himself. At the Extraordinary Synod of 1985, called to commemorate twenty years since the closing of Vatican II, I cheered when I read Archbishop Frank Rush's final remark: "The Church needs to search for and shape an answer to the only ultimate question: Who is Christ for the world of today?"[27]

Both for students and teachers of religion and for ordinary readers, I have repeatedly tried to answer that question and not least through articles in *America* magazine and *The Tablet*, as well as through entire books.[28] If by this present work, I help readers to "know Jesus more clearly, love him more dearly, and follow him more nearly" (from a prayer of St. Richard of Chichester), I will be more than satisfied. I passionately believe that the teaching of Vatican II can help bring about that happy result.

2

FACILITATORS
OR GATEKEEPERS?

> The best preparation for the new millennium...can only
> be expressed in a renewed commitment to apply, as faith-
> fully as possible, the teachings of Vatican II to the life of
> every individual and of the whole Church.
>
> John Paul II, *Tertio Millennio Adveniente*, 20

At the Second Vatican Council the bishops showed a practical concern for the implementation of the documents for which they
voted. Thus in their very first document, the Constitution on the
Sacred Liturgy of 1963, they mandated that national conferences of
bishops and particular dioceses should set up, where they did not
already exist, liturgical commissions (nos. 22, 44–45). Even before
the council closed in December 1965, such commissions and other
bodies were at work to implement the conciliar teaching and
decrees. This chapter will sketch what various institutions both in
Rome and around the world have contributed and continue to contribute to the living reception of Vatican II.

The Liturgy

Some offices of the Roman Curia, the institution that serves popes
in their ministry for the worldwide church, were called at once to
play their part in carrying out the changes mandated by the council. In the area of the liturgy, the Congregation for Divine Worship
(which Pope Paul VI created in May 1969 and to which he amal-
gamated the already existing Congregation for the Discipline of the

Sacraments that had been founded in 1908) worked for years to carry out the conciliar desire for reforms that would help Catholics understand more clearly and participate more fully in the sacred celebrations. Thus the Congregation for Divine Worship published in May 1969 a new rite for the baptism of children (mandated by *Sacrosanctum Concilium*, 67–69), in August 1969 a new order for Christian funerals (mandated by *Sacrosanctum Concilium*, 81–82), in February 1970 a new rite of religious profession for men and women (mandated by *Sacrosanctum Concilium*, 80), in August 1971 a new rite of confirmation (mandated by *Sacrosanctum Concilium*, 71), and in January 1972 the Rite of Christian Initiation of Adults. This rite (mandated by *Sacrosanctum Concilium*, 64) renewed in a revised form the practice of the early church of preparing candidates in stages for their receiving during the Easter Vigil the sacraments of baptism, confirmation, and Eucharist. In December 1972 the Congregation for Divine Worship issued a new rite for the sacrament of the anointing of the sick (mandated by *Sacrosanctum Concilium*, 74–75), and in December 1973 a new rite of penance with rites of reconciliation for individual penitents and groups of penitents (mandated by *Sacrosanctum Concilium*, 72).

Another office of the Roman Curia, the Congregation of Rites, promulgated in March 1969 the new rite for celebrating marriage (mandated by *Sacrosanctum Concilium*, 77–78). All this work by the Congregation for Divine Worship and the Congregation of Rites was made possible by the Council for the Implementation of the Constitution on the Sacred Liturgy that Paul VI had set up in January 1964. A direct line led from *Sacrosanctum Concilium* through this council to the rites promulgated by the two congregations. This council was integrated into the Congregation for Divine Worship in 1969.[1]

All the above reforms came during the pontificate of Paul VI and with his authority. He lent that authority even more to three further significant steps in liturgical renewal. Chronologically the first was the revision of the rites of ordination (mandated by *Sacrosanctum Concilium*, 76). In 1968 the pope used his supreme authority to decree the new rites of ordination to the diaconate, the presbyterate, and the episcopate. Simpler, clearer, and doctrinally richer, these new rites centered around the laying on of hands and the consecratory prayer that follows.

Second, the pope announced in April 1969 the publication of the new *Roman Missal*, which followed from a number of decrees of Vatican II (*Sacrosanctum Concilium*, 50–58), appeared in March 1970, and replaced the *Tridentine Missal*, which that had been introduced in 1570. The Roman rite originally developed in fourth-century Rome and southern Italy; missionaries and such powerful rulers as Charlemagne (d. 814) and St. Henry II (d. 1024) spread the Roman-style liturgy and liturgical books. Long before the time of Charlemagne the eucharistic prayer (or "canon" because of its unchanging nature) for the Roman Mass had become fixed, and in a virtually identical form was accepted as the only eucharistic prayer used throughout Western Christianity. For more than a thousand years, from around 800 until after Vatican II, priests recited the Roman Canon in a whisper. In 1967 Paul VI authorized the audible recitation of the Canon and the use of its translation into the vernacular. The new *Roman Missal* of 1970 contains four eucharistic prayers: Prayer I the Roman Canon in a slightly revised version, Prayer II an adaptation of the eucharistic prayer found in the early third-century *Apostolic Tradition* of St. Hippolytus, Prayer III a modern composition, and Prayer IV an adaptation of the "anaphora" or eucharistic prayer of St. Basil (d. 379).

Paul VI promulgated in 1970 a revised form of the divine office (also mandated by *Sacrosanctum Concilium*, 83–101). For this "Liturgy of the Hours" a community gathers at different times of day or night to hear passages from the scripture (and from other spiritual sources, especially the works of the fathers of the church) and to recite or sing together psalms and other prayers. The prayers, hymns, and readings are adapted to the liturgical feasts and seasons of the year. In the West, under the form of the "breviary," the divine office is used for daily prayer by priests, male and female religious, and a considerable number of laypersons. Our next chapters will evaluate more fully the reception of this and other liturgical reforms mandated by the council, carried out by Paul VI and his official collaborators in Rome, and implemented at the national and local levels.

In summarizing the reform of sacramental rites, other "orders of worship," and the Liturgy of the Hours introduced by Paul VI and the offices at his disposal in Rome, I have illustrated how these changes adhered closely to the decrees of the council's Constitution on the Sacred Liturgy. Vatican II, by and large, was more precise about specifics when it dealt with liturgical matters. The institutions handling postconciliar liturgical reforms in Rome received a clear account of what was required of them. In Rome that adaptation and renewal of Catholic worship continued into the third millennium, not least through the work of Archbishop Piero Marini, the pope's master of ceremonies. On October 19, 2003, dozens of television networks carried around the world the Mass at which Mother Teresa of Calcutta was beatified in St. Peter's Square. During that Mass graceful Indian girls in saris danced as they scattered petals and carried flowers and burning incense to the altar. Marini let the world see how Catholic liturgy has become inculturated in India.

Other Roman Congregations

What of the central institutions in Rome administering other, non-liturgical areas of renewal mandated by Vatican II? Here a number of bodies, either already existing or newly created, were and remain involved. Various congregations of the Roman Curia were obviously responsible for implementing the teaching and decrees of Vatican II: the Congregation for the Doctrine of the Faith, the Congregation for the Causes of the Saints, the Congregation for the Oriental Churches, the Congregation for Bishops, the Congregation for the Evangelization of the Peoples, the Congregation for Institutes of Consecrated Life and for Societies of Apostolic Life, the Congregation for the Clergy, and the Congregation for Catholic Education—to use their current names rather than those in use back in 1965. I leave to the research of later historians any full-scale answers to the question: To what extent and in what ways did these eight congregations or central offices of papal administration facilitate and guide the implementation of the teaching and decrees from Vatican II? In the meantime, however, we can fix on some details that should enter any full accounting of their performance.

When reforming the Congregation for the Doctrine of the Faith (hereafter CDF) on December 7, 1965, and so on the eve of the council's closing, Paul VI charged this institution not only with "defending the faith" but also with promoting Catholic teaching and theology. How far has the post-Vatican II history of the congregation been marked with shadows as well as lights in carrying out the papal mandate? The CDF's contribution to the reception of conciliar teaching has depended obviously on the quality of those who work for it in either a full-time or a part-time capacity.

The first World Synod of Bishops (1967) suggested the formation of a body "composed of theologians of diverse schools... whose duty it will be, acting with all lawful academic freedom, to assist the Holy See and especially the Sacred Congregation for the Doctrine of Faith, in connection with questions of greater importance." To provide himself and the CDF with the services of such experts who represent various schools of Catholic thought, Paul VI in 1969 established the International Theological Commission as an adjunct to the CDF. In its early years the Theological Commission included among its thirty members such outstanding scholars as Hans Urs von Balthasar, Walter Burghardt, Yves (later Cardinal) Congar, Bernard Lonergan, Henri (later Cardinal) de Lubac, Gerard Philips, Karl Rahner, Joseph Ratzinger (later a cardinal, then Pope Benedict XVI), Rudolf Schnackenburg, and Jean-Marie Tillard. In the early years those on the commission were all male and clerics, as well as being mostly European. Members of the commission appointed later have included more representatives from around the world and a few laymen but, until 2004, never a woman (either lay or religious). Overall, when compared with the seventies, there has been a decline in quality, in part because the commission's members have been largely recruited from the ranks of "conservative" theologians and do not represent the theological pluralism that the Synod of Bishops asked for in 1967 and Paul VI "willingly allowed" in his inaugural address to the commission. The result is that the commission has not played its expected vital role in implementing and applying the teaching of Vatican II; its statements are normally cautious, often do little else than repeat official positions, and—with one or two exceptions such as the 2002 statement on the diaconate—are widely ignored.[2]

The post-Vatican II history of the Pontifical Biblical Commission, another group that advises the pope and the CDF, has proved, however, much more positive. Founded in 1902 by Pope Leo XIII, the Biblical Commission, after acting for decades as little more than a vigilance committee that hampered teaching and scholarship, underwent a remarkable change in the aftermath of Pope Pius XII's 1943 landmark encyclical on promoting biblical studies, *Divino Afflante Spiritu*. Its 1964 instruction, "On the Historical Truth of the Gospels," provided principles for interpreting the gospels that Vatican II adopted a year later in *Dei Verbum*. The 1993 document from the commission, *The Interpretation of the Bible in the Church*, in turn built on *Dei Verbum* to evaluate a whole range of methods and approaches in biblical interpretation, proposed some central characteristics of Catholic interpretation of the Bible, and encouraged the active appropriation of the scriptures in the life of the church. The very wide and positive reception within Catholic Christianity and beyond that this 1993 document has enjoyed matches the high scholarly quality and Catholic commitment of the commission's members.[3]

But what of the CDF itself, the institution that the International Theological Commission and the Pontifical Biblical Commission are intended to serve? Has it been notably successful in defending and promoting the teaching of Vatican II? Truth, as an old proverb has it, is the daughter of time. At this point, early in the twenty-first century, no well-informed answer can be given. Yet a priest who has served for many years as a consultor on the CDF admitted to me that he "wondered whether the CDF has done more harm than good." Three things might have fueled his hesitancy: a certain lack of love, justice, and balanced membership in the CDF. Where John Paul II echoed and extended Vatican II's teaching on Jesus Christ right from his first encyclical of 1979 and his stress on "the tremendous mystery of love" effectively revealed in Christ (*Redemptor Hominis*, 9), some of the CDF documents seemed far more concerned about truth than about love. Thus the controversial declaration of September 2000 on the universal saving work of Christ, *Dominus Iesus*, wrote of "truth" and what is "true" forty-five times, but invoked "love" only four times. The declaration repeatedly cited and referred to the pope's 1990 encyclical *Redemptoris*

Missio (The Mission of the Redeemer), but fell far short of imitating that encyclical, which appeals thirty-one times to love and twenty-five times to truth. A poor ratio between concern for love and concern for truth played its part in creating the negative tone that many commentators sensed in *Dominus Iesus*. Then one wonders about the fairness of the procedures followed by the CDF when investigating theologians whose views have been challenged for failures in orthodoxy. In a widely reproduced article, the Washington-based canon lawyer Ladislas Örsy showed how the procedures to which the CDF subjects theologians are hardly in accord with proper principles of justice: for example, the right of the accused to be present, to meet his/her accusers, to be given in writing well beforehand their complaints, and to be represented by someone of his or her choice, right from the time when the case begins to be heard.[4] My acquaintance in the CDF may also have been set wondering by the somewhat one-sided selection of his fellow consultors. One could hardly describe them as "theologians of diverse schools." Notoriously, when an institution is not strengthened by appropriate diversity, it lacks the internal criticism that can lend more balance and wisdom to what it does and what it publishes.

Let me be brief in raising some further significant questions that later historians might use when assessing what the other congregations of the Roman Curia achieved toward implementing the teaching and decrees of Vatican II.

The universal call to holiness, the theme of its chapter 5, proved to be one of the many features of the council's Dogmatic Constitution on the Church that impressed commentators and many Catholics. *Lumen Gentium* stated clearly the vocation of all the baptized: "All of Christ's faithful in whatever state or walk of life are called to the fullness of Christian life and the perfection of love" (no. 40). In the longest section of this chapter the council spelled out a wide range of "conditions, commitments, and circumstances" of life in which the baptized may find themselves (no. 41). The chapter ended by reiterating that "all the faithful are invited and obliged to the pursuit of holiness and perfection in their own state of life" (no. 42). How effective has this call to pursue holiness in every state of life proved? Later chapters of this book will here and there offer partial answers to this question. One might argue that it will only be at the final judgment of all human beings and all Christians that a clear and full answer will emerge to the question: What was in fact the response after Vatican II called all the baptized to holiness and the perfection of Christian life?

One element in the whole picture was the desire of Pope John Paul II to "raise to the altars" by canonizing or at least beatifying many Catholics from all walks of life and from many countries around the globe. Ever since he was elected pope in October 1978, he wanted to bring holiness home to the world and offer a wide range of models by officially recognizing the heroic virtues of numerous men and women. By the end of his life, he had canonized or declared to be saints 482 men and women, and beatified—a stage before possible canonization—a total of 1,338. Many of those beatified or canonized had died a martyr's death, including 103 Koreans whom he canonized during his visit to Seoul on March 6, 1984, the 459 beatified and 12 canonized who were martyred in the Spanish Civil War (1936–39), and the 120 canonized on October 1, 2000, who had been martyred in China between 1648 and 1930.[5] In implementing this policy of showing how lives of heroic love are possible everywhere and for everyone, the pope needed the constant help of the Congregation for the Causes of Saints, as well as the prior work of local bishops and their collaborators. They initiate the "process" or possible path to beatification by thoroughly investigating locally the life and works of those being promoted for their outstanding holiness. All the relevant documents are then sent to Rome for examination by the Congregation for the Causes of Saints. If and when the results are positive, the congregation then proposes the candidates for beatification by the pope. Some have pointed out that since the Congregation was set up in 1588, John Paul II made more saints and blesseds than all his predecessors created: 300 saints and 1,310 blesseds.

I beg to differ from some cardinals and other critics, who think that sheer numbers have cheapened the "honors" of canonization and beatification. The Holy Spirit operates powerfully everywhere, and one can rightly suppose that many of the faithful have responded courageously to the call to universal holiness, which Vatican II recognized and proclaimed. To say otherwise would be to demean the work of the Spirit and Christ's call to heroic discipleship, and even to picture real sanctity as something that happens only far away and long ago. The truth was stated on May 4, 2003, by a huge banner in Madrid's Plaza de Colón when John Paul II came to canonize five twentieth-century Spaniards: "You too can be a saint." Karl Rahner's view of a deep experience, even mystical experience, of our gracious God being universally possible underpins the practice of recognizing officially the widespread presence of truly saintly lives.[6]

If there is any criticism to be made, it might be that those beatified and canonized still include a disproportionate number of European religious, especially French, Italian, and Spanish founders and foundresses of religious institutes. But the Congregation for the Causes of Saints and the pope himself depend on the local churches to examine and promote candidates who represent all ways of life within the church. If more married, single, and widowed laypersons were put forward by dioceses and bishops around the world, a better balance would be achieved and the line between *Lumen Gentium*'s universal call to holiness and the work of the congregation would be even clearer.

In the case of the other six congregations in the Roman Curia, one could assess their active reception of the teaching and decrees of Vatican II by examining their performance in the light of conciliar documents that are peculiarly relevant to them. The Decree on the Pastoral Office of Bishops, *Christus Dominus*, as well as the passages on bishops in *Lumen Gentium*, obviously provide a template for evaluating the postconciliar work of the Congregation for Bishops. Has the congregation effectively encouraged and helped bishops to shape their lives according to that Vatican II teaching: for instance, by fulfilling what *Lumen Gentium* characterized as their "outstanding" duty of preaching the gospel and being "heralds of the faith" (no. 25)? Or has the congregation favored the choice of good administrators over inspiring preachers and teachers? Since the assassination in San Salvador of Oscar Romero in March 1980, other bishops (in Africa, Central America, the Philippines, and South America) have also been martyred as shepherds who were "not afraid to lay down their lives for their sheep" (*Lumen Gentium*, 41). Does this postconciliar development owe something to the work of the Congregation for Bishops in selecting and supporting bishops around the world?

With its Decree on the Training of Priests, *Optatam Totius*, and the Declaration on Christian Education, *Gravissimum Educationis*, the council provided a program for the Congregation for Catholic Education. We can partly gauge its performance toward renewing Catholic education in general and theological education in particular by scrutinizing its major postconciliar documents in the light of the relevant Vatican II texts. Such a scrutiny would take us through "Certain Norms" for ecclesiastical studies (May 1968), the "Study of Philosophy in Seminaries" (January 1972), "Theological Formation of Future Priests" (February 1976), the April 1979 "Apostolic Constitution on Ecclesiastical Universities and Faculties" (*Sapientia Christiana*, Christian Wisdom) promulgated by Pope John Paul II, "The Basic Plan for Priestly Formation" (March 1985), a circular letter on "Some of the More Urgent Aspects of Spiritual Formation in Seminaries" (January 1980), an "Instruction on the Study of Fathers of the Church in the Formation of Priests" (November 1989), and the August 1990 Apostolic Constitution on Catholic Universities (*Ex Corde Ecclesiae*, From the Heart of the Church) promulgated by Pope John Paul II. Unquestionably such documents had to take into account not only the Vatican II decrees but also the changing contexts and challenges of the last decades of the twentieth century. Nevertheless, the conciliar texts on education remain a major template for evaluating the work of the Congregation for Catholic Education as a pontifical institution responsible for part of the application of the teaching of Vatican II.

In this way, specific Vatican II documents supply or should shape the particular agenda for eight of the nine congregations in the Roman Curia that assist the pope. In the case of CDF, we might say that it works or should work as the theological conscience, concerned with the living reception of all the theological teaching found in various documents of the council. We have raised a few questions about the performance of the Roman congregations in receiving and implementing the conciliar teaching and decrees. The postconciliar documents, gathered and published by Austin Flannery, yield some insight into the ways in which the congregations promoted and applied the council's decisions and doctrine.[7] Obviously only later historians will be in a position to assess thoroughly how each of the nine congregations of the Roman Curia have carried out (or failed to carry out) what the council taught and decreed.

Pontifical Councils

Such an evaluation, even at this point in history, is somewhat easier in the case of what are now called pontifical councils. Some of these Roman institutions were created at the time of Vatican II and have played a worldwide role in implementing what the council wanted.

The Pontifical Council for Promoting Christian Unity, which was founded in preparation for Vatican II by Pope John XXIII in June 1960 as the Secretariat for the Promotion of the Unity of Christians, has been responsible for relations with non-Catholic Christian communities and with Judaism (through the Commission for Religious Relations with Jews). This secretariat, which was renamed in 1988 the Pontifical Council for Promoting Christian Unity, received its brief from Vatican II through two documents: the Decree on Ecumenism, *Unitatis Redintegratio,* and the second half of the Declaration on the Relation of the Church to Non-Christian Religions, *Nostra Aetate* (nos. 4–5). *Unitatis Redintegratio* depended on *Lumen Gentium,* which recognized how "many elements of sanctification and truth are found outside the visible confines" of the Catholic Church (no. 8) and listed the many ways in which the Catholic Church is "joined" with other Christians (no. 15).

In the aftermath of Vatican II, the Council for Promoting Christian Unity has encouraged and guided Catholics around the world in starting or joining dialogues and consultations with the vast majority of other Christians. By 2002 twelve such official international dialogues or consultations were in progress with the Orthodox Churches, the Ancient Oriental Churches, the Anglican Communion, the Lutheran World Federation, the World Methodist Council, the Disciples of Christ, the Pentecostals, the World Evangelical Fellowship, the World Alliance of Reformed Churches, the Mennonites, and the World Baptist Alliance.[8] In other ways, the Catholic Church also has contacts with such groups as Old Catholics, Quakers, the Salvation Army, and Seventh-day Adventists.

The Council for Promoting Christian Unity, headed by such outstanding ecumenical figures as Cardinal Augustin Bea (until 1968), Cardinal Johannes Willebrands (until 1989), Cardinal Edward Cassidy (until 2001), and Cardinal Walter Kasper (from 2001), has directed on the world level the Catholic Church's ecumenical outreach, which includes participating in many World Council of Churches programs, although without being a member of the WCC.[9] The Catholic Church does belong to the theological subunit of the WCC, Faith and Order, and the Catholic representatives have played their part in producing some outstanding consensus papers on issues that have divided Christians. The Faith and Order Paper No. 111, which was published after a 1982 meeting in Lima (Peru), *Baptism, Eucharist and Ministry*, transmitted to churches around the world for their official response an agreed statement on these three sacraments (even if some churches do not consider ordained ministry a sacrament).

The Council for Promoting Christian Unity has been heavily involved in forwarding bilateral dialogues, which have sometimes resulted in official agreements. An Anglican-Roman Catholic International Commission (ARCIC) was set up in 1970, and produced agreed statements on the Eucharist, ministry and ordination, and authority, which were all published together as the *Final Report* of 1982. This was offered to the Churches of the Anglican Communion and to the Roman Catholic Church for their serious consideration. At its 1988 Lambeth Conference, the Anglican Communion declared that the ARCIC statements on both the Eucharist and ministry and ordination were "consonant with the faith of Anglicans" and recognized a convergence in understanding authority. The Roman Catholic response was delayed until 1991 and came from the CDF. It welcomed "the achievement of points of convergence and even of agreement which many would not have thought possible before the Commission began its work," but noted that "substantial agreement" had not yet been reached "on all the questions studied by the Commission." In particular, the CDF wanted some points relating to the Eucharist and the ordained ministry clarified (ND 931, 932h). Some commentators questioned, however, whether the language used in this official response followed the recommendations of Pope Paul VI and Archbishop

Michael Ramsey. In setting up ARCIC they had hoped that the Commission would go beyond expressions that had emerged in situations of controversy and with an ecumenical spirit would seek formulations out of a common heritage. Regardless of the language used, the long delay in the official response was one of the impulses that prompted the Church of England into going ahead with the ordination of women. ARCIC continues its work, even with further "obstacles" to growth in communion occasioned not only by the Anglican ordination of women to the priesthood and episcopate but also by the 2003 ordination as a bishop of an Episcopalian priest living openly in a gay relationship. George Carey, the former archbishop of Canterbury, in a letter to *The Times* of London (November 6, 2003) deplored that ordination as, among other things, doing "incalculable" damage to ecumenical relations.

Under the auspices of the Secretariat for Promoting Christian Unity, an international Catholic-Lutheran theological dialogue began in 1967. Catholics and Lutherans have always officially agreed that the saving gift of righteousness that makes human beings acceptable to God comes through faith in Jesus Christ. Lutherans have, however, stressed the justifying verdict passed by God on those who have sinned, whereas Catholics (and Orthodox) have highlighted the grace received that actually transforms sinners through the Holy Spirit. Many of these and other differences can be seen as complementary approaches rather than mutually exclusive positions. Thus the Catholic-Lutheran dialogue in 1999 produced its "Joint Declaration on the Doctrine of Justification," which contains forty-four common statements covering basic truths regarding justification. This was accepted by the Catholic Church and the Lutheran World Federation. The head of the Pontifical Council for Promoting Christian Unity, Cardinal Cassidy, joined leading Lutherans in Augsburg for a formal signing of the "Joint Declaration" on October 31, 1999 (ND 527, 940, 2000k–s). The cardinal summed up the momentous nature of that achievement by remarking that when asked on the day of judgment to give an account of himself, he would simply say that he had signed the "Joint Declaration."

Let us offer one even more dramatic example of an ecumenical agreement guided to a happy conclusion by the Pontifical

Council for Promoting Christian Unity: the Common Christological Declaration signed in 1994 by Pope John Paul II and Mar
Dinkha IV, the Patriarch of the Assyrian Church of the East (ND
683). This church, which courageously spread Christianity in the
early centuries to India, China, and other parts of Asia, became
more isolated from the rest of Christianity after the Council of
Ephesus in 431 and its condemnation of the patriarch Nestorius.
Controversy, sometimes bitter, continued for centuries over the
right language to use about Christ's being divine and human and not
being divided into two persons (the Son of God and the Son of
Mary). Through joint meetings convened by the Council for
Christian Unity and such other bodies as the Pro Oriente movement (promoted by Cardinal Franz König of Vienna), a common
text that combines theological precision with a deep Christian love
emerged. The declaration not only laid to rest debates about the
expression of faith in Christ as the Son of God come to save us but
also provided for ongoing ecumenical cooperation in catechesis and
clergy training. The goal of full, organic unity has not yet been
reached, but a truthful and healing resolution has been reached
about doctrines that seemed to divide permanently the Catholic
Church and the Assyrian Church of the East.[10]

Many other documents record the painstaking work in carrying
out the ecumenical commitment of Vatican II, expressed in *Unitatis
Redintegratio* and personified by the presence of 167 non-Catholic
"observers" and 22 "guests" at the council. At the council the
observers were given front-row seats, received all the "secret" documents, shared in discussions organized by the Secretariat for
Promoting Christian Unity, and had their influence on the work
of the council, not least on the Decree on Ecumenism, *Unitatis
Redintegratio*. I must recall also such documents produced by the
Pontifical Council for Promoting Christian Unity as the ecumenical
directories (1967/1970, and 1993) and the 1995 encyclical *Ut Unum
Sint* (That They May Be One) written by John Paul II but with substantial help from the Pontifical Council itself (ND 935a–937a). The
Directory for the Application of Principles and Norms on Ecumenism (ND
932a–g, 1850–52), approved by the pope in March 1993, has sup-
planted the first directory (which had been published in two parts—
in 1967 and 1970), and provides a clear framework and much

inspiration for interchurch activities. The encyclical *Ut Unum Sint* spelled out the Catholic Church's commitment to ecumenism, the fruits already achieved by dialogue, and the path that lies ahead. The catalogue of progress made since Vatican II records what the pope and the Pontifical Council had done not only through the ecumenical dialogues that have produced some notable agreements but also through pilgrimages, visits of Christian leaders, ecumenical prayer, and cooperation on behalf of justice, peace, and the integrity of creation. Such cooperation did not slacken, as one sees from the common declaration on environmental ethics issued in June 2002 by Pope John Paul II and the Ecumenical Patriarch Bartholomew I, the head of Orthodox Christians.

Right from the start of his pontificate John Paul II set himself to heal the gaping wounds between Jewish people and Christians—not least through such visits as those to Auschwitz (1979), the synagogue of Rome (1986), and the Holy Land (2000). At Yad Vashem Holocaust Memorial in Jerusalem, the pope once again called Catholics to repent for their sins against Jews and joined Vatican II's *Nostra Aetate* in deploring "the hatred, acts of persecution and displays of anti-Semitism directed against the Jews by Christians at any time and any place." Cardinal Cassidy was at the pope's side in Yad Vashem, as president of the Commission for Religious Relations with the Jews, a department that, as we saw above, is attached to the Council for Promoting Christian Unity. Through that commission, Cardinal Cassidy, his colleagues, and successors have played their part in fulfilling the mandate of *Nostra Aetate*. As part of a penitential preparation for the celebration of the Jubilee Year of 2000, the commission issued in 1996 *We Remember: A Reflection on the Shoah*, a call to Catholics and other Christians to recall with deep sorrow their part in the terrible suffering of Jews and to pray for the grace to never let the seeds of anti-Judaism and anti-Semitism take root again in their hearts.

In the last few pages I have been recalling some items that should enter into any accounting of how the Council for Promoting Christian Unity, along with its Commission for Religious Relations with the Jews, has carried out the mandate it received not merely from Paul VI and John Paul II but even more from two documents of the Second Vatican Council. One could practice the same method of evaluation by confronting the achievements of other pontifical councils with the texts from Vatican II that should inspire their work. Two such councils were founded by Paul VI in January 1967—with a view to implementing certain aspects of conciliar teaching. The Pontifical Council for the Laity bears particular responsibility for nurturing the apostolate of laymen and laywomen and, specifically, their sharing in the life and mission of the church, whether they do this as members of apostolic associations or as individuals. This council finds its Magna Carta in Vatican II's *Lumen Gentium* (nos. 30–38) and the Decree on the Apostolate of Lay People (*Apostolicam Actuositatem*), as well as drawing much inspiration and direction from what *Gaudium et Spes* taught on such matters as the family (nos. 47–52), economic and social life (nos. 63–72), and the political community (nos. 73–76). As part of its work in receiving the conciliar teaching, the Council for the Laity promoted a world meeting in Loreto (November 1995), which resulted in the joint volume, *"Gaudium et Spes": Thirty Years Later.*[11]

The Pontifical Council for Justice and Peace bears particular responsibility for promoting justice and peace—in the light of the church's social teaching. Its commitment to furthering the observance of human rights and the progress of all peoples includes collaborating with various non-Catholic groups in achieving those ends. The Constitution on the Church in the Modern World (*Gaudium et Spes*) remains the major charter for guiding the Council for Justice and Peace and for appraising its contribution toward implementing Vatican II. The council has been blessed by outstanding leaders such as Cardinal Roger Etchegaray (president 1984–98), Cardinal François-Xavier Nguyên Van Thuân (president 1998–2002), and Cardinal Renato Martino (president from 2002). The council has worked for justice as a constitutive part of the gospel and practiced a preferential love for the poor and oppressed. In Rome and around the world, the Society of Jesus and some other religious institutes have also been at the forefront of these emphases. The martyred bishop of San Salvador, Oscar Romero, gave his life for the promotion of justice and peace.

The Synods of Bishops

Before leaving the institutions in Rome and their special responsibility for carrying out the teaching and various mandates from Vatican II, I recognize how much more would need to be examined and retrieved before reaching any well-balanced answer to the question: To what extent have the offices of the Roman Curia facilitated and creatively furthered the reception of the council? Or how far have they been reluctant gatekeepers and tightly controlled what they let through? These questions are peculiarly relevant to the functioning of the world synods of bishops, mandated by the Second Vatican Council's Decree on the Pastoral Office of the Bishops in the Church (*Christus Dominus*, no. 5) and organized (many observers say manipulated) by a permanent secretariat in Rome. As much as any post-Vatican II developments these synods have raised the question: To what extent has the collegiality (or shared responsibility for the universal church) of the world's bishops been seriously implemented? Thus far seventeen such synods have taken place in Rome, from 1967 to 2001.

From the first meeting in 1967, these world synods have addressed a variety of topics: for instance, priesthood and justice (1971), evangelization (1974), catechesis (1977), the Christian family (1980), penance and reconciliation (1983), the Second Vatican Council (1985), the laity (1987), priestly formation (1990), and religious life (1994). The 1971 synod published, with the approval of Paul VI, an official document on justice in the world (*De Iustitia in Mundo*) that taught that action on behalf of justice and for the liberation of people also belongs to the mission of the church: "Action on behalf of justice and participation in the transformation of the world fully appear to us a constitutive dimension of the preaching of the Gospel, or, in other words, of the Church's mission for the redemption of the human race and its liberation from every oppressive situation" (ND, 2159; see also 2160–64). After the debacle at the 1974 synod described by Jacques Dupuis in an appendix to this book, the synods published only interim messages, leaving it to the pope to issue a statement in the light of the synods' deliberations and proposals. Paul VI and then John Paul II published the postsynodal documents in the form of apostolic exhortations: in 1975 on evangelization, *Evangelii Nuntiandi*

(ND, 672–73, 884–85, 1036, 1149, 1158–60, 1259, 1336, 1751, 2167–71), in 1979 on catechetics, *Catechesi Tradendae* (ND, 163a, 259, 1161), in 1981 on family life, *Familiaris Consortio* (ND, 1843–44, 2181, 2236), in 1984 on reconciliation and penance, *Reconciliatio et Paenitentia* (ND, 887–88, 1673–76e, 2067a–67e), in 1988 on the laity, *Christifideles Laici* (ND, 894–96a, 1448, 1758), in 1991 on priestly formation, *Pastores Dabo Vobis* (ND, 183a–b), in 1996 on religious life, *Vita Consecrata.*

As can be seen, except for *Vita Consecrata*, all the apostolic exhortations contained at least one and often several sections that contributed something new to the post-Vatican II doctrinal teaching of the Catholic Church. The synods and then the apostolic exhortations took up themes already addressed by the council, dealt with them in changed contexts (for instance, in Western Christianity the dramatic exodus from priesthood and religious life in the postconciliar years), and made some contribution to a healthy development of doctrine that one expects from Catholic Christianity. Jacques Dupuis and his team of collaborators found some fresh items in these texts to add to the seventh edition of *Christian Faith* (ND), which sets out doctrinal documents of the Catholic Church—from the beginning of Christianity until 1999.

Beyond question, the synods and the postsynodal documents could have been more fruitful. The preparatory documents, sent to the bishops before they arrived or waiting for them when they reached Rome, have been at times woefully weak. Once the synod opens, some procedures have involved serious loss of time—as still happens in many other organizations. Despite the invention of photocopying machines, precious time is wasted and keen interest dissipated by long speeches being relentlessly read to a captive audience of synodal bishops.

With a view to the Great Jubilee Year 2000 and the start of the third millennium, special synods of bishops from each of the five continents took place in Rome: the Assembly for Africa (1994), America (1997), Asia (1998), Oceania (1998), and Europe (1991 and 1999). The apostolic exhortations that John Paul II published later on the basis of the synods' work and recommendations mirrored the present state and future hopes of the Catholic Church around the world: *Ecclesia in Africa* (1995), *Ecclesia in America*

(1999),[12] *Ecclesia in Asia* (1999),[13] *Ecclesia in Oceania* (2001), and *Ecclesia in Europa* (2003). In part because these assemblies did not address particular themes of Vatican II, there are fewer formal links made with conciliar teaching. *Ecclesia in Africa*, for instance, refers to or quotes from the council's documents only thirty-one times, including nine references to or quotations from *Lumen Gentium*, and eight each in the case of *Ad Gentes* and *Gaudium et Spes*. This compares with seventy-six references to or quotations from encyclicals, apostolic exhortations, apostolic letters, homilies, and addresses of John Paul II. Thirty years after the council closed in 1965, in his 1995 postsynodal exhortation, *Ecclesia in Africa*, the pope drew more than twice as many times on his own magisterial teaching than on the conciliar documents. In *Ecclesia in Europa* the proportion is even more startlingly different: John Paul II cited or referred to his own teaching sixty times, but cited or referred to Vatican II teaching only thirteen times.[14]

Ecclesia in Europa contains, however, two striking passages that could serve for an examination of conscience in all Roman institutions. It calls the whole church to be "at the service of love" and so become a believable sign "of an existential and experiential love, to lead men and women to an encounter with the love of God and Christ, who comes in search of them" (no. 85). An earlier paragraph invites all members of the church in Europe to "enter the new millennium with the Book of the Gospels" and find "through the careful study of God's word" daily "nourishment and strength to carry out our mission" (no. 65). These two passages raise questions for members of the Roman Curia: Are they "at the service of love" and believable signs of a love that will lead people to "encounter the love of God and Christ"? Is their work nourished and strengthened through the constant study of the gospels? To these questions we might add the practice of transparent accountability to which John Paul II appealed years ago in an address to journalists (January 27, 1984): "The Church tries and will try more and more to be a glasshouse where everyone can see what is happening and how she fulfills her own mission in fidelity to Christ and the Gospel message." The pope's words raise a question for all Roman institutions: Are they "glasshouses where everyone can see what is happening" and how do they fulfill their "mission in fidelity to Christ and the Gospel message"?

Canon Law and the Catechism

Before leaving Rome to examine the reception of Vatican II around the world, we should recall three postconciliar documents: two codes of canon law and a catechism. When convoking the council in January 1959, John XXIII also announced a revision of the Code of Canon Law for the Western Church. Through long consultations with bishops, episcopal conferences, and experts, the new Code of Canon Law was promulgated by Pope John Paul II in 1983. It contains, 1,752 canons arranged in seven "books," as compared with the first Code of Canon Law promulgated by Pope Benedict XV in 1917, which contained 2,414 canons in five "books." The 1983 code expressed in juridical terms the teaching of Vatican II and its subsequent implementation. A decade after Benedict XV promulgated the Code of 1917, work began on a code of canon law for the Eastern churches in union with Rome. Various drafts were prepared before and after Vatican II. Eventually John Paul II promulgated in 1990 the Code of Canons for the Oriental Churches.

Right from the fourth century, ecumenical or general councils of the church not only taught doctrine but also regularly enacted legislation in the form of "canons" or their equivalent. Thus the first such ecumenical council, Nicaea I (325), legislated against newly baptized being "promoted" at once to the priesthood and episcopate, strongly denounced the habit of some bishops, priests, and deacons who moved from one city to another, and supported the practice of standing during liturgical prayer (against those who knelt to pray on Sundays and during the days of Pentecost). Nicaea I also introduced canons about such matters as the admission to clerical status of good candidates who had suffered castration at the hand of barbarians, the presence of several bishops at an episcopal consecration, the treatment of those who had lapsed during the recent Roman persecutions, the pastoral care of the dying, and similar matters. Thus the post-Vatican II codes of 1983 and 1990 enjoyed conciliar precedents in the long story of the church. But they went beyond these precedents, inasmuch as they systematically legislated for numerous aspects of Catholic life and worship—from the election of popes to the baptism of babies.

The *Catechism of the Catholic Church*, also prepared with the approval of Pope John Paul II and first published (in French) in October 1992, forms a compendium of Catholic teaching and is intended to guide bishops in preparing local catechetical programs. It is divided into four parts: the profession of faith (in which the Apostles' Creed provides the central structure); liturgical celebration (in which the seven sacraments enjoy prime importance); life in Christ (in which a presentation of the Ten Commandments forms the main road map); Christian prayer (in which the Our Father receives particular attention). Being published after the two codes of canon law, the *Catechism* refers to and quotes from them many times, but not nearly as frequently as the scriptures. Biblical references and quotations outnumber the use of all the other sources put together; those other sources include documents from councils and popes and a generous selection of Christian writers from St. Clement of Rome in the first century to St. Teresa of the Child Jesus in the nineteenth. The *Catechism* lives up to the expectations that the bishops at Vatican II expressed in *Dei Verbum*—that catechetics, along with all other forms of Christian instruction, should be "healthily nourished" by the Bible (no. 24). Yet one notices how the use of scriptures at times leaves something to be desired: for instance, the difference between the more "historical" Gospels of Matthew, Mark, and Luke and the more "theological" Gospel of John tends to be glossed over.

Being officially promulgated exactly thirty years after the opening of Vatican II, the *Catechism* encourages the reception of the teaching of the council. In particular, it draws extensively from two documents on the church, *Lumen Gentium* and *Gaudium et Spes*, and from the Constitution on the Sacred Liturgy, *Sacrosanctum Concilium*. In the whole history of the twenty-one general councils of the church, the *Catechism* enjoys only one prototype, the *Roman Catechism* issued on papal authority in 1566. Although called for at the Council of Trent as early as 1546, only one year after the council opened, the Roman Catechism could not be prepared and published until Trent had concluded its work of clarifying Catholic doctrine and practice and had closed in 1563. Its somewhat polemical context and motivation set the 1566 catechism apart from its successor in 1992. The *Roman Catechism* was intended, at least in part, as a Catholic counterpart to the many Protestant and Anglican catechisms, of which the most famous was proving to be Martin Luther's *Small Catechism* of 1527. But when expounding the essential "marks" or characteristics of the church, in particular its unity, the 1992 *Catechism* drew on Vatican II's *Lumen Gentium* and *Unitatis Redintegratio* to describe the separated "Churches and ecclesial communities" with serene love and hope (nos. 817–22).

Around the World

This chapter has set itself to sketch the ways in which various official bodies in Rome, led by Pope Paul VI and Pope John Paul II, have contributed to the reception of Vatican II's teaching and the implementation of its reforms. What of the institutional reception of the council in the wider Catholic world? That reception was furthered through national episcopal conferences, particular dioceses (or eparchies among Eastern Catholics), parishes, universities, colleges, seminaries, hospitals, schools, the houses and monasteries of religious men and women, and Catholic journals and publishing houses.

From the end of the second century, provincial and regional councils brought bishops together. Sometimes their teaching proved enduringly important for the life of Catholic Christianity: for instance, in the case of early councils held in Carthage (North Africa), Orange (France), and Toledo (Spain). Over the centuries and in various numbers, patriarchs, diocesan bishops, and other official leaders have come together, in emergency situations or on a regular basis. In their Decree on the Pastoral Office of Bishops in the Church, the bishops at Vatican II recalled with gratitude this "pooling of resources" between individual dioceses through synods, provincial councils, and plenary councils, and the "outstanding examples of a more fruitful apostolate" and collaboration shown by the episcopal conferences that by the 1960s had already come into existence in different countries. Thus the first national conference

of bishops in the United States met in September 1919; this episcopal conference flourished, and has come to be known, since the
year 2000, as the United States Conference of Catholic Bishops. At
Vatican II the bishops passed various decrees on the nature and
work of episcopal conferences. They judged it to be "in the highest
degree helpful if in all parts of the world the bishops of each country or region would meet regularly, so that by sharing their wisdom
and experience and exchanging views they may jointly formulate a
program for the common good of the Church" (*Christus Dominus*,
36–38). In the postconciliar church the work and even the competence of the national and international conferences of bishops have
experienced many tensions and struggles—within the conferences
themselves and between the conferences and Rome.

After the council closed in December 1965, the existing and
the newly formed episcopal conferences and the episcopal synods
of Eastern churches have played a major role in handling the
implementation of the conciliar teaching and decrees about such
matters as liturgical reform, ecumenical relations, social action, the
training of candidates for the priestly ministry, interreligious dialogue, family life, and catechetical instruction. The 1983 Code of
Canon Law for the Latin Church (nos. 447–59) largely followed
Christus Dominus in its prescriptions for episcopal conferences. But
matters did not rest there, since the 1985 Synod of Bishops discussed the theological and juridical nature of these conferences.
Eventually in 1998, by his "motu proprio" *Apostolos Suos*, John Paul
II limited the powers of episcopal conferences by decreeing that,
for their doctrinal declarations to be authentic teaching, such conferences need the unanimous agreement of all the bishops, or—in
the case of a two-thirds majority—the approval of the Holy See. In
effect, this decision strengthened the authority not only of the
papacy but also of the bishops of individual dioceses. One should
also recall that at Vatican II, despite overwhelming votes for the
final texts, no doctrinal document was approved unanimously or
literally by all the bishops. There were always at least a very few
who voted "no."

As it carefully pointed out, *Apostolos Suos* did *not* apply to
Eastern churches led by a patriarch, and to major archiepiscopal
churches headed by a major archbishop (who enjoys almost all the

prerogatives of a patriarch). These churches are governed by their episcopal synods, which have legislative, juridical, and, in some cases, administrative power. These synods differ from the episcopal conferences of the Latin Church.

When Vatican II ended, its implementation was institutionally administered also at the level of particular dioceses. Where they did not already exist, diocesan pastoral councils and commissions were established to deal with liturgical matters, ecumenical relations, issues of justice and peace, education, and so forth. Within individual dioceses, as at the national level, the degree of vibrant reception of the conciliar reforms has depended not only on the bishops themselves but also on the quality of the various commissions that collaborate with them.

Any summary of the institutions that furthered the renewal required by Vatican II must also pay attention to the contribution that came from such international bodies as the Consejo Episcopal Latinomericano (CELAM), the Federation of Asian Bishops' Conferences (FABC), the Council of European Bishops' Conferences, and the six international unions of episcopal conferences in Africa. Let me comment on the first two such international bodies.

CELAM was a preconciliar foundation, having been organized by the Brazilian Dom Helder Camara (d. 1999) in 1955, in the wake of a General Conference of Latin American Bishops that met in Rio de Janeiro. Camara himself served as vice-president of CELAM from 1958 to 1965. Its aim was to study challenges facing the church in Latin America and coordinate Catholic activities throughout the continent. The social concerns of such outstanding champions of justice and peace as Dom Helder himself fed into the commitment to help poor and afflicted people expressed by Vatican II's *Gaudium et Spes* (for example, nos. 27, 69). Camara and his colleagues hoped to transform Latin America with its impoverished majority into a more humane society by eliminating structures of injustice and encouraging governments to introduce social reforms. CELAM organized general conferences of Latin American bishops in Medellín, Colombia (1968), Puebla, Mexico (1979), and Santo Domingo, Dominican Republic (1994). Camara at times summed up the opposition he faced both in working for social reform in the impoverished northeast of Brazil and in bringing the suffering of third world peoples to the attention of affluent nations: "When I give food to the poor, they call me a saint. When I ask why the poor have no food, they call me a communist." The social reforms that Camara and like-minded bishops expected were hampered not only by some of their own colleagues but also by the military coups in Argentina (1976), Bolivia (1971), Brazil (1964), Chile (1973), Ecuador (1976), and Uruguay (1973)—with those in Argentina and Chile being particularly bloody. Nevertheless, the work of CELAM in implementing the hopes of Vatican II for such vital areas of Catholic life as liturgy, education, peace and justice, and family life has been an inspiring model for regional and continental conferences of bishops that emerged after the council.

Unlike CELAM, FABC was a post-Vatican II creation, which held its first plenary session in 1974. A transnational episcopal structure, it brings together fourteen bishops' conferences from such countries as India, Indonesia, Korea, Japan, and the Philippines. Unlike Latin America where two languages predominate in a continent shaped by the colonial powers of Spain and Portugal, the bishops of FABC represent many language groups and a wide variety of cultural traditions. Add too the fact that, except for the Philippines, Catholics form only a minority, sometimes a tiny minority, in their countries. Right from their 1974 session in Taipei (Taiwan) on "Evangelization in Modern Asia," the bishops and their theological advisors have consistently committed themselves to promoting a shared vision of being the Catholic Church in Asia—the church on mission and in dialogue. They drew initial inspiration and encouragement from Vatican II's Decree on the Relation of the Church to Non-Christian Religions, and from the ecumenical commitment of the council and Pope Paul VI. FABC has forged closer understanding and cooperation with the Christian Conference of Asia, which represents most of the Anglican, Protestant, and Orthodox Churches in Asia. It has consistently encouraged a threefold dialogue with the wider Asian world: a dialogue with the religions of Asia, with the cultures of Asia, and with the poor of Asia. In receiving and going beyond Vatican II, FABC strikingly exemplifies the creative reception of a council, to which we will return in chapter 3, as well as the Asian value of harmony.[15]

Laypeople and Religious

Thus far this chapter has offered a broad survey of the impact Vatican II made (or failed to make) through institutions led by bishops and cardinals. What has been done by local communities, especially by parishes and parish councils (*Apostolicam Actuositatem*, 10)? How too has the council helped and inspired those innumerable devoted laymen and laywomen, who are often neither members of their parish councils nor members of various lay movements? Such laypersons have their stories to tell, whether they are old enough to have experienced the preconciliar church or have known the church only in the postconciliar situation. Any adequate assessment of Vatican II's contribution to holy living among laypersons needs to scrutinize the council's influence on such men and women and not limit itself to movements.

The movements, of course, are also part of the story, whether we examine postconciliar movements or such preconciliar ones as the Focolare ("fireplace" or "hearth") Movement (founded by Chiara Lubich and approved by Rome in 1962) and Opus Dei (founded by St. Josemaría Escrivá de Balaguer y Albás and approved in 1950). The Focolare Movement started in 1943 when Italy was being ravaged by war, strives for unity based on mutual love, and now enjoys over two million male and female members and sympathizers attached to communities around the world. The Focolare constitution requires that the president be a woman. Opus Dei began in 1928, is primarily as a movement for laypersons, and now has nearly 100,000 lay members, dedicated to the sanctification of the world through their holiness lived out at their place of work. Some movements were founded during or after the council, such as L'Arche—an ecumenical and interfaith movement started in 1964 by a Canadian professor of philosophy, Jean Vanier, that provides family-style households for people with intellectual and physical disabilities served by those who live, work, and pray with them. The name comes from the house used by the members of the first community, "Noah's Ark." Vatican II taught that the "charisms" or special gifts of the faithful were vital for the life of the church (*Lumen Gentium*, 12)—a teaching that inspired and encouraged the Charismatic Renewal Movement, which emerged on some American university campuses in 1967 and spread rapidly through prayer groups around the world.

A worldwide account of the living impact of the council would also examine how men and women living a consecrated life of community (involving chastity, poverty, obedience, and common life under a superior) have implemented the conciliar teaching. Such an examination would cover not only such long-standing orders as the Benedictines, Carmelites, Cistercians, Dominicans, Franciscans, Jesuits, and so forth, but also the new religious communities that have come into existence after Vatican II. How have those following religious life put into practice not only the Decree on the Up-to-date Renewal of Religious Life but also the total range of the council's teaching? Have their lives been deeply shaped, for instance, by that constant contact with the scriptures that *Dei Verbum* in its closing chapter expected from all Catholics? Many religious men and women have retrieved and put into practice today the spiritual vision of their founder or foundress. To a lesser extent they have come to live lives based more clearly on the Bible. Some religious have proved outstanding leaders in implementing the teaching and mandates of Vatican II: for instance, about service in the cause of justice and peace.

Another fascinating but neglected way of evaluating the reception of Vatican II would be to examine Catholic journals and newspapers around the world. More and more run by lay editors, such publications have often operated as effective channels for the renewal that the council dreamed of. But we lack any serious studies of postconciliar contributions from such printed sources and their associated institutions. Many journals that one might examine, such as the *Catholic Biblical Quarterly* published by the Catholic Biblical Association since 1939, preexisted the council and helped to prepare its way. Other publishing ventures were postconciliar developments, such as those sponsored by the Catholic Biblical Federation (founded in 1969 and now present in at least 126 nations). The CBF collaborates with other biblical societies in spreading the scriptures everywhere and encouraging all Christians to live that scripturally based existence encouraged by *Dei Verbum* in its final chapter.

From among the scholarly quarterlies let me take one published by the institution where I have spent most of my teaching

life, the *Gregorianum*. The 1966 issues of the *Gregorianum* contained six articles dealing with the conciliar documents. Then followed a 1968 article by René Latourelle (on Vatican II and the signs
of revelation); eight articles on the council's documents appeared in
the *Gregorianum* for 1969. After that promising start, for nearly
twenty years the quarterly published little by way of interpreting,
receiving, and applying the council: two articles (in 1971 and 1973)
on Vatican II's teaching about scripture as the "soul of theology"
and a 1975 article on the meaning of "charism" for the council.
From 1976 the *Gregorianum* began publishing the documents from
the International Theological Council—at best only an indirect
way of promoting the conciliar teaching. Things changed in 1987,
under the new editor (Jacques Dupuis). To help prepare the
October 1987 synod on the "Vocation and Mission of Lay People
in the Church and the World," the *Gregorianum* issued a double
number on "lay people in the Church today," which included four
articles on interpreting and applying relevant aspects of Vatican II's
teaching. Two years later the journal carried a piece on the role of
theologians at the council and three long articles by Angel Antón
on a development fostered by Vatican II: episcopal conferences.
Antón returned to this theme in the *Gregorianum* for 1994, 1995
(two articles), 1996, and 1999. Dialogue with other religions, as
stemming from the conciliar teaching, featured in three articles:
one by Dupuis himself in 1994 and two by Peter Phan (in 2000 and
2002). As the new millennium opened, Jared Wicks published articles in the *Gregorianum* on the origins of the council's Constitution
on Divine Revelation: two articles in 2001 and one in 2002. In 2003
he also wrote a long article for the journal on Yves Congar's contribution to Vatican II. Since the journal had carried only three
articles on Vatican II from 1970 to 1986 inclusive, it hardly functioned as a means for promoting the council's teaching for those
seventeen years. By publishing twenty articles on Vatican II from
1987 to 2003 inclusive, the *Gregorianum* began once again to function as a quarterly concerned to receive and live the conciliar teaching—a change attributable at least partly to the fact that Dupuis
served as editor from 1985 to 2002. Any scholarly study of what the
Gregorianum contributed to the reception of the council would
need, of course, to examine and evaluate in depth the content of

those thirty-eight articles: the fifteen up to 1969, the three from 1970 to 1986, and the twenty from 1986 to 2003.

Receiving a Council

In spelling out the roles that various institutions and individuals in Rome and around the world have played and continue to play in implementing the teaching of Vatican II, I have often linked their work to the provisions of various conciliar documents. But receiving the council was more than a straightforward execution of some mandates or a mere repetition of the council's teaching. John Paul II, in his reception of the council, has repeatedly shown what a creative reception entails in such areas as social teaching, ecumenical relations, and interreligious dialogue. Changing situations call for fresh emphases and developments. The long history of Catholic Christianity shows repeatedly that it takes creative fidelity to effect a rejuvenating reception and promote true development. Both fidelity and creativity have been regularly involved: a fidelity that does not decline into rigidity and a creativity that does not lose its roots in the mainstream tradition. Since I wish to invoke these two elements in later chapters, it would be good to illustrate what I mean from Christian history. A fourth-century family group, known as the Cappadocians, provides a shining example of such creative fidelity. Their performance in the aftermath of Nicaea I (325) yields several principles that set out clearly what drives this creative fidelity. This I shall consider in my next chapter.

Note: For many of the points raised and briefly discussed in this chapter, fuller treatment and bibliographies are available in the *New Catholic Encyclopedia* (Washington, DC: Catholic University of America, 2nd ed., 2003). See "Assyrian Church of the East," vol. 1, 805–8; "Bea, Augustin," vol. 2, 167; "Camara, Helder Pessoa," vol. 2, 899–901; "Charismatic Renewal, Catholic," vol. 3, 392–93; "Consejo Episcopal Latinoamericano (CELAM)," vol. 4, 157–58; "Consilium," vol. 4, 164–65; "Council of European Bishops' Conferences," vol. 4, 296–98; "Curia, Roman," vol. 4, 438–40; "Episcopal Conferences," vol. 5, 299–301; "Federation of Asian

Bishops' Conferences," vol. 5, 660–62; "Focolare Movement," vol. 5, 785–86; "International Commission on English in the Liturgy (ICEL)," vol. 7, 523–25; "International Theological Commission," vol. 7, 527–29; "Liturgy, Articles On," vol. 8, 725–27; "Liturgy of the Hours," vol. 8, 729–36; "Opus Dei," vol. 10, 616–18; "Pontifical Biblical Commission," vol. 11, 476–79; "Pontifical Council for Interreligious Dialogue," vol. 11, 479–80; "Pontifical Councils," vol. 11, 480–83; "Romero, Oscar A.," vol. 12, 365–66; "Saints and Beati," vol. 12, 607–8; "Synod of Bishops," vol. 13, 683–94; "Synod of Bishops, Assemblies," vol. 13, 688–94; "Vatican Council II," vol. 14, 407–18.

3

RECEIVING A COUNCIL
WITH CREATIVE FIDELITY

> As the Arians in denying the Son deny also the Father, so
> also these men [the Pneumatomachians] in speaking evil
> of the Holy Spirit speak evil also of the Son.
>
> St. Athanasius, *Letter to Serapion*

Let me at this point take a long step back in time and examine an outstanding example of receiving and living a general council from a fourth-century family of saints—the Cappadocians. The children of a wealthy landowner, St. Basil the Great (d. 379), his brother St. Gregory of Nyssa (d. ca. 395) and his sister St. Macrina (d. 380), together with St. Gregory of Nazianzus (d. 389), who had studied with Basil in Athens, made up the core of a special group living in Roman Cappadocia in modern Turkey. None of them had been present at the First Council of Nicaea of 325, but all of them were committed to receiving and living its teaching. They did so in a creative way that prepared the ground for the next general council, Constantinople I in 381, at which two of them were major figures, Gregory of Nazianzus and Gregory of Nyssa. They give a wonderful example of what it means to implement conciliar teaching with creative fidelity. Those readers who do not want to take up this historical example and feel that they may lose the Vatican II plot should move at once to chapter 4.

Four Challenges

In the early fourth century Arius, a priest of Alexandria, disturbed the unity of the church just when it was emerging from a time of persecution into unexpected freedom under Emperor Constantine I (d. 337). Arius held that the Son of God was created "out of nothing," and so was neither eternal nor truly divine. He expressed his beliefs in catchy songs that were sung by his followers in church and along the streets. An unimaginative ascetic, Arius assumed that any "generation" of the Son must be just like human generation, in which parents exist *before* their children and then beget them through a physical division of matter. Around 230 bishops assembled at the First Council of Nicaea and all but two of them condemned the views of Arius. From the council came the familiar words of the creed—that Jesus Christ is "God from God, Light from Light, true God from true God, begotten, not made, of one Being *[homoousios]* with the Father." Thus the Son of God is not less than God; in the eternal generation (not creation) of the Son, the "Being" or substance of the Father has been fully communicated; and the Son is co-eternal with the Father.

Against the false teaching of Arius and his followers, Nicaea spoke out clearly for Christ's divinity, but its teaching and terminology continued to run into difficulties for years after the council. The story of what happened to Nicaea's teaching during the decades up to the First Council of Constantinople illustrates the creative fidelity shown by the Cappadocians within a changing situation. Let me pick out four challenges that they had to meet in the years leading up to 381.

1. After the Council of Nicaea, Arius and the Arians did not disappear overnight, but enjoyed wide support among rank-and-file Christians and some church leaders. They continued to reject the true divinity of the Son, holding him to be created out of nothing and hence not co-eternal with the Father. After Arius died (ca. 336), other Arian leaders emerged, such as Eunomius (d. 394), a controversial bishop who spent a lifetime demanding clear and exact beliefs and dismantling

anything mysterious in God. He developed the "Anomean (dissimilar)" doctrine, according to which the Son is a creature who is simply "unlike" the Father and thus radically inferior.

2. Then there were bishops and other Christians who were happy to confess that Jesus Christ is "God from God" but remained uneasy with the Nicene term, *homoousios* (of one being or substance with the Father). It was not biblical. Furthermore, it could be interpreted in a false, "modalist" sense, as if "Father" and "Son" were only different ways or "modes" in which God acts externally and do not express any personal distinctions within God's inner life.

   Related to this terminological problem was the way in which the Council of Nicaea took *ousia* ("being," "essence," "substance") as equivalent to *hypostasis*, itself still an ambiguous term. From the third century into the fourth century, *hypostasis* could mean either (a) essence, or (b) the individuating principle, subject, "sub-sistence," or, as we would say, "person." The upshot for Nicaea of this inherited ambiguity about *hypostasis* was that, by taking *ousia* and *hypostasis* as equivalents, the council ran the risk of *homoousios* being understood in a modalist way. Father and Son are not only of the same being, substance, or essence but are also the same "subsistence"—in sense (b) of *hypostasis*. Then there would be no real distinction between Father and Son; they would not be distinct, individual subsistences or persons.

3. At the Council of Nicaea, the humanity of Christ had not been an issue. Apollinarius of Laodicea (d. ca. 390) put it on the agenda by pushing faith in Christ's divinity to an extreme. A forceful defender of the council and sharp critic of Arius, he held that when the Word of God "became flesh" (John 1:14), the Word assumed a human body but itself took the place of the rational, human soul. In other words, a unilateral defense of

Christ's divinity led Apollinarius to maintain that Christ did not have a rational soul and so did not fully share our human condition. By rigidly defending Nicaea's teaching, Apollinarius finished up holding Christ to be truly divine but not completely human. One finds here a vigorous but spurious reception of conciliar teaching that in fact corrupts orthodox teaching.

4. At the Council of Nicaea the divine identity of the Holy Spirit was not an issue. Arius had almost nothing to say about the Spirit. Hence the Nicene Creed was content to end very briefly: [We believe] "in the Holy Spirit." Since the creed explicitly recognizes the divinity shared by Father and Son, it implies that the Spirit, who is also the object of Christian faith, shares in the same divinity. In the aftermath of Nicaea the divine identity of the Spirit came, however, under explicit fire. Various Pneumatomachians ("fighters against the Spirit") emerged during the second half of the fourth century to question and deny the divinity of the Holy Spirit. Arians, like Eunomius, since they held the Son to be a creature and radically inferior to the Father, argued even more for the created, inferior status of the Spirit.

The Response of the Cappadocians

The Cappadocians grappled with all four challenges, of which the first two had been explicitly met at the Council of Nicaea and the other two surfaced in the decades that followed.

1. As regards the first challenge, Basil and the two Gregorys saw Bishop Eunomius with his extreme Arian doctrine as their primary theological opponent. They all wrote works against him. The two Gregorys proved more penetrating than Basil in their analysis and rejection of the teaching of Eunomius and his followers. These Arians were particularly strong in Constantinople, where Gregory of Nazianzus went as bishop in

378. He preached five sermons (his *Orations* 27–31) against a large number of Eunomians and encouraged the minority of orthodox Christians to remain faithful to the teaching of Nicaea. Around the same time Gregory of Nyssa wrote treatises against Eunomius himself. Clearly the two Gregorys faced in Eunomius a subtler and more brilliant adversary than Arius had ever been. Gregory of Nazianzus had to probe carefully into the eternal generation of the Son, while also insisting on this divine generation as an incomprehensible heavenly mystery that should be "honored by silence" (*Orations* 3, 4, 8–10). He concluded this sermon by basing his belief in the Son's divinity on the witness of the scriptures (ibid., 17–20).

2. The Cappadocians obviously took the biblical witness to be normative and to support authoritatively the Nicene confession of Christ's divinity. Terminology did not, however, enjoy such ultimate normativity, and they felt free to introduce modifications. As regards the one nonbiblical term adopted in the Nicene confession, *homoousios* (of one being), and the difficulties it triggered, Basil helped to sweep aside some misinterpretations. But then he and his colleagues made a new move in language: There is an identity of being or essence (*ousia*) between Father, Son, and Holy Spirit. But they are distinct *hypostaseis* (subsistences or, as we would say, persons) (*Letter* 210,5).

In this letter we find Basil not only faithfully championing the teaching of Nicaea I but also partially switching away from the council's terminology. No longer are *ousia* and *hypostasis* being used as equivalents. Like Gregory of Nazianzus, Basil writes of one *ousia* (the one, identical being or essence of God) or one *physis* (nature) and three *hypostaseis* or *prosôpa* (individual, personal subsistences, subjects, or persons) in God (*Letters* 51 and 52).[1] This trinitarian terminology was to be adopted by a synod of 382 that followed the Council of Constantinople. In its letter to Pope Damasus, the synod confessed "one divinity, power or essence *[ousia]*" in "three most perfect *hypostaseis*, that is, in three perfect *prosôpa*."[2] Through the Cappadocians the distinction between *ousia* and *hypostasis* prevailed as the standard terminology.

3. Against Apollinarius's misguided attempt to defend the Nicene Creed by affirming Christ's true divinity at the expense of his complete humanity, Gregory of Nazianzus insisted that the Word of God assumed the full human condition at the incarnation (*Letter* 101). In 381 the First Council of Constantinople, at which he presided for some time, condemned the errors of Apollinarius (DzH 151; ND 13). After the council a letter sent to Pope Damasus by a synod held in 382 called Christ "perfect" or "full man."[3] Several years after the Council of Constantinople, Gregory of Nyssa followed up the refutation of Apollinarian errors in what remains the most important extant work against that heresy, *Antirrheticus adversus Apollinarem*.

4. The Cappadocians refuted the Pneumatomachians or those who wrongly understood the Holy Spirit to be only a creature who differed from other creatures merely in rank and not in nature. This meant springing to the defense of the divine identity of the Holy Spirit. Basil did this in a work (*De Spiritu Sancto*) in which he also engaged in polemic against the Arians for denying the divinity of the Son (8.20). Basil knew that a true doctrine of the Holy Spirit stood or fell with a true doctrine of the Son, and vice versa. Believers could not know or say anything of the Spirit apart from the Spirit's relationship with the Father and the Son. The Father and the Son are necessarily involved in any reference to the Spirit. This conviction about the relationship between the Father, Son, and Holy Spirit underpinned the Cappadocians' belief

about the inseparable quality of the Trinity's activity. Each act of God, as Basil put it, is "initiated by the Father, effected by the Son, and perfected by the Spirit" (*De Spiritu Sancto*, 16.38). Both in activity and being, each of the three persons is totally related to the other two.

To what extent was this championing of the Holy Spirit and, more widely, the trinitarian theology of the Cappadocians reflected in the Creed of Constantinople? The council retained the Nicene language about the Son as *homoousios* or "of one being" with the Father, but refrained from applying this term to the Holy Spirit. The divinity of the Spirit was confessed by the language of being "worshipped" and "glorified" together with the Father and the Son. The Spirit, who "proceeds from the Father," receives the adoration due only to God. The council may well have adopted more guarded speech about the Holy Spirit, in order to avoid the controversies that using *homoousios* to express the Son's divinity provoked after Nicaea I. The bishops at Constantinople I probably hoped that their totally biblical language about the Holy Spirit might win over at least some of those who had been denying the Spirit's divinity.

To sum up, in the aftermath of the Council of Nicaea, the Cappadocians continued to support the rejection of Arius and the Arians, but they felt free to change the terminology of Nicaea (which used *ousia* and *hypostasis* as equivalents). They met the new challenge coming from Apollinarius's one-sided orthodoxy, which tampered with the full human condition of the incarnate Son. They also met the new challenge of those who denied the divinity of the Spirit, and supported some relevant additions to the creed. This record illustrates what it means to speak of a conciliar reception being characterized by creative fidelity.

But what inspired the Cappadocians (and others like Athanasius) to oppose the Arians, the Apollinarians, and the Pneumatomachians and insist on the divinity of the Son and the

Spirit and the completeness of the humanity assumed by the Son at the incarnation? What gave them the freedom to modify the conciliar language of Nicaea and even add what was almost a new article to the Nicene Creed?

Principles for Reception

The Cappadocians shared four deep commitments, three of which fed into and shaped their doctrinal teaching and the fourth of which empowered their social teaching and practice. These commitments concern, respectively, the saving work of Christ and his Holy Spirit, the worship of the community, the normative authority of the scriptures, and Christ's call to minister to the sick and destitute. We can distinguish but never separate these four commitments. They overlap obviously and persistently, just as the doctrine and practice of the Cappadocians are distinguishable but not separable.

1. Basil and others showed persistent sensitivity to what the Son and the Holy Spirit have done and continue to do for our salvation. Apropos of the Holy Spirit, Basil pointed to the sanctifying work of the Spirit that reveals a divine identity (*De Spiritu Sancto*, passim). Since God alone is holy by nature, only a divine agent can bring us the reality and the experience of being made holy. Long before the fourth century, such an experience of salvation had already fueled the confession of the divinity of the Son. He must be divine, St. Irenaeus of Lyons (d. ca. 200) argued, if he were "to give us salvation" (*Adversus Haereses*, 3.18.7). The same experiential argument drove the Cappadocians: Experiencing through Christ the forgiveness of sins, the new life of grace, and the hope of glory, they insisted on his divine identity. Only God could bring about this experience. It took one who is by nature Son of God to have effected what they experienced: the unmerited status as God's adopted sons and daughters who share in the divine life itself. This experience of

being "divinized" through the Son and the Holy Spirit mobilized the Cappadocians in opposition to Arians and Pneumatomachians, groups who challenged the true divine identity of Christ and his Spirit.

In the case of Christ, the Cappadocians' sensitivity to what he had done for human salvation also involved the human condition he had assumed at the incarnation. They knew that he had taken on the whole human condition, because they experienced the fullness of salvation *also* coming through his humanity. Unless the Son had assumed a complete humanity including a rational soul, their rational souls could not have experienced full salvation. Gregory of Nazianzus summed up this conclusion in his lapidary phrase: "the unassumed is the unhealed" (*Letter* 101, 32). Basil wrote similarly of Christ needing to take on true humanity if he were to do what we know him to have done—namely, destroy the power of sin and death "from the inside" (*Letter* 261, 2). A sensitive reflection on their experience of salvation supported the faith of the Cappadocians that they were saved both "from the (divine) outside" (through the divine persons of the Son and the Spirit) and "from the (human) inside" (through the full human condition of the Son). As Gregory of Nazianzus put it, for sinful human beings to be "fashioned afresh," this needed to be effected "by one who was wholly man and at the same time God" (*Letter* 101, 15).

2. The Cappadocians were inspired to receive and live the teaching of Nicaea through their awareness of the redeeming work of Christ and the Spirit in Christian worship. Their experience of baptism, confirmation, and the Eucharist supported their fidelity and productive freedom. The baptismal profession of faith in God as one and three, along with the eucharistic "remembering" (*anamnesis*) of Christ's life, death, and resurrection, the invocation (*epiclesis*) of the Holy

Spirit, and the concluding *doxology* or giving glory to God the Father, provided for them "the law of praying" that is "the law of believing" (*lex orandi lex credendi*)—a "law" of trinitarian praying that shaped a "law" of trinitarian believing. The principle was to be formulated in the following century by St. Prosper of Aquitaine (d. ca. 463),[4] but the Cappadocians and others in the fourth century already sensed that liturgical prayer was the heart of their Christian life and played an essential role toward interpreting their faith in God as tripersonal and the challenges that faith met.

When opening his treatise on the Holy Spirit, Basil reported how he himself prayed; later in the same work he gave "glory to the Father and to the Son and to the Holy Spirit" (27.68). The early church had developed for their worship what came to be known as the "subordinate" doxology: "Glory to the Father *through* the Son and *in* the Holy Spirit." When Arians abused this doxology to argue that the Son was inferior to the Father and that the Spirit was inferior to the Son, Basil encouraged a "coordinate" doxology, which had already existed in the third century: "Glory to the Father with *[meta]* the Son, together with *[sun]* the Holy Spirit." Eventually the "coordinate" doxology prevailed in general liturgical usage as "Glory be to the Father and to the Son and to the Holy Spirit." Basil believed that this form of the doxology met and overcame the errors of the Arians and Pneumatomachians. Praising the Son and the Holy Spirit equally "with" the Father acknowledged the divinity of the Son and the Spirit. Worship guided Basil's account of his faith in the tripersonal God.

3. The inspired biblical texts, without which community worship was unthinkable, provided a further, decisive norm when the Cappadocians expounded their trinitarian faith against Arians and Pneumatomachians. Thus Gregory of Nazianzus ended his third oration

with the authoritative scriptural witness for his case that the Son shares one and the same nature with the Father (*Orationes*, 17–20). While they did not minimize the difficulties that faced those who interpret scripture,[5] they gave their unqualified loyalty to the biblical witness and its first-order language. Hence they felt free in their usage of second-order, philosophical terminology. The classic example of this freedom came with their willingness to move beyond Nicene teaching and distinguish *ousia* (being or essence) from *hypostasis* (subsistence or person).

4. Along with their experience of salvation and community worship (which drew constantly on biblical texts), the discerning and innovative fidelity of the Cappadocians can be recognized in what it led them to do: in that service of the suffering where the "law" of praying and the "law" of believing move into the "law" of living and acting (*"lex orandi, lex credendi, lex vivendi/agendi"*). In the New Testament and the works of early Christian writers, *leitourgia* referred both to Christian worship and to the obligation to meet the material needs of others. The double usage of this term suggests the essential bond between worship and social action through the service of the suffering.[6] Those whom Jesus expected his followers to help included the hungry, the thirsty, strangers, the naked, the sick, and prisoners (Matt 25:31–46). This list of suffering people with whom Christ identified himself did not explicitly include a typical Old Testament pair of sufferers: widows and orphans. But the list was obviously open-ended. Christ's parable of the Good Samaritan powerfully illustrated what he wanted from all: the willingness to help any human being in distress (Luke 10:30–37). The words of Jesus from Matthew 25 and Luke 10, along with the parable of the rich man and the poor Lazarus (Luke 16:19–31), have influenced and disturbed the conscience of Christians

down through the centuries—not least, the conscience of the Cappadocians.

When a very severe famine struck Cappadocia in 368, Basil spent his money in providing for the hungry and homeless and encouraged others to engage in famine relief. His sister Macrina was outstanding in service to the starving poor. When the famine eased, Basil built a hospice on his family's country estate and staffed it with doctors, nurses, cooks, and other servants to provide medical care for the sick, housing for needy travelers, and food for the hungry. His brother Gregory of Nyssa and his friend Gregory of Nazianzus joined Basil in preaching on true love for the poor and starving. Other fourth-century Christian leaders shared their practical concern for the destitute, and Basil's hospice was not unprecedented. Nevertheless, his Cappadocian family was second to none in alleviating the sufferings of the sick and starving. To mobilize further relief and overcome the selfish opportunism of those who had hoarded grain supplies to keep prices high, Basil, Gregory of Nazianzus, and Gregory of Nyssa preached vigorous sermons on the sufferings of the hungry and sick.[7] The love of neighbor that they and Macrina practiced also vindicated the creative fidelity with which they received the teaching of the Council of Nicaea. "By their fruits" we can know them in their authentic reception of the council.

Thus we may glean from the Cappadocians four tests of creative fidelity in the reception of conciliar teaching and decrees: (1) a deeper experience of salvation that comes through real sensitivity to the work of Christ and the Holy Spirit; (2) a richer experience of life-giving worship in the community; (3) fidelity to biblical witness; and (4) a generous service of those who suffer. These are still four daunting tests in the twenty-first century when we commit ourselves to living by the teaching of Vatican II. When we follow some particular path in receiving and living Vatican II, the example of the

Cappadocians raises the questions: Does *this* way of receiving the council involve our being led by the Holy Spirit and by Christ? Does it help us to worship better? Is it being illuminated and supported by prayerful reflection on the scriptures? Does it lead us to a more generous service of the needy?

I am not alleging that these four questions can be answered easily and at once. But if we do not even ask these questions, it becomes much harder to discern and practice the creative fidelity that Vatican II requires. In my next chapter I will reflect on something very dear to the Cappadocians, the rejuvenating experience of liturgical reform in the aftermath of the council.

4

LITURGICAL PROGRESS

The first and indispensable source of the true Christian spirit is the active participation of the faithful in the most holy mysteries and in the public and solemn prayer of the Church.

> St. Pius X, *Tra le sollecitudini* (1903), introduction

In the liturgy God speaks to his people, and Christ is still proclaiming his Gospel.

> Vatican II, *Sacrosanctum Concilium*, 33

Over the years we have experienced the various changes in liturgy, language, and sanctuary layout imposed by priests, religious and activist members of the laity.

> Denis O'Leary, *The Tablet*, March 1, 2003

What liturgical renewal has happened and is happening in the Catholic Church around the world? What might be my dreams for liturgical celebration in the years to come?

On Not Ignoring the Eastern Catholic Churches

Although I am writing this chapter about the Roman rite and the Catholic Church of the West, I want to start with the Eastern Catholic churches. The story of their liturgical life, both before and after Vatican II, is very different from that in the West. Eastern Catholic churches enjoy different and richer liturgical resources and traditions. It is no surprise, then, that the Eastern churches have introduced more limited liturgical changes in the aftermath of Vatican II.

Members of the Roman rite have regularly forgotten to recall the long experience of vernacular and the variety of eucharistic prayers in Eastern Catholic churches. It can be useful to remind many Western Catholics who speak, with praise or criticism, of "the changes in the liturgy after Vatican II," that they are speaking only of the Roman rite or the Western Church and not of the very different history and experience of worship among the Eastern Christians. They are also probably unaware that the majority of the changes in the Latin liturgy implemented after the council show direct influence from the Eastern Catholic churches, which have preserved early liturgical traditions of Catholic Christianity: for instance, celebrating the liturgy in the vernacular, concelebration of the Eucharist, having communion under both species, and changing the rite for the sacrament of penance to allow for the confessor and penitent to sit face-to-face.

Progress Made in Western Catholicism

In pre-Vatican II days the people of God were assembled but separated within the one church building. Many Western Catholics spoke of "going to Mass" or "hearing Mass." Except in those countries (for example, Germany) where solid liturgical renewal had preceded the council, people assisted at the liturgy but hardly participated in it. Some used their own missal to follow what the priest whispered at the altar; others said the rosary or adopted traditional prayers to fill in the time from the sermon to holy communion. Although assembled within the one church building, the faithful pursued their private prayers and separate devotions. An altar rail physically separated the priest in the sanctuary from the people in the body of the church. Priest and people were also divided by language, with the priest reciting in Latin the entire Mass (including the readings from scripture). The people of God were assembled within the one church building but separated from the priest.

On weekdays, in those churches or colleges that had a number of priests on the staff, altar boys would lead individual priests out of the sacristy to side altars. Four or five "private" Masses could be simultaneously and inaudibly going on at the same time. There was no concelebration that could have expressed visibly how those ordained are united in the one priesthood of Christ and minister together to all the people of God.

But now the local languages have been introduced and made it easier for everyone to participate more fully in public worship.[1] We saw that the Eastern Catholic churches have a richer tradition. Now the West has been enriched by three eucharistic prayers added in 1969 alongside "the Roman Canon" or First Eucharistic Prayer. In 1974, two eucharistic prayers for reconciliation and three for children were introduced, and were used "experimentally" by many episcopal conferences until 1980. John Paul II then extended the permission indefinitely.

The revised lectionary, published in the local languages, has enriched the Liturgy of the Word by letting the congregation hear readings from the entire Bible: for instance, by drawing the gospel passages from all four evangelists. This was a most welcome improvement over a situation in which St. Mark was neglected and with monotonous regularity certain passages from St. Matthew were read (in Latin) at Mass. For instance, the parable of the wise and foolish virgins (Matt 25:1–13) was repeatedly prescribed for feasts of women saints. Now the lectors, who are normally laypeople, read a passage from the Old Testament, a responsorial psalm, and a passage from one of the New Testament epistles. Deacons or priests proclaim or sing the gospel. One particularly welcome change comes on Palm Sunday when the version of Our Lord's passion from Matthew, Mark, or Luke is now proclaimed as the gospel. Rather than providing only once a year (on Good Friday) the passion account of John, Holy Week begins with the story of Christ's suffering and death from one of the Synoptic Gospels. This sets the religious tone for the week that follows.

Instead of being received kneeling at the altar rail and on the tongue, holy communion is normally received standing and in the hand—a dignified and more adult practice retrieved from early Christianity. Lay ministers assist the celebrant in distributing communion, as well as in bringing communion later to the sick and aged. We are fed by God's word and then by God's meal. Through the Liturgy of the Word and the Liturgy of the Eucharist, God works on us and in us. Both the Liturgy of the Word and the Liturgy of the Eucharist should receive their appropriate weight.

What does a well-prepared Sunday Mass look like in the three continents where I have spent most of my life: Europe, North America, and Australia? Even before the Mass begins, the gathered community appreciates, with various degrees of awareness, that its coming together symbolizes a basic presupposition for worship. They have assembled for the unique privilege of praising God as a community united by faith and baptism. Led by a crossbearer, altar boys and girls, and the adults who will act as readers and eucharistic ministers (officially called "extraordinary ministers of holy communion"), and often flanked by a married deacon, the parish priest (or associate pastor) enters the main door or aisle of the church, while the congregation is directed by a cantor in singing an opening or "gathering" hymn. In a unified liturgical space, the altar, presidential chair, and ambo stand out and fit visually together. Candles and flowers enhance the significance of the altar, and do not detract from its role in symbolizing Christ and the peace he brings.[2]

Two servers with candles often flank the deacon or priest when he proclaims the gospel. Incense may be used to express and heighten a perception of the holiness of the altar, of the gospel book, of the gifts brought up at the offertory procession, of the president of the liturgical assembly, and of the entire congregation gathered in worship. During the institution narrative of the Eucharistic Prayer, bells can intensify faith in the presence of Christ, provided this does not give the impression that the rest of the Prayer (in particular, the *epiclesis* or invocation of the Holy Spirit and the doxology to God the Father) is somehow less significant.[3] The sign of peace given to each other by the entire congregation dramatizes a loving communion between priest and faithful, and among all the faithful—a union with Christ and one another expressed and enacted at once in holy communion.

At the end of Mass, servers, readers, the cantor, the deacon, and the eucharistic ministers flank the priest at the closing blessing, which is carried out to sick members of the parish by eucharistic ministers when they now leave to bring holy communion to the shut-ins. Quite visibly that final blessing, with its associated dismissal, conveys a sense of the Eucharist or *leitourgia* empowering the service or *diakonia* of others. During the Mass the second invocation of the Holy Spirit or *epiclesis* has gifted the liturgical assembly to act as the body of Christ for others in daily life.[4] At the final blessing and dismissal we can sense how that service of others is about to begin at once.

As we saw in chapter 3, *leitourgia* denoted in the early church both worship and the service of those in need. On October 19, 2003, the beatification of Mother Teresa of Calcutta in Rome delivered another vivid instance of the union between worship and service. Front seats in St. Peter's Square were reserved for 3,500 poor people. After the Mass they were invited to have lunch in the Hall of Paul VI with Sister Nirmala Joshi, Mother Teresa's successor as the superior general of the Missionaries of Charity. The meal was served by ambassadors of the UN Food and Agriculture Organization. Such an integration of worship with a life of service and justice is proposed at "ordinary" Masses in parishes, when the intercessory prayers remind us of the whole world and its needs and so call on the worshippers to use their worldly goods for the benefit of the entire human family. Some parishes in wealthier communities practice a union of worship and service by being twinned with parishes in the developing world.

In very many parishes, the beauty, rhythm, and simplicity of Sunday Masses glorify the tripersonal God and work to save, serve, and sanctify human beings. Yet, what needs yet to be done if the far-reaching liturgical renewal mandated by Vatican II is to be fully accepted, absorbed, and implemented at all levels?

Dreams for the Priesthood

In the performance of the Eucharist and the other sacraments, the central protagonist is the risen Christ, who through the Holy Spirit worships the Father and brings salvation to human beings. At public worship, priest and people enter a situation shaped in the most vivid way by the tripersonal God. Not a simple social event in which a human community merely celebrates itself, the liturgy enlists the worshippers in a sacred drama that is essentially fashioned by the Father, Son, and Holy Spirit.[5] The Mass opens with the sign of the cross and closes with the blessing, both of which invoke the names of the Trinity. The collects are normally addressed to God the Father through Christ in the Holy Spirit. The creed, with an article dedicated to each divine person, reminds those assembled for Sunday worship of their trinitarian faith. The eucharistic prayers are shaped by the *anamnesis* and *epiclesis* as they lead up to the *doxology*. The *anamnesis* as "remembering" brings to mind God's saving actions in history, especially in Christ's passion, death, resurrection, and glorification. The first *epiclesis* asks that the Holy Spirit descend to change the gifts of bread and wine into the body and blood of Christ; the second *epiclesis*, after the words of institution, asks the Spirit to make the communicants live as the body of Christ in the world. Then the *doxology* or "giving glory" to God completes the Eucharistic Prayer by directing "all glory and honor" to God the Father through Christ and in the unity of the Holy Spirit. The eucharistic worship of believers is unthinkable without the trinitarian *anamnesis*, *epiclesis*, and *doxology* into which they devoutly enter.

What are my dreams for priests? What should a reformed and renewed priesthood achieve in and for the liturgy? Six suggestions can be made.[6]

First, a liturgically committed priest would have convened a liturgical committee for the parish or community, and would regularly meet with them. He would hear what they have to propose about their common worship and share with them in preparing it, especially the Sunday liturgy. I remember one chaplain of a student community at a famous German university. His preaching was dull and ineffective, until he began studying the readings with the students, listening to their insights, and allowing them to shape his homilies. They helped him to achieve a dramatic improvement in what he said on Sundays.

Second, a priest who cares about the liturgy would never celebrate Mass without having read through the collect and other prayers and "set up" the missal by putting the markers carefully in place. He could not allow himself to stand at the altar thumbing through the missal in search of a preface, while he distractedly addresses the people with the preliminary "The Lord be with you" and "Lift up your hearts."

Third, homilies should be filled with the intense power of God and respond to the questions, fears, and hopes of the people. Homilies will certainly fail to convey the presence of the risen Christ and his transforming grace, as *Sacrosanctum Concilium* expected (no. 33), if the preacher neglects to spend time in serious preparation. One American parish priest, when welcoming young assistant priests, used to tell them, "Each week you must take one day off for relaxation, and you must spend one day preparing your homily for the following Sunday." If pleased by the first rule of the rectory, the young priests were startled at the second rule, but soon came to appreciate its value.[7] The Liturgy of the Word leads up to the homily, which too often is still a whimper rather than a bang. We need far more Christ-centered, imaginative, and well-aimed preaching that can touch and change the lives of people.

Too often homilies fail through two faults. They become tedious exercises in moralizing, summed up years ago by a poet as little more than the exhortation, "Be good, be kind, and God save the Queen." Or else preachers cover a range of topics and do so in a highly superficial manner. The wife of one Lutheran pastor would chide her husband afterwards, "You were trying once again to present the whole of salvation history."

Fourth, my ideal priest will also want his deacons and readers to prepare carefully their assigned texts and proclaim them effectively. A priest should make much of the blessing that introduces men and women into the ranks of readers ("lectors") and acolytes, and consult with them about the formal attire suitable for their ministry. The eucharistic ministers also play a key liturgical role. It is impossible to take too much trouble over their preparation, the ceremony that introduces them into the ministry, and their appropriate attire. That might include a suitable sash or an eye-catching medal, which is given them at their initiation into the ministry and worn when they exercise their ministry.

Fifth, the priest of my dreams will celebrate the Eucharist and the other sacraments reverently and audibly. The divine company he is keeping at Mass should be reflected in the way the priest delivers his words and holds his body. He will never render the eucharistic drama banal and verbose by capitulating to the desire to explain everything; he will never trivialize the texts by any "chatty" additions and alterations.[8] The awed silence that precedes the opening collect helps worshippers to realize that they are in God's presence. One can also experience an awesome numinosity in the two offertory prayers, recited when the priest holds up the bread and then the wine. If the presiding celebrant races through these two prayers or combines them in a "time-saving" fashion, the people lose a sense of a solemn address to the first person of the Trinity, the source of all existence within the Godhead and beyond. The divine company he is keeping at Mass should be reflected in the way the priest delivers his words and holds his body.

What one expects from the presiding priest or bishop is not simply a matter of communication skills, although they obviously help. What is to be expected from those who preside at the Eucharist (or other forms of worship) is that they preside prayerfully in the presence of God and show a transparent care and compassion for their fellow men and women.

Sixth, my ideal presiding priest will be even more sensitive than most people to the fact that many young people find the normal liturgy removed from their lived experiences. The young often declare Mass to be "boring" rather than an indispensable source of power and light for their daily existence. Through what they see, hear, smell, touch, and taste, they will be enabled to "connect" and enjoy a sense of belonging at the liturgy. Some parishes use audiovisuals to accompany the homily and general intercessions. Others enhance the offertory procession with symbolic dance drawn from different cultures. I have seen effective liturgical dance done by Africans coming down the aisle to drumbeats and by Indian women in saris dancing with lights and flowers.[9]

Most of all, the young want to be involved in the liturgy—by carrying candles, reading lessons, leading the congregation as cantors, singing in the choir, playing musical instruments, ringing bells, swinging thuribles full of incense, and acting as ushers. One parish I know was blessed by a young woman flautist who accompanied an Indian priest when he sang the Eucharistic Prayer. She rejoiced in contributing her talents, and the whole congregation grew in devotion to the Mass. Each Pentecost in Rome, at the end of a hearty liturgy young firemen climb up on the outside of the Pantheon, and through the opening at the top of that old temple shower down on the congregation red rose petals to symbolize an outpouring of the Holy Spirit. I have never known a more cheerful ending to the Mass.

On a visit to California in 2003, I asked two outstanding lay Catholics what advice they would give to those concerned to serve the young. "Change the music and make the youth Masses even better," they told me. Their response echoed the practice of John Paul II in ministering to the young, with the highlight being the World Youth Days that he started back in 1986. More than a million young people came to Rome, for example, to celebrate the Jubilee Year with him in the summer of 2000 (August 15–20). The city of Rome hung banners and flags along the streets leading to the major churches and most significant monuments. Special posters and tapestries adorned the cathedral of St. John Lateran and St. Peter's Basilica. The celebration ended with a megagathering: an all-night vigil and a Sunday morning Mass with the pope on the grounds of a university on the outskirts of Rome. As a young bishop during the Second Vatican Council, John Paul II got to know the monks of Taizé through praying and eating with them in their small apartment in Rome.[10] For sixty years their monastery in France has been a mecca for young people of all persuasions. In summer the surrounding fields fill up with tents, and young men and women learn to love the meditative music of the eighty monks. Set to simple tunes and repeated with harmonies provided by voices and instruments, the texts linger in the memory—like the Spanish melody sung at the end of the day in the candlelit church: "By night, by night, we journey—simply to find the source. Only our thirst lights the way, only our thirst lights the way."

All these helps toward participating "knowingly, actively and faithfully" (*Sacrosanctum Concilium*, 11) aim at nothing less than enabling the young to encounter Jesus. If/when they experience him, they will not find him "boring." The Mass is charged with the powerful presence of the crucified and risen Christ. He is present through such symbolic objects as the altar, the crucifix, and the Easter candle. His presence is conveyed by the scriptural readings and the homily. Through the invocation of the Holy Spirit and the words of consecration, he becomes present under the appearances of bread and wine. Christ is present as his brothers and sisters gather to celebrate the liturgy and bring with them their sufferings and hopes. But nothing puts Christ more vividly before the eyes of the young and others than the presiding priest radiant with and enthusiastic at what he celebrates: the crucified and risen Christ who can powerfully change our lives forever. He has encountered Jesus and lives by his good news. He shares Jesus with the young and with all the members of his congregation. His attitude charges the atmosphere with Christ.

In many countries around the world young Catholics, especially when compared with an earlier generation that lived through the Second World War (1939–45) and the postwar years that led up to Pope John and his council, have a weaker sense of being affiliated institutionally with the church. Many of them rightly feel that they were deprived of a solid religious education. Too often the classes they attended aimed at promoting their human development without also helping them to understand the meaning and life-giving nature of basic Catholic and Christian beliefs. But many remain firm about such doctrines as the divinity of Christ, his real presence in the Eucharist, and life after death. Many identify positively with some aspects of Catholicism, but they define Catholicism in their own terms. When it comes to making important personal decisions, they do not automatically accept official Catholic teaching as authoritative but rely on their own experience, education, and conscience. Nevertheless, where they find thoughtful homilies, good music, and a sense of community, the parish Eucharist will continue to be the center of their Catholic spirituality and life. The quality of the liturgy is often the decisive factor in the decision to attend.[11]

Augustine Birrell, the British Secretary to Ireland (1907–16), was asked once by the government in London to report on the level of faith and practice among the Irish. For many decades at home and around the world Catholic teachers were to quote his reply: "It is the Mass that matters." Birrell's remark has lost none of its force. When they are fed from the bread of the scriptures and the bread of the Eucharist, the Mass provides Catholics, young and old, with a deep and transforming experience of the living Christ. It focuses and fosters their commitment to him and to one another. Through his powerful presence they are strengthened to renew the church, work for the good of all human beings, and bring to the world the ultimate good news that is Christ himself. If he were alive today, Birrell might have said, "The Mass puts a tiger in the tank."

I do not want, however, to indulge excessively idealistic expectations about the celebration of the Eucharist, either with the young or with others. John's Gospel proves helpful here, with its theme of "disturbed" meals that runs through the narrative. A "misunderstanding" occurs between Jesus and his mother at a marriage feast when the wine runs out (2:3–4). The miraculous feeding of the five thousand (6:1–15) leads into a beautiful discourse about the bread of life, but that ends with many disciples leaving Jesus and with the first warning about Judas's treachery (6:25–71). A later meal proves the occasion of deadly threats against Jesus, and disputes about "wasting" precious nard to anoint his feet (12:1–11). The betrayal of Jesus casts its shadow over the Last Supper (13:21–30). The crises associated with all these meals warn us that the saving presence of Jesus in the eucharistic meals in the coming history of the church may also involve disturbances, misunderstandings, and even painful crises.

Five Dreams for Bishops and Liturgical Commissions

Thus far my liturgical dreams have circled around the local parish community and its presiding priest. Let me move to the level of the cathedral and the bishop, the chief liturgist in the diocese. *Cathedral,* as many readers will know, comes from a Latin word that was taken over from a Greek word with the same meaning, *cathedra* or chair. Here it refers to the chair on which the bishop sits and from which he exercises his role as teacher, pastor, and chief liturgical celebrant for the whole diocese. Vatican II left us a lovely paragraph about cathedrals being the central churches of their dioceses. Cathedrals focus the faith of the local community, especially when people gather with their priests and other ministers around the bishop who presides at the Eucharist (*Sacrosanctum Concilium,* 41). In celebrating with priests and people at the Chrism Mass on Holy Thursday, the Easter Triduum (Good Friday, Holy Saturday, and Easter Sunday), ordinations, confirmations, and other ceremonies for the diocese, the bishop gives an indispensable liturgical lead to all his flock. At this level he should work closely with those who staff the cathedral, with his diocesan liturgical commission, and with the national liturgical commission of the episcopal conference. But what specific dreams do I entertain for those who lead liturgically at the diocesan and national levels?

My first dream concerns the missal and the rituals being translated into the local languages. Episcopal conferences have repeatedly asked the central Roman authorities to let them go ahead in translating and approving the liturgical texts themselves. This permission has been repeatedly refused. In an interview published by *Famiglia Cristiana* on December 14, 2003, the Japanese Cardinal Stephen Fumio Hamao, the president of the Pontifical Council for the Pastoral Care of Migrants and Itinerants, declared, "One doesn't understand why the translations of the liturgical texts ought be approved by Rome. Here no one knows Japanese. Yet before being used, a text in this language must be examined by the Roman Curia." He recalled what other bishops had said earlier: "Remarks like these have been made many times at the Synods [of Bishops], but without any effect." The authority of bishops to legislate about liturgical matters in their different countries became an issue when the council in its first session took up the reform and renewal of the liturgy. *Sacrosanctum Concilium* left matters open: "Regulation of the sacred liturgy belongs solely" to "the Apostolic See and, as law may determine, to the bishop." It added: "In virtue of power granted by law, the regulation of the liturgy within defined limits belongs also to various kinds of territorial episcopal conferences" (no. 22). As a peritus at Vatican II who was involved in the making of the Constitution on the Sacred Liturgy wrote, the years since the council have seen "an ongoing tug of war between Roman authorities and national conferences of bishops in the area of liturgy."[12] According to the 1983 Code of Canon Law (no. 838, #3), bishops' conferences are responsible for translating liturgical texts. The Congregation for Sacraments and Divine Worship has, however, been accused of attempting to take these translations out of the hands of the bishops.[13]

In the English-speaking world recent years have witnessed debates between those who want to follow "functional" or "dynamic equivalence" in translating the original Latin texts of the Roman rite and those who champion a "sacral" translation, "liturgical vernacular," or even "timeless English." As regards the former option, it can turn out to be "beautiful" but not sufficiently "faithful" to the original text. No translation, of course, does full justice to the original; as the Italians say, "*Traduttore traditore* (the translator is a traitor)." But it does not seem justified to blur the distinction between what the text says and what it is understood to mean, a blurring that turns translations into commentaries. A desire to render the text clearly can lead to paraphrases and to supplying the readers/hearers with what the translators think the text should have said and/or meant. But should prioritizing clarity and intelligibility override fidelity? To be sure, we need accessible, idiomatic translations for our liturgy. Yet rendering too freely liturgical images, which very often draw on biblical images, may mean dropping such particular images as "Lord," "kingdom," "sheep" and their "shepherd," "glory," and "blood," which enjoy a long and privileged place in the history of God's revealing and saving activity.

As regards those who champion sacral translations, some examples they have offered do not inspire enthusiasm: for instance, replacing the words of the Third Eucharistic Prayer, "And so, Father, we bring you these gifts. We ask you to make them holy by the power of your Spirit" with "Therefore, Lord, we humbly beseech you, deign to sanctify by the same Spirit these gifts we have brought before you to be made holy."[14] Some of the words (for instance, *beseech* and *deign*) chosen for this translation no longer belong to spoken English, including the English of those who use the language with correct and polite formality. Is the aim to introduce a strangely formal and old-fashioned language that priests and people use only when talking to God? Will the health of the English-speaking areas of the church be promoted or even maintained by a special sacral language that sounds remote, archaic, and awkward? Such language hardly agrees with the kind of language for prayer used and recommended by Jesus himself. He spoke to God and about God in a simple, direct, and familiar way: "Abba (Father dear)," "your kingdom come," "deliver us from the evil one," and so forth. It is very difficult to imagine Jesus encouraging us to start using words like *beseech* and *deign*.

Those who champion the use of sacral translations also frequently oppose gender-inclusive language and play down the many ways in which a moderate use of inclusive language has replaced an outdated, gender-specific language. In this context it is worth recalling the practice of Pope John Paul II and his commitment to inclusive speech. Immediately after his election on October 16, 1978, he addressed the crowd gathered in St. Peter's Square as "my brothers and sisters." He seems to have been a factor in Italians shifting from *fratelli* (brothers), which they had considered to include both men and women, to the papal style of address, *fratelli e sorelle* (brothers and sisters). Non-inclusive language can carry some odd implications: for instance, when the Revised English Bible (REB) translates James 5:15 as "the prayer offered in faith will heal the sick man, the Lord will restore him to health." This translation could be taken to imply either that women are not expected to fall ill or that, if they do, they cannot expect to be restored to health. The New Revised Standard Version (NRSV) avoids this false implication by using an inclusive plural: "The prayer of faith will save the sick, and the Lord will raise them up." The REB, likewise, limits the scope of Jesus' invitation to Simon and Andrew by translating Matthew 4:19 as "Come with me, and I will make you fishers of men" and thus ignoring the fact of the Greek being *anthrôpôn* (human beings) and not the gender-specific *andrôn*. This translation could imply that the mission of apostles will exclude women. The NRSV avoids any "males-only" implication by using an inclusive plural: "I will make you fish for people." A further example comes from 1 Timothy 2:5. The NRSV translation ("there is also one mediator between God and humankind") respects the fact that the Greek text uses *anthrôpôn* and avoids the males-only implication of the REB ("there is one mediator between God and men").[15]

For the task of liturgical translation, what is needed above all is the help of truly great writers, those who have expertise not only in Latin but also, and even more, in the nuances of their own languages. Those who read Seamus Heaney's prizewinning translation of *Beowulf* will learn just what an ear he has for language. When preparing the 1966 Jerusalem Bible, the publishing house of Darton, Longman & Todd enlisted the help of literary advisors such as J. R. R. Tolkien (d. 1973). He helped in the translation of the Book of Jonah, and some of the good current English in which this text was rendered reflected his vigorous narrative style:

> Jonah *decided to run away* from Yahweh, and to go to Tarshish. He went down to Joppa and found a ship *bound for* Tarshish; he *paid his fare* and went *aboard*, to go with them to Tarshish, to *get away* from Yahweh. But Yahweh *unleashed a violent wind* on the sea, and there was such a great *storm* at sea that the ship *threatened* to break up. The sailors *took fright*, and each of them called on his own god, and to lighten the ship they threw *the cargo overboard*. (Jonah 1:3–5; italics added)

Tolkien knew well the King James Bible of 1611 (also known as the Authorized Version), which for centuries was very widely used in the English-speaking world and had as good a claim as any version to have been written in "timeless English." The expressions in italics show how Tolkien and those he worked with introduced energetic, modern language,[16] which clearly improved on the now archaic expressions of the King James Version: "decided to run away from Yahweh, and to go to Tarshish" (in place of "rose up to flee unto Tarshish from the presence of the Lord"), "a ship bound for Tarshish" (in place of "a ship going to Tarshish"), "went aboard" (in place of "went down into it"), "to get away from Yahweh" (in place of "to go...from the presence of the Lord"), "unleashed a violent wind on the sea" (in place of "sent out a great wind into the sea"), "a great storm"(in place of "a mighty tempest"), "the sailors took fright" (in place of "the mariners were afraid"), and "they threw the cargo overboard" (in place of "cast forth the wares that were in the ship into the sea."). Even where the 1966 Jerusalem Bible resembled the King James Version, one spots the improvements: "he paid his fare" (in place of "he paid the fare thereof"), and "the ship threatened to break up" (in place of "the ship was like to be broken").[17] Undoubtedly his collaborators and perhaps Tolkien himself knew the Revised Standard Version of 1952 and other modern translations of the Bible. But the King James Version was well known to them, and they broke away from familiar expressions to produce a robust, contemporary translation. (I am not so sure that the few, slight modifications introduced in the 1985 New Jerusalem Bible's version of Jonah render the original Hebrew more accurately and elegantly than Tolkien and his collaborators did in 1966.)

A second dream of mine involves ecumenical editions of hymns, which could be used on a national and even an international basis. This has already happened in some countries.[18] My hope is that Christians who sing together will come together. In producing such an ecumenical hymnal, Catholic bishops and liturgical experts would be forced to hear and take advice from their Anglican, Orthodox, and Protestant counterparts, who sometimes show much better musical taste than Catholics. The hymnal would include the best of the old (for example, from Gregorian chant, Christmas carols, Methodist hymns, and the work of J. M. Neale) and the best of the new (for instance, from the work of Lucien Deiss, Joseph Gelineau, Graham Kendrick [see his "Servant King"], the Taizé monks, Weston Priory, Christopher Willcock, and Brian Wren).[19] Such a hymnal could carry a notice indicating that it has been officially approved by a given list of Christian churches. By encouraging Christian congregations to sing the same hymns when they worship, it could play its part in bringing organic unity closer. In many countries Christians sing the same carols during Advent and at Christmas. A common hymnal could spread throughout the year the harmonious concord that the season of Christmas already fosters and prays for: in the words of "O come, O come Emmanuel, / Bid now our sad divisions cease."

Third, the diocesan liturgy commission, working in harmony with its national counterpart and with local parish commissions, obviously has much to do when new churches are built and old ones restored. But those in charge need to involve as many of the parishioners as possible at all stages of building and renovating, so as to facilitate their input or at the very least to avoid their feeling simply manipulated or imposed upon. Around the world, bishops and their liturgical experts often work well with parish priests in ensuring appropriate church buildings and a harmonious rapport among the baptismal font, the altar, the presidential chair, the ambo, the crucifix, the tabernacle for reserving the Blessed Sacrament, and statues and images of the Virgin Mary and of other saints. But are the "ordinary" parishioners normally enabled to contribute to the planning of places for worship—for instance, through courses in their own parish (or elsewhere) or guided visits to churches that "work well" liturgically?

Fourth, bishops and their commissions have a special responsibility toward discerning, fostering, and leading something that can deeply enrich the life of their dioceses: popular religiosity, with its world of devotions, processions, and pilgrimages.[20] The feasts of local saints, pilgrimages, home altars in the kitchen,[21] and other manifestations of such religiosity can help put all times, places, and activities in relationship with Christ. There is an intimacy, warmth, and immediacy to popular religiosity that touches the heart and can contribute much to the life of ordinary people, as well as to the struggles of indigenous groups and others needing strength to vindicate their human rights. In Italy, to single out the country where I have spent more than thirty years, on February 5 the annual feast of St. Agatha in Catania brings out the whole population to celebrate exuberantly their favorite saint. They do so in ways that are directly accessible to everyone: through twenty-four-hour processions, prayers, fireworks, flowers, eating customs, and Masses. Around the corner from where I live in Rome is a church dedicated to St. Rita of Cascia (d. 1457), whose dreadfully hard life has made her the patron saint for all manner of desperate cases. On her feast day, May 22, devotees come to pray in her church and receive red roses with which she is particularly associated. Things that we see, hear, smell, taste, and touch, like red roses, can bring us something of the power and truth of our all-loving God.

In recent years pilgrimages for all manner of Catholics and other Christians have been enjoying a fresh burst of popularity. In the Middle Ages, the village of Walsingham (in Norfolk, England) ranked fourth as a place of pilgrimage, after Rome, Jerusalem, and Compostela. It was the only one of the four to be dedicated specifically to Our Lady and dates back to the middle of the eleventh century. Each year thousands of pilgrims now visit the Shrine of Walsingham, alone or in busloads of groups. In the summer the fields around the Shrine of Walsingham fill up with tents and caravans, when innumerable young people come to pray and renew their Christian faith. The New Dawn in the Church Conference, a charismatic gathering, attracts several thousand people for five days of prayer at the shrine. At Walsingham six chapels of different denominations (two Catholic, two Anglican, one Methodist, and one Orthodox) show the ecumenical outreach of what is once again the main center of pilgrimage in England. When I went to pray at Walsingham in mid-1968 after completing my doctorate at the University of Cambridge, the other doctoral student who drove me there was Peter Carnley, future Anglican archbishop of Perth and primate of Australia. At the end of the Second World War, American servicemen organized a special Mass there, and led to the Shrine of Our Lady of Walsingham being created in Williamsburg, Virginia.

On their roads through France and northern Spain to Compostela, the traditional burial place of St. James "the Great," thousands of pilgrims share food and lodgings. Walking together, they find a fresh relationship with themselves, with God, with other human beings, and with the earth over which they travel. At the height of the summer more than a thousand pilgrims arrive each day at Santiago de Compostela and ask for the official certificate to show that they have completed the pilgrimage.[22] A cousin of mine told me recently of a woman friend who a few years ago started her pilgrimage from Paris to Compostela. Each year she spends her two-week vacation on the road, taking up again her *camino* at the *refugio* where she had stopped the previous year.

Since the Middle Ages many other places of pilgrimage have emerged, especially such Marian shrines as those of Aparecida (Brazil), Czestochowa (Poland), Fatima (Portugal), Guadalupe (Mexico), Loreto (Italy), and Lourdes (France). Bishops and priests often lead groups on visits to these shrines, and at times experience surprisingly open contacts with the young people who join them on pilgrimage. The popular religiosity of a pilgrimage offers an easy way of demonstrating that official leaders are also Christian pilgrims on their *camino* with all the baptized.

My fifth and final dream for bishops and their diocesan liturgical commission affects how they might revive the sacrament of reconciliation of individual penitents. The Second Vatican Council recognized that the scriptures have "the greatest importance in the celebration of the liturgy," and mandated that scriptural readings be restored to the "sacred celebrations" (*Sacrosanctum Concilium*, 24, 35). Unfortunately in the revised Rite of Reconciliation for Individual

Penitents, the reading of the word of God remains optional,[23] and in my experience very few priests begin the administration of the sacrament with an appropriate text of scripture that proclaims God's mercy and calls human beings to conversion. In the case of the other sacraments the reading of the scriptures is prescribed and enjoys its essential place. But when "hearing confessions," the overwhelming majority of priests neglect to introduce the inspired scriptures. As a confessor I always begin with a reading from the Bible and can testify to the way in which the word of God repeatedly enlightens and heals penitents, sometimes in a striking fashion. At the moment many bishops around the world are aware of the social and ecclesial nature of sin and reconciliation (*Lumen Gentium*, 11) and yet frustrated in their attempts to revive the use of the sacrament of reconciliation that is not "private" and even "furtive" but visibly involves the whole community.[24] While waiting for better days, they might think of encouraging their priests and people to value the role of the scriptures in the performance of this sacrament and not ignore as a mere optional extra the reading of the word of God. The Bible is the book of the whole church, and its powerful presence in the administration of all the sacraments vindicates itself in practice.

Since this chapter has discussed liturgical progress made and yet to be made in the Catholic Church of the Roman rite, it has been directly concerned with my second criterion for putting Vatican II's teaching into practice: a richer and more grace-filled worship. What of the other three criteria drawn from the Cappadocians and also proposed at the close of chapter 3? A sensitivity to the transforming presence of the risen Christ and his Spirit (criterion 1) prompted a number of the "dreams for the priesthood" just suggested above. Love for the scriptures (criterion 3) encouraged, for instance, my fourth dream for priests and my first and fifth dreams for bishops and their liturgical commissions. The desire to serve well those who suffer (criterion 4) lay behind what was said about *leitourgia* at the end of the second section of this chapter ("Progress Made") and behind several of my dreams (for example, the desire to minister more effectively to young people and the encouragement given to popular religiosity).

Once again let me insist that it is not easy to apply the four daunting tests I gleaned from the practice and teaching of a shining, fourth-century group of Christians, the Cappadocian saints. Nevertheless, it is essential to raise the questions they provoke. What happens when these questions are not even raised was reflected in a report by Elena Curti in the London *Tablet* (June 28, 2003) and the letters published in subsequent issues. In all that debate about the values and disvalues involved in maintaining the Tridentine form of the Latin Mass, no one on either side, at least in what they said and wrote, asked the Cappadocian-style questions: Does the inspiration for *this* way of celebrating the liturgy come from the risen Jesus and the Holy Spirit? Is it prompted by fidelity to the biblical witness? Does it lead us to a more generous service of those who suffer? Ultimately I have, of course, no other conscience to examine but my own. But, in a very particular way, I did and do miss the Cappadocian questions in recurrent liturgical debates. After sharing my hopes for the liturgy, let me turn next to the reception of the council's moral teaching in the church in the third millennium.

Note: For further themes of interest for liturgical renewal and practice see Cardinal Joseph Bernardin, "New Rite of Penance Suggested," *Origins* 13 (1983), 324–26; P. Bradshaw, ed., *The New Westminster Dictionary of Liturgy and Worship* (Louisville, KY: Westminster John Knox, 2002); M. Drumm, *Passage to Pasch: Revisiting the Catholic Sacraments* (Dublin: Columba Press, 1998); M. F. Mannion, *Masterworks of God. Essays in Liturgical Theory and Practice* (Mundelein, IL: Hillenbrand Books, 2004); K. Perry et al., eds., *The Blackwell Dictionary of Eastern Christianity* (Oxford: Blackwell, 2001); the following works by Keith Pecklers: *Dynamic Equivalence: The Living Language of Christian Worship* (Collegeville, MN: Liturgical Press, 2003); *Worship* (New York/London: Continuum, 2003); and as editor, *Liturgy in a Postmodern World* (New York/London: Continuum, 2003); and the following entries in the 2003 edition of *The New Catholic Encyclopedia:* "Bugnini, Annibale," vol. 2, 676–77; "Rites, Congregation of," vol. 12, 256; "Roman Rite," vol. 12, 327–29; and many relevant entries in vol. 8, 617–736.

5

RECEIVING THE COUNCIL'S MORAL TEACHING

Modern society is earmarked for a great material progress to which there is not a corresponding advance in the moral field. Hence there is a weakening in the aspiration towards the values of the spirit.
                    Blessed John XXIII, Christmas Day 1961

Jesus' way of acting and his words, his deeds and his precepts, constitute the moral rule of Christian life.
                    John Paul II, *Veritatis Splendor*, 20

The wars affecting our region are dividing our people, sowing a culture of violence and destroying the social and moral fabric of our societies.
                    Bishop Nicolas Djomo Lola of Tshumbe, Congo,
                    November 11, 2003

Before the Second Vatican Council, those who taught and wrote (frequently in Latin) moral theology aimed to train about-to-be-ordained clerics for the ministry of the confessional. The approach was rational rather than biblical, individual and private rather than ecclesial and communal. Seminary training, admittedly, often gave considerable time to spirituality, but it was treated separately from moral theology. The virtues, especially justice, were studied, but much of the agenda consisted of examining specific moral situations or "cases" in order to resolve an individual's doubts and decide on a particular course of action. William Spohn, a moral theologian teaching at Santa Clara University (California), sums up what was lacking in that preconciliar situation: "The older moral theology operated in a theological vacuum, virtually untouched by any reference to Christ, the role of the Spirit, sanctification, or discipleship."[1]

The council helped to transform that situation not only through its Pastoral Constitution on the Church in the Modern World, but also through its teaching in its other fifteen documents. The ground for a more biblically based and experiential morality that stressed personal conversion and responsibility had been prepared by moral theologians such as Bernard Häring (1912–98). His three-volume *Law of Christ*, published originally in German in 1954, was translated into eleven other languages. It caused a theological revolution by putting Christ at the center of moral theology. Häring served as an expert at Vatican II, and played his part in preparing *Gaudium et Spes.*[2]

Vatican II on the Moral Life

In the late twentieth century John Paul II emerged as the great champion of human rights. It was a huge change for the Catholic Church, sparked off by Pope John XXIII, who gave official recognition to some approaches for renewal that had been developing for decades and that reflected a deep concern for the dignity of the human person that had been massively violated in the Second World War. The notion of human rights, as we now understand them, had medieval roots, and early intimations can be found in the writings of the Dominican activist and theologian Bartolomé de Las Casas (1484–1566). In modern times John Locke (1632–1704) and some other philosophers found a basis for human rights in a version of the natural law. But leaders of the Catholic Church, with some notable exceptions like the German Bishop Wilhelm Emmanuel Ketteler (1811–77) and the English Cardinal Henry Edward Manning (1808–92), remained suspicious of secular doctrines of human rights; they distrusted the Enlightenment thinkers and the French Revolution from which modern formulations of such rights sprang. The change is startling.

The breakthrough came with Pope John's 1963 encyclical *Pacem in Terris*, which drew from the dignity of the human person created in the divine image an extensive treatment of such natural rights as the rights to life, to basic education, and to religious freedom. These rights, which "the Creator of the world" has written into the natural order of things, imply a corresponding set of duties (DzH 3956–72; ND 2026–42), and apply also to the actions of civil authorities and to relations between sovereign states. Vatican II's *Gaudium et Spes* took further the theme of *dignity*[3] and value of the human person and endorsed Pope John's plea for the universal *common good* (no. 26),[4] which demands—among other things—a just international socioeconomic development (nos. 63–72) and an end to war through peaceful methods for settling conflicts between nations (nos. 77–82). Following the example of John XXIII, the council addressed the message of *Gaudium et Spes* to the whole human family (nos. 2, 92). It wanted to further dialogue and make common cause with all the groups and individuals working for the common good. This broke with the tradition of "the Church" offering the world a package of political and social teaching, as had been the case even with such an enlightened encyclical as Leo XIII's *Rerum Novarum* (1891). Rather than handing down magisterial teaching from on high, Pope John and then the council preferred dialogue on issues that affect the welfare of the whole human race and put the "signs of the times" firmly on the agenda.

When tackling such matters of "universal concern" as "marriage and the family, human progress, life in its economic, social and political dimensions, the bonds between the family of nations, and peace," *Gaudium et Spes* wanted to be led by "the light" not only of the gospel but also of "human experience" (no. 46). The council expected experience to play its part in yielding insights into moral truth and action. Factual truths known through experience can help ground value judgments.

Such an appeal to experience will, however, inevitably prompt some readers into asking: Whose experience? How much experience? How does one go about discerning the experience? It is obvious that one may have significant experiences but miss much of their meaning, truth, and value. Or else the full meaning of some experience may call for years of exploring before we can find and appreciate it.[5] Nevertheless, the challenge of interpreting experiences never excuses us from dismissing or ignoring them. By introducing human experience and the gospel, Vatican II showed its desire to develop not only an ethic with a specifically Christian configuration but also one grounded in our common experience.

So in reflecting at length (*Gaudium et Spes*, 46–92) on matters of "universal concern," the council drew on the lessons of human experience to ground its value judgments, together with the "universal, natural law and all-embracing principles" that enjoy "a perennial binding force" for everyone. Human "conscience" gives an "ever more emphatic voice to these principles" (no. 79). An appeal to "the voice of conscience" revealing the universal law inscribed in human nature turned up much earlier in *Gaudium et Spes*: "In the depth of their conscience human beings detect a law which they do not make for themselves but which they must obey. Its voice always summons them to love and to do what is good and to shun what is evil" (no. 16). This is the law "written by God" in their heart.[6]

Vatican II's Declaration on Religious Freedom, promulgated on the same day as *Gaudium et Spes* (December 7, 1965, the final day of the council), develops further the theme of human conscience responding to the truth of divine law. First, "the highest norm of human life is the divine law...whereby God orders, directs and governs the entire universe and all the ways of the human community by a plan conceived in wisdom and love." Second, human beings "can perceive and acknowledge the imperatives of the divine law through the mediation of conscience" (*Dignitatis Humanae*, 3). They all share in this law by which, in wisdom and love, God guides human life and the whole cosmos to an ultimate fulfillment.[7]

In *Gaudium et Spes*, the council recognized that conscience may inculpably, or without any personal fault, often go wrong: "conscience frequently errs from invincible ignorance without losing its dignity" (no. 16). This is to recognize the integrity not only of individuals who honestly practice what is objectively wrong but also of groups who honestly seek what is true and good but may come to false conclusions. But there is another side of the issue. The council was sadly aware that there are many, both inside and outside the Catholic Church, who "take little care to seek what is true and good" and whose conscience "through a habit of sin" gradually becomes "almost blind" (ibid.). They can hardly appreciate what is normatively human and acknowledge the guidance of common values and principles. Faced with moral challenges and dilemmas, such people could have known better and ought to have known better. But they have culpably let their conscience become deaf to the divine voice of conscience. Here the council's moral teaching begins to take on a distinctively Christian configuration. Common human experience shows the evil inclinations of human beings that can disrupt their proper relationship to God, to themselves, to other men and women, and to all created things. Human beings experience their divided selves, caught in a dramatic struggle between good and evil. It takes the self-revelation of God in Christ to explain and illuminate the mystery of human beings in their "call to grandeur and depths of misery" (ibid., 13, 22). Harmed by sin, human beings need to be "redeemed by Christ and made new creatures in the Holy Spirit," if they are to treat all creatures with loving "respect and reverence" and to realize their destiny (ibid., 37). The council's teaching on sin and transforming grace goes beyond any merely human ethic.

A Christian moral configuration also comes through the call to be converted and follow Christ. Accepting the call to conversion and faith in Christ initiates one into the Christian life and worship (*Sacrosanctum Concilium*, 9; *Ad Gentes*, 7, 13). Discipleship is a deep personal relationship to Christ that shapes the moral behavior and ethic of Christians and that is nourished liturgically and biblically. Through the Eucharist and the other liturgical celebrations, God is glorified and human beings are sanctified (*Sacrosanctum Concilium*, 10). Disciples show through the holiness of their lives what, or rather whom, they receive in all the sacraments, and especially the Eucharist. Consistent with its biblical orientation, the council mandated that in the formation of priests "special attention needs to be given to the perfecting of moral theology" through its being "more thoroughly nourished by the teaching of the Holy Scripture" (*Optatam Totius*, 16). This emphasis on a biblical teaching that feeds moral thought and practice entails a Christ-centered vision of the Bible and hence the conviction that Christ should be the very soul of moral reflection and conduct. A Christ-centered morality is necessarily biblical and vice versa. As the council put matters in *Dei*

Verbum, through the "frequent reading of the divine Scriptures" all the faithful should learn the "excellent knowledge of Christ" (no. 25, with reference to Phil 3:8).

Inevitably Vatican II summed up its moral message in terms of "the first and greatest commandment," love for God and love for one's neighbor (*Gaudium et Spes*, 24; see also 16, 38). Such love responds to God who has first loved us (*Perfectae Caritatis*, 6) through the coming of Christ and the outpouring of the Holy Spirit. The Decree on the Apostolate of Lay People, *Apostolicam Actuositatem*, emphasized how this "greatest commandment" rests upon what Christ said and did (no. 8). This "new" commandment of love is deeply personalized by the example of Christ: "Love one another, just as I have loved you" (see John 13:14–15, 34–35). Jesus is love incarnate or the love of God in person.[8]

Vatican II yields then an intriguing blend of a common human ethic, which treats universal natural law, conscience, and experience, with some distinctively Christian elements: the self-revelation of God in Christ who illuminates the enigma of human destiny, sin, and redemption; the call to the following of Christ, a call nourished by the scriptures and by all the sacraments, especially the Eucharist, and summed up by the commandment of love. In many ways the council did not propose a special moral agenda. It listed, for instance, fundamental human rights and condemned those practices that "violate the integrity of the human person," such as murder, genocide, abortion, and euthanasia (*Gaudium et Spes*, 27, 29, 51). Christian identity, at least for the council, did not seem to add much normative content to common human morality, based on natural law and human reason. Obviously it went beyond a widely acceptable human ethic by seeking to implement the agenda in a distinctively Christ-centered vision of the world. The teaching and practice of Jesus gave a particular urgency to the "inescapable duty of making ourselves the neighbor" of all who are in great need and distress (*Gaudium et Spes*, 27). The faithful and creative reception of Vatican II's moral teaching in these and other areas was to encounter huge changes and challenges around the world.

Four Areas of Challenge

BELIEF SYSTEMS

After Vatican II ended nearly forty years ago, four global changes have come to shape the context for human and Christian moral behavior. The first concerns seismic shifts in belief systems. When Vatican II opened in October 1962, the Cuban missile crisis had brought the United States and the Soviet Union to the brink of a nuclear war. John XXIII, who had called together the council, played a key role in defusing that crisis. Few would have thought then that, in Europe at least, the Communism of Joseph Stalin (1879–1953) would officially end when the Berlin Wall came down in 1989 and the USSR (the Union of Soviet Socialist Republics) was dissolved in 1991. The sudden collapse of European Communism and the Soviet Union was perhaps the most surprising event in the entire twentieth century.

As I write this chapter, the cold war has long ago ended and the United States has emerged as the sole military and economic superpower. The moral and ideological climate of the world's international order has dramatically changed since the council ended in 1965. Communism was then still offering a master story of emancipation and progress: Humankind was to liberate itself, enjoy socialist freedom, and "annihilate" God in order to create the perfect society. Back in the 1960s there were also various "liberal" thinkers and leaders who still espoused their alternate master story, an optimistic belief in progress and the perfectibility of human beings. Yet nowadays master stories seem an endangered species. Indeed, some so-called postmodern philosophers would deny that there is any universal reason to which we could appeal in proposing a common ethic and constructing a master story. Many in the Western world appear content with an individualistic relativism—in the spirit of "You have your story and experience and I have mine; if you feel good about something, do it, provided you don't hurt anyone else." At the same time, the spread of some interpretations of Islam has brought a new conservative, even repressive morality in many parts of the world. The global moral climate has undergone some dramatic shifts after 1965—since the collapse of Communism in 1989 and its aftermath.

Faced with such changes in beliefs and moral codes, leaders and members of the Catholic Church have vigorously endorsed and practiced dialogue and collaboration with those of other religions (see chapters 2 and 6). They constantly recall the "authentic values grounded in the universal moral law written in the heart of every man and woman" (*Ecclesia in Europa*, 116).[9] These values include the "inalienable dignity of the human person, the sacredness of human life and the centrality of the family, the importance of education and freedom of thought, speech and religion, the legal protection of individuals and groups, the promotion of solidarity and the common good, and the recognition of the dignity of labor" (ibid., 19). Above all, the Catholic Church continues to proclaim its master story of the crucified and risen Christ, and its attendant vocation "to lead men and women to an encounter with the love of God and of Christ, who comes in search of them" (ibid., 85).

POPULATION EXPLOSION

My second global change concerns the world population, which stood at three billion in 1960, passed the six billion mark in October 1999, and by late August 2004 stood at 6,380,041,000. Rising numbers, along with new means of communications, have disrupted the age-old autonomy of village life almost everywhere. The demographic explosion, which has taken place above all in Latin America, Africa, and Asia, has worsened things and not been accompanied by any real improvement in the appalling conditions of life that Vatican II already denounced. An unjust economic situation has made rich nations and persons even richer and the poor even poorer.[10] A report released on November 25, 2003, by the United Nations Food and Agriculture Organization illustrated this global inequity. It reported that, despite such astounding successes as the Green Revolution, hunger, after falling steadily during the first half of the 1990s, grew during the second half of the decade. The report found that more than 840 million persons are still chronically hungry around the globe.[11] Hunger is worsening worldwide, often spread by wars, lack of access to markets through trade barriers, other structures of economic exploitation,[12] and the AIDS pandemic. By November 2003 forty million people were suffering from HIV/AIDS. In July 2003 a visit by President George Bush focused world attention momentarily on Botswana, the former British protectorate of Bechuanaland that became independent in 1966. In many ways this tiny republic of less than two million people has proved a solid democracy, but every day twenty-five children are born HIV positive and seventy-one inhabitants die from AIDS. (In the United States this would be the equivalent of losing fifteen thousand people a day.) The average life expectancy has fallen from sixty-five to forty years, and 38.8 percent of people between the ages of fifteen and forty-nine are HIV positive.

One hundred million children live on the streets of the world. Up to ten thousand street and underprivileged children die each year in Lima alone; around the world eleven million children under the age of five die of hunger every year. Malaria, now a disease forgotten in developed countries, remains endemic in many developing nations and kills a million or more people a year, including 700,000 African children. Over one billion people in the world do not have access to safe drinking water, about two and a half billion do not have adequate sanitation, and by 2025 two-thirds of the world population will live in countries with a major water shortage problem. Quetta, the capital of Pakistan's Baluchistan Province, has one million inhabitants who depend on two thousand wells pumping water from an underground supply that will probably be exhausted by 2010. Deserts are spreading alarmingly in China, Iran, Nigeria, Sudan, and elsewhere. In China, for example, the Gobi Desert is growing at the rate of four thousand square miles a year.

Deforestation and selfish exploitation of fossil fuels have led to global warming and climate changes that have tripled the number of droughts, floods, and other natural disasters since the 1950s. Through pollution and global warming human beings have been steadily destroying marine ecosystems, as well as ravaging the supply of fish through overfishing. Those who earn massive fortunes in the petrol industry have not been prominent in actively trying in any serious way to develop alternatives to fossil fuel. The moguls of the energy industries seem to wage war against the environment of a now highly populated world. Pollution and the reckless squandering of natural resources threaten everyone, perpetrators and victims alike. Our environment must be protected if it is to continue being a habitat for humans. John Gummer, the former minister for environment in the British government, has rightly called on constituents everywhere to pressure administrations to take decisive steps toward protecting the world in which we live.

SCIENTIFIC REVOLUTION

Along with the growth in disinherited and hungry masses since Vatican II closed in 1965, there have also been amazing scientific and technological advances, symbolized by the first human visit to the moon in 1969 and the arrival of *Spirit* on the surface of Mars in January 2004. Christiaan Barnard performed the first heart transplant in 1967, and since then thousands of heart transplants have been successfully done—not to mention very common transplants of kidneys, livers, and other organs. Reproductive technologies have also undergone a revolution. Born in July 1978, Louise Brown was the first human being to be conceived outside her mother's body through an in vitro process in which the gametes of her parents were fused in a test tube. Genetic engineering on human beings is deeply problematic, but similar technologies applied to plants and animals raise fewer ethical questions.[13] Genetically modified plants and animals have come to stay. Technology has brought a revolution in global communications and transport. In 1970 the introduction of the Boeing 747 initiated travel on large jet airliners with a capacity for several hundred passengers. We live in the brave new world of mass tourism, cell phones, e-mails, and computers.

The stunning progress in science and technology since 1965 raises many moral questions, not least the basic issue of human survival. How high are our survival prospects? Neanderthals emerged and flourished for over 200,000 years, arriving in Europe around 300,000 BC, becoming extinct around 30,000 BC, and playing no part in the genetic makeup of modern humans. Homo sapiens, now roughly 200,000 years old, arrived in Europe from Africa around 45,000 BC. On the earth itself life began 3.6 billion years ago, and we might expect it to last another six billion years until the sun becomes a red giant—provided, of course, that Homo sapiens lives up to the "wisdom" of that name and his/her maximum potential. At the University of Cambridge in 1973 Dr. Brandan Carter developed the Anthropic Principle, which emerges from the fact that in our present universe the development of carbon-based life and eventually of self-conscious, human life has depended on certain physical quantities having the precise values they actually do have. If they had been only slightly different, the development of galaxies and planets would have been very different and have ruled out the possibility of life developing on earth. Their "anthropic" quality suggests that the laws of the universe were finely tuned to effect the appearance of human life. The scientific work of Carter and others[14] made human beings look less like cosmic accidents and more like the results of divine planning. After helping to further thinking about the origins of the universe and human life, Carter turned his attention to the future. In 1981 (the year he became a Fellow of the Royal Society) he launched discussion on the doomsday argument that concerns the possibility or probability of the world ending soon. Global disaster could be caused by an all-destroying bubble born inside particle accelerators or calamitous overheating coming from a runaway greenhouse effect. Could tragic mistakes in academic or commercial experiments turn this twenty-first century into our final century? Do governments have the moral responsibility to ban potentially disastrous research as well as to commit themselves effectively to reduce global warming? In any case, evil and/or irrational governments, no less than terrorist groups and even iniquitous loners, could shut down human life on our planet.[15]

CHALLENGES TO LIFE

One can hardly sum up the world's history since 1965 as showing greater respect for human life. Issues involving abortion, euthanasia, embryo research, capital punishment, and war illustrate how in the post-Vatican II years old moral challenges have been renewed and new challenges have emerged.

Abortion

From ancient times the practice of inducing abortion to terminate unwanted pregnancies was widespread, but before the nineteenth century was not always criminalized.[16] The Soviet Union legalized abortion in 1920, and from the 1960s abortion began to be legalized in other countries. In the United Kingdom (with the exception of Northern Ireland and the Channel Islands) the 1967 Abortion Act permitted abortion under certain circumstances up till the twenty-fourth week of pregnancy. Some who supported the act did so because they hoped to eliminate "backstreet" abortions, limit the circumstances under which abortion would be legal, and reduce the overall number of abortions. But the legislation opened the way, more or less, to abortion on demand. Something similar happened in the United States after the 1973 case *Roe v. Wade* (and then its companion case *Doe v. Bolton*) opened the door to legalized abortion. In December 2003 the High Court in Britain granted an appeal by a newly ordained Anglican priest, Reverend Joanna Jepson, to review a decision by the West Mercia Police not to prosecute the doctors who aborted a child beyond six months' gestation. The mother, after taking advice from her doctor, did not want to give birth to a baby with a cleft palate. The baby was deemed too defective to live a meaningful life. Jepson herself had been born with a similar defect, which appropriate surgery remedied. In an article for *The Sunday Telegraph* (December 21, 2003) she wrote of current society's ruthless "readiness to refuse life to those who are less than perfect." Parents can be put under various forms of pressure if they refuse an abortion when abnormalities are detected before birth. What Jepson opposed goes hand in hand with the leap to "designer babies" or embryos selected for their desirable attributes. Such developments seem a new form of eugenics, or updated ways for altering the human race by breeding for inherited characteristics deemed desirable and eliminating those deemed to be unwanted. Embryos are to be selected for implantation or destroyed, because they display the "right" or the "wrong" characteristics, respectively.

Euthanasia

Many Western countries (or particular states of those countries) have officially or unofficially legalized euthanasia and physician-assisted suicide. Euthanasia entails bringing about death through a direct act on the part of another when the person affected requests such an *action:* for instance, a lethal dose of sleeping pills. Physician-assisted suicide refers to the situation where a patient requests the *means* for directly bringing about his or her death and the physician supplies those means: for instance, a lethal injection. In both cases, death is directly and deliberately brought about for patients who have given their consent. It may take little to persuade them to accept such a decision. Stroke patients and the senile often have no choice; their death can result when others decide to terminate their life directly. This is called involuntary euthanasia, as death does not result from the request and/or action of the patient. Members of the medical profession have crossed a major line into morally unacceptable killing when they claim the right, even in conjunction with patients and their relatives (the case of euthanasia) and in conjunction with pregnant mothers and their partners (the case of abortion), to decide which lives are not worth living and then deliberately to bring about the death of the old, the incurably ill, and the unborn. They collaborate in a culture of death, which "puts down" the defenseless, both those who are not yet born and those whom old age or sickness have made a "burden" to family and society. A quiet, bespectacled British doctor, Harold Shipman, went further in what he arrogated to himself over matters of life and death. He used deadly injections to kill at least 215 patients and possibly as many as 260 over a period of twenty-three years. In January 2004, he took his own life in prison.

Embryo Research

Vatican II labeled infanticide and abortion as "abominable crimes" (*Gaudium et Spes*, 51). But it had nothing to say about experiments with human embryos, which had not yet begun in the United States and elsewhere. In July 2001 the news broke that the Jones Institute for Reproductive Medicine in Norfolk, Virginia, was creating human embryos for the sole purpose of dismembering them for their stem cells (undifferentiated cells from which specialized cells develop). Immediately after that it was learned that a laboratory in Worcester, Massachusetts, was aiming to grow cloned human embryos to produce stem cells. The same laboratory three years earlier had produced a hybrid human-cow embryo. In November 2003 the issue of therapeutic cloning and reproductive cloning (or producing a baby identical to its genetic parent) came up for debate at the United Nations. (The UN does not have the authority to ban such research, but the nations who sign a convention are expected to follow through with legislation.) Therapeutic cloning is a procedure in which stem cells are removed from human embryos with the intention of producing replacement tissue or even a whole organ for transplant into someone who supplies the DNA. Since the embryo is destroyed, there is nothing therapeutic about the process itself, and the term *therapeutic cloning* is a misnomer. The procedure yields material, which might be used later for therapeutic purposes. Supporters argue that the end (a potential medical value) justifies the means (experimenting with human embryos). The research might one day come up with cures; the *might* is worth stressing. Even the *New York Times* left vague the prospects of future results from such research: "*Some* scientists *believe* it is *possible* that cells *could* be transformed into new tissue that *could* be used to treat diabetes, spinal cord injuries and *perhaps* Alzheimer's and Parkinson's diseases" (November 27, 2003; italics mine). In other words, why snuff out promising medical research by imposing moral restraints? In any case, is it commonly or even universally accepted that experimenting with human embryos is wrong?[17] In his 1995 encyclical *Evangelium Vitae* John Paul II took a clear stand on these post-Vatican II issues by calling "the use of human embryos or foetuses" for experiments "a crime against their dignity as human beings who have a right to the same respect owed to a child once born" (no. 63).

Even if they do not endorse the pope's teaching, some opponents of stem-cell research point out that supplies of such cells might be available from noncontroversial sources—from umbilical cords and even from the bodies of adults. Certain ordinary body cells might be induced to have the same properties as embryonic stem cells. Moreover, while potential medical findings from stem-cell research may be considerable, actualizing them in therapeutic practice remains doubtful, even highly doubtful.[18] The ethical debate flared up around the world in February 2004, when the news came that some scientists in South Korea had created human embryos through cloning and then extracted embryonic stem cells. To make these stem cells useful for therapy, they would then have to be turned into such particular types of cells as brain cells or heart cells. The moral objection remains the same: Such experiments create human lives with the purpose of destroying them in research. Human life is being used as a mere object or as a means to an end.

Death Penalty

To punish serious crimes many public authorities have inflicted the death penalty, using a variety of means such as hanging, the guillotine, firing squads, gas chambers, electric chairs, and lethal injections. In Britain the death penalty, previously imposed for a wide range of offenses, was limited in the nineteenth century to cases of treason and murder, and in 1965, the year Vatican II ended, it was abolished for murder. Many countries in the West and elsewhere have dropped the death penalty, but it continues in Russia, China, a number of states in the United States, and some other countries. The traditional teaching of the Catholic Church, maintained even as late as the 1992 *Catechism of the Catholic Church* (nos. 2266–67), accepted the death penalty, provided that it was inflicted on those whose guilt for murder and other serious offenses had been judicially established. However, notorious miscarriages of justice that led to the execution of the innocent, the possibility of imprisonment bringing murderers to true repentance, the fact that secure prisons defend the public from dangerous criminals, and further considerations (for example, that the threat of capital punishment is not an effective deterrent against murder) have convinced many Christians and others to support the abolition of the death penalty.

In the Catholic Church, after he became pope in 1978, John Paul II led the way with his almost unqualified opposition to capital punishment. In *Evangelium Vitae* he excluded the death penalty, "except in the case of absolute necessity," or "when it would not be possible otherwise to defend society." The pope added: "Today, however, as a result of steady improvements in the organization of the penal system, such cases are very rare, if not non-existent in practice" (no. 56). John Paul II's concern for a coherent ethic of life led him also to repudiate abortion as a "grave moral disorder" and a decision "against the weakest and most defenseless of human beings (ibid., 28, 62, 70) and euthanasia as "a grave violation of the law of God" (ibid., 17, 64–66). His ethic of life emerged also in his teaching and practice in the service of peace.

War

As a bishop at the Second Vatican Council, John Paul II had shared in the making of the Constitution on the Church in the Modern World, which devoted a whole chapter to the fostering of peace and establishing an effective community of nations (nos. 77–90). The council, in the face of modern weapons that "can inflict immense and indiscriminate havoc," called for "a completely fresh appraisal of war," and endorsed condemnations of "total war" (condemnations that had already come from Pius XII, John XXIII, and Paul VI) and of "the indiscriminate destruction of whole cities and vast areas." *Gaudium et Spes*, along with a radical concern to "curb the savagery of war," nevertheless, acknowledged that, "as long as the danger of war persists and there is no international authority with the necessary competence and power, governments cannot be denied the right of lawful self-defense, once all peace efforts have failed" (no. 79). This was tantamount to accepting the possibility of a just defensive war (to be distinguished from "preventive war"), provided certain stringent conditions were met.[19] During Vatican II some supporters of pacifism and nonviolence, like the Americans Dorothy Day and James Douglass with his wife Shelley, lobbied the bishops to take an unconditional antiwar stance. In the decades since the council the world has continued to suffer from the scourge of wars, some of them very long lasting.

In Guatemala thirty-four years of conflict finally came to an end with the 1996 peace agreement. No fewer than 200,000 Guatemalans, mostly Mayan Indians, had been killed—not to mention innumerable cases of rape, torture, and the destruction of property. Between 1979 and 1992, El Salvador was devastated by a civil war characterized by ferocious military and paramilitary repression. After a civil war in the Sudan that lasted twenty years and left nearly two million dead, peace seemed to have come at the end of 2004, at least in the South. In Liberia nearly fourteen years of civil war lasted up to November 2003. The 1992–95 wars in former Yugoslavia meant well over 200,000 dead. In Rwanda at least 800,000 people, largely Tutsis, were slaughtered in 1994 by predominantly Hutu supporters after the president of Rwanda died in a plane crash. The Indonesian occupation of East Timor, which began in 1975 and ended only in 1999, cost 200,000 lives. As I write this chapter, ruthless suppression of the local population goes on in Aceh (Sumatra, Indonesia), and of the Chechen people in the Caucasus Mountains. The intifada or Palestinian uprising in the Israeli-occupied West Bank and Gaza Strip, which began in 1987, regularly brings terrorist atrocities and savage reprisals. The American occupation of Iraq continues, with daily casualties on both sides: More than 100,000 have died. The war in Afghanistan seems far from over. These are only some of the wars that have devastated many countries after Vatican II closed in 1965.

Among the many horrible features of these wars are the use of such weapons as cluster bombs and millions of land mines, as well as the recruiting of children as soldiers. In November 2003, according to "Go Between," a UN nongovernmental liaison service, about 300,000 child soldiers, some as young as eight years of age, are engaged in over thirty conflicts around the world. A large number of these have been orphaned by war and have no other family than the armies or guerilla groups to which they belong. Add, too, the way these and other wars have driven millions of people out of their homes into refugee camps or permanent exile. When speaking in Washington on November 11, 2003, to the U.S. Conference of Catholic Bishops, the president of the Episcopal Conferences of Central Africa, Bishop Nicolas Djomo Lola, reported how "the wars affecting our region" were "destroying the social and moral fabric of our societies."

Addressing the diplomats accredited to the Holy See on January 12, 2004, John Paul II once again expressed his conviction: "War never resolves conflicts among peoples." Once more he called for a global rule of law and "a more effective collective security system that gives the United Nations its proper place." This means that the authority to judge the legitimacy of aggressive military action resides with the UN Security Council. Right through his long pontificate (1978–2005), John Paul II followed the lead of Paul VI in urging the principles of international law, the removal of injustices that cause conflicts, and effective economic aid toward development, "the new name for peace." In his teaching and personal witness, John Paul II stressed the need for forgiveness between nations and all groups at odds with each other. As he put it in his Message of the World Day of Peace in 2002, "No peace without justice. No justice without forgiveness." One can express this same message as "if you seek peace, work for justice and forgiveness."[20]

I have painted with broad strokes the global moral scene, highlighting some major shifts since 1965: the end of European Communism, the growth of the world population, the revolutionary scientific and technological advances, and the continual threats to human life at every stage. Apropos of the last theme, I indicated how issues about abortion, euthanasia, embryo research, capital punishment, and war have flared up.[21] We have looked briefly at the teaching of John Paul II in those four areas to see how Vatican II's moral teaching was implemented and developed. *Gaudium et Spes* wanted our moral behavior to be led by the "light of the Gospel" (no. 46)—that is to say, by Jesus who is the gospel in person. John Paul II declared in *Veritatis Splendor:* "Jesus' way of acting and his words, his deeds and his precepts, constitute the moral rule of Christian life" (no. 20). What then was Jesus' "moral rule of life"? What should we retrieve from Jesus and his earliest followers, if we want to let his teaching shape our lives?

The Moral Teaching of Jesus

From some points of view, Jesus did not change very much in the area of morality and seemed to keep the best of existing Jewish teaching. The Wisdom of Solomon, written only a few years before the birth of Jesus, pictures poignantly the reasoning of sensual and ungodly sinners (Wis 1:16—2:24). They think of themselves as being "born by mere chance" and of death as the end of their existence. Life has no ultimate meaning for them, and they give themselves up to sensual satisfaction—even at terrible cost to others. The Book of Wisdom allows us to overhear their talk and thoughts: "Let us oppress the righteous poor man; let us not spare the widow or regard the gray hairs of the aged. But let our might be our law of right" (Wis 2:10–11). The Jewish prophets also denounce the oppression of helpless, righteous people. But Wisdom goes further in depicting dramatically the way in which wicked sinners urge each other to live frivolously and persecute mercilessly. Their wickedness has blinded them; their sin clouds and corrupts their reasoning; they know neither God nor "the secret purposes of God" (Wis 2:21–22). Jesus likewise saw that sin comes from within a person (Mark 7:20–23). Along with the author of Wisdom, he knew that something goes wrong in the human mind and heart even before sinners commit evil actions. Yet he differed from the author of Wisdom through the personal authority with which he offered his teaching. Thus he quoted traditional Jewish teaching against acts of murder and adultery, proscribed murderous and adulterous thoughts, and yet did so in terms of "But I say to you" (Matt 5:21–22, 27–28).

Jesus also built on a moral tradition by upholding the Ten Commandments (Mark 10:19) and following the prophets in stigmatizing social injustice, especially the failure to act justly and lovingly toward those like Lazarus who suffer and are in terrible distress (Luke 16:19–31). But Jesus went so far, according to one tradition, as to make the final judgment depend simply on our practical concern for the hungry, the sick, prisoners, homeless persons, and others in great need (Matt 25:31–46). This included in Jesus' teaching something no prophet ever taught: He identified himself with the hungry, the sick, and others in terrible distress. Moreover, his table fellowship with the pariahs of his society took Jesus beyond anything the prophets ever taught or practiced.[22]

Jesus also broke new ground by linking together the commands to love God and to love our neighbor (Mark 12:28–34). Here he maintained some central moral teaching he had inherited from the Jewish scriptures, but innovated by putting together into one love command the hitherto distinct commandments to love God

(Deut 6:5) and to love one's neighbor (Lev 19:18). He also introduced something startlingly new by teaching love for one's enemies (Matt 5:43–48). Here we reach what have been called "the hard sayings" of Jesus: "love your enemies"; "do not resist an evildoer. But if anyone strikes you on the right cheek, turn the other also"; "do not refuse anyone who wants to borrow from you" (Matt 5:38–42). These and other hard sayings are heroic ideals that go beyond any commonsense morality that might be established on reasonable grounds. A dramatic example comes from what Jesus said to someone who had invited him to a meal: "When you give a luncheon or a dinner, do not invite your friends or your brothers or your relatives or rich neighbors.... But when you give a banquet, invite the poor, the crippled, the lame, and the blind" (Luke 14:12–13). Such a practice obviously went above and beyond the call of duty and what would have seemed reasonable to any ordinary "good" person. It was not simply that such hard sayings spoke out against a self-centered policy in life. They were part and parcel of a new life of discipleship that gave total allegiance to Jesus himself. After announcing his coming suffering and death, he added, "If any want to become my followers, let them deny themselves and take up their cross and follow me" (Mark 8:34).

Both then and now, those who do not pay allegiance to Jesus will hardly find any grounds for accepting such heroic demands and putting them into practice. Jesus endorsed the Ten Commandments, which exhort us to do what in any case is morally good and to avoid what in any case is immoral. But he went further to inculcate the heroic morality involved in becoming his disciple. He encouraged his listeners to change their moral perception of the world and to do so by accepting permanent relationship with him—in other words, by accepting a relational, instead of a self-regarding, sense of their moral identity and so asking, "*Whose* am I?" rather than "*Who* am I?"

If we look to Jesus for specific instructions about moral behavior, we find that he forbade certain types of actions. He condemned, for instance, retaliation or paying back in kind those who have harmed us (Matt 5:38–42). Yet he appears to have taught little about particular issues of human behavior, and obviously offered no complete and detailed moral code. What he did was to inculcate certain attitudes and dispositions, and left it to his followers to work out the detailed consequences. Take the parable of the Good Samaritan. The lawyer who provoked Jesus into telling the story asked the question, "Who is my neighbor?" because he wanted to "justify himself." He was anxious to establish his right to eternal life by specifying (or having Jesus specify) exactly his duty toward his neighbor and then by proving that he had carried it out. In that case he would be shown to be "righteous" or acceptable to God. But, instead of engaging in such specifics, Jesus gave an example of helping another human being whom we come across in great distress, and added, "Go and do likewise" (Luke 10:29–37). As far as Jesus was concerned, our neighbors are any human beings who desperately need our help, no matter who they are in their ethnic, national, or religious identity. If we share Jesus' general vision of the world and accept his call to be "perfect as your heavenly Father is perfect" (Matt 5:49), we will set no limits to our goodness since God's goodness knows no limits. Then we will constantly open our eyes to what happens around us, appreciate the decisive values involved, and discern an appropriate response.[23]

The Followers of Jesus

The followers of Jesus, who led the church that emerged after his resurrection and Pentecost, summoned their communities to a different way of living that came from the new life "in Christ" and the guidance of the Holy Spirit, through whom "God's love has been poured into our hearts" (Rom 5:5). Through celebrating together the Lord's Supper, they were expected to let their lives be characterized by hospitality, fundamental equality, and peacemaking (1 Cor 11:18–34). Paul's letters illustrate how sin threatened the life of the church, especially when believers turned back to the lifestyle of the "old self" that they had renounced at baptism (Rom 6:6). Believers could become once again envious and quarrelsome (1 Cor 1—4). Paul admitted that he was afraid to visit the Corinthians a third time, since he might encounter "quarreling, jealousy, anger, selfishness, slander, gossip, conceit, and disorder" (2 Cor 12:20). Vatican II retrieved this sense of the social and ecclesial dimensions of sin—for instance, in its teaching about sin "wounding" the church (*Lumen Gentium*, 11). So too did John Paul II in his 1984 apostolic exhortation, *Reconciliatio et Paenitentia* (Reconciliation and Penance), when he observed how "every sin has repercussions on the entire body of the Church and on the whole human family" (no. 16).

The last paragraph has brought us beyond Jesus to those like Paul who left us the inspired New Testament record, which together with the books of the Old Testament make up the authoritative canon of the scriptures. Here we come to another question based on what I drew from the Cappadocians in chapter 3: What moral decisions and behavior would be illuminated and supported by prayerful reflection on the biblical witness?[24] It is worth starting with the conviction developed by St. Augustine of Hippo: The purpose of scripture is the love of God and neighbor (*De Doctrina Christiana*, 1.84–85). Augustine forcefully reminds us that any use of the Bible in moral argument must be a loving use, a use inspired by the twofold commandment of love proposed by Jesus and repeated, as we saw above, by Vatican II. Having said that, we are still faced with the issue of discerning in and through the scriptures the appropriate response that disciples of Jesus should make when faced with particular moral problems.

Two Principles

Vatican II (*Gaudium et Spes*, 27) and John Paul II in his 1979 encyclical *Redemptor Hominis* (no. 16) applied the parable of the rich man and the poor Lazarus (Luke 16:19–31) to the modern situation of world poverty and hunger. This is a transposition from the level of individuals (the well-fed rich man and the hungry Lazarus) to that of the international order of rich nations and poor nations. Contemporary moral issues often call for such transpositions of scriptural teaching through using *analogical reasoning* and imagination—a principle that still proves its ethical worth. Poor nations, crippled by huge debts and economically deprived of access to the necessary markets by rich nations, resemble Lazarus lying hungry and sick at the door of the wealthy man's home. In the parable of the Good Samaritan, Jesus ends the parable in effect by recommending such analogical thinking: "Go and do likewise" (Luke 10:37). It is up to each Christian group and person to work out in different situations what it is to "do likewise" by serving the needy in ways that cancel boundaries and no longer decide to include some people (neighbors whom enlightened self-interest urges us/me to care for) and exclude others (non-neighbors who have nothing to offer us/me and whom we/I do not have to bother about). In discerning thoughtfully and imaginatively what it would be like in a very different world to "do likewise," the use of analogical reasoning in moral decision making will also be guided by the moral demands implied through the celebration of the Eucharist (see chapters 2 and 3), the lives of saintly men and women (see chapters 1 and 3), the official teaching of those in authority, and the teaching on a virtuous life coming from such classical authors as Aristotle and St. Thomas Aquinas.

Along with such analogical thinking about the parable of the Good Samaritan and further moral teaching from Jesus, a second principle seems important in applying New Testament teaching to the current situation—what we might call *the principle of a further rationale.* Jesus opposed divorce on the grounds of its being against the divine intentions in creating the two sexes. In marriage two "become one flesh"; hence "what God has joined together, let no one separate" (Mark 10:2–9). Jesus linked marriage and the family to a transcendent principle of legitimation, God's original plan in creating the human race. One can add further considerations by reflecting on the functioning of marriage and the family. Let me develop a little the relevance of such analogical thinking and further rationale.

Advanced industrial nations are presently enjoying an age of affluence and general excess that bears comparison with the situation of the rich man, his family, and his friends in the parable of Jesus. We can fill out the laconic picture of the rich householder "feasting sumptuously each day," and add a further rationale to the lesson(s) of the parable. Binge drinking and alcoholism, for instance, appear nowadays to be on the increase. Excessive drinking is often regarded as an indispensable element in college and higher education—part of good-natured fun. Habitual heavy drinkers can be taken as comic or at least routine. Excessive drinking currently costs Western nations billions of dollars in absenteeism, family breakdowns, crime, and pressure on health services.

Alcohol-related illnesses seem to be spiraling out of control. At the end of 2003 it was reported in the United Kingdom that cases of liver disease caused by overdrinking have soared by 75 percent in six years and now cost the National Health Service more than sixty-five million pounds a year. A September 2003 government report in the UK estimated that seventeen million working days were lost each year to hangovers. Excess in the consumption of alcohol offers an analogy to the habits of the rich man in Jesus' parable. One could draw out a similar, even more painful analogy by introducing the current consumption of drugs and its results. Such contemporary parallels to Jesus' story of the rich man raise similar questions: Is such a lifestyle meaningful? Or does it poison your life here and hereafter by doing harm to yourself and to others?

When defending marriage, Jesus was content to quote the words of Genesis about the God-given impulse that draws men and women away from their parents to establish a new life together (Gen 2:24). Vatican II would call the "partnership" or "companionship" of man and woman "the primary form of communion between persons" (*Gaudium et Spes* 12)—in other words, a unique relationship of love. The council made a crucial advance in official teaching on marriage by adding a further rationale to Jesus' defense of marriage. Vatican II placed love between the couple on a par with the generation of children (ibid., 47–52, esp. 49).

We may develop this rationale even further. Men and women experience a profound human yearning for lasting love; they want to commit themselves permanently to a caring relationship and to raising children together. Religious and civil marriage brings a range of practical benefits to the couple, their children, and the state. Marriage is the foundation of organized society; the future of nations depends on the health of family life. The common good requires the state to protect and encourage strong, stable marriage as the favorable setting for child rearing; children do better in the family environment when reared by their biological mother and father. Broken marriages and single-parent families often leave the offspring with serious, lifelong problems.[25] Sadly in modern society an adult-focused view of marriage sees it largely or simply as a relationship between consenting adults with a bundle of their rights and privileges. Since, however, children are the future of society, the state cannot afford to take a merely adult-focused view of marriage, but must encourage and facilitate the begetting of off-spring and their healthy education within the family and society.

Same-Sex Unions

What then of "same-sex marriages," a social experiment that goes beyond "civil partnerships" and redefines marriage as it has been long understood? This means more than merely extending the public benefits of a registered and legally recognized "civil part-nership" to same-sex couples and to other domestic partners. Same-sex marriages would mean that same-sex couples have the right to marry and make that exclusive and permanent commit-ment that the states have so far normally limited to partners of a different sex. In the name of the dignity, equality, and legal rights of all, advocates for same-sex marriages want to alter legally the institution of marriage. Two individuals of the same sex who wish to marry, it is claimed, should be able to do so and enjoy all the pro-tections, benefits, and obligations that have been so far conferred by civil marriage on married couples of the opposite sex.

Many argue, rightly I believe, that such a redefinition would undermine the institution of (heterosexual) marriage and damage the family, the basic unit on which the future of civil society depends. It would be a declaration on the part of society that it is entirely indifferent as to whether women marry men or marry other women. Society would be saying to young people in school, "It is entirely up to you whether you marry people of the same sex or of the other sex. Both are perfectly equal and acceptable lifestyles." I do not think the future good of society allows the state to endorse such a stance. The state and all its citizens should respect the private lives and choices of people, and not capitulate to ugly, homophobic prejudices and to any kind of "unjust discrimi-nation" (*Catechism of the Catholic Church*, 2358). But that is not the same thing as introducing same-sex marriages as a totally accept-able alternative to other-sex marriages.[26]

On certain issues like same-sex marriages some Christians want to rework the moral teaching inherited from the scriptures and the mainstream tradition and make it more acceptable to "current thinking" and so render Christianity more "credible" to the modern world. But what is ultimately at stake is responsibly discerning the mind of Christ and following the prompting of the Spirit. Where and how in the questions of today and the signs of the times do we experience the guidance of Jesus and the Spirit, who hold together the key to being truly human? The context has to be found in the inspired witness of the scriptures, in common worship (which reformulates and recontextualizes the scriptures), and in generous service of the needy.

Thus we are brought back to four questions of chapter 3, which do not appear to be always raised when some Catholics and other Christians discuss vexing moral questions of today. Does this or that decision involve our being led by the Holy Spirit and by Christ? Does it enrich our common worship and is it prompted by the Eucharist? Is it supported by prayerful reflection on the scriptures? Does it lead us to a more generous service of the needy? Once again let me admit that it is not always easy to answer these four questions. But if we do not even ask them, it is doubtful that in our post-Vatican II situation we will discern and practice a Cappadocian-style creative fidelity in our moral lives.

Note: For a fuller treatment of many points discussed in this chapter, see the *Catechism of the Catholic Church*, 1700–2557, and various articles in the NCE: "Abortion," vol. 1, 24–35; "Capital Punishment," vol. 3, 84–89; "Contraception," vol. 4, 218–23; "Euthanasia," vol. 5, 457–59; *"Evangelium Vitae,"* vol. 5, 476–77; "Homosexuality," vol. 7, 66–71; *"Humanae Vitae,"* vol. 7, 179–81; "Pacificism," vol. 10, 744–48; *"Veritatis Splendor,"* vol. 14, 451–52; "War," vol. 14, 634–44. See also the 1999 encyclical of John Paul II, *Veritatis Splendor* (The Splendor of Truth) and some commentaries: M. Allsopp, ed., *Veritatis Splendor: American Responses* (Kansas City, MO: Sheed & Ward, 1995); J. A. DiNoia and R. Cessario, eds., *"Veritatis Splendor" and the Renewal of Moral Theology* (Princeton, NJ: Scepter, 1999); M. Elsbernd, "The Reinterpretation of *Gaudium et Spes* in *Veritatis Splendor,"* *Horizons* 29 (2002), 225–39; R. Hütter and

D. Dieter, eds., *Ecumenical Ventures in Ethic:. Protestants Engage Pope John Paul's Moral Encyclicals* (Grand Rapids, MI: Eerdmans, 1998); J. A. Selling and J. Jans, eds. *The Splendor of Accuracy: An Examination of the Assertions Made in Veritatis Splendor* (Kampen, Netherlands: Kok Pharos, 1994); J. Wilkins, ed., *Considering Veritatis Splendor* (Cleveland: Pilgrim Press, 1994).

6

RELATIONS WITH OTHERS

We must force ourselves to overcome every barrier with
incessant prayer, with persevering dialogue and with a
fraternal and concrete cooperation in favor of the poor-
est and the most needy.

> John Paul II, during the Week of Prayer
> for Christian Unity, 2003

Thanks to Vatican II, the Catholic Church is irrevocably
committed to meeting other believers.

> Francis Cardinal Arinze,
> *Vatican II: Forty Personal Stories*, 176

One of the great things to be encouraged systematically by the
Second Vatican Council was the openness of the Catholic Church
to relations with other Christians, Jews, Muslims, and members of
other religions. Receiving and living the teaching of the council
entails persevering dialogue and cooperation with these "others,"
and very much requires a spirit of creative fidelity. The election to
the papacy of John Paul II in 1978, the collapse of European
Communism in 1989 and of the Soviet Union in 1991, and the ter-
ror attacks on the United States of September 11, 2001, are only
some of the major events that have changed the post-Vatican II climate and context in which the whole Catholic Church is called to
practice loving relations with all "other" men and women. A rich
quarry of documents and events opens up for those who wish to
explore the story of those relations since 1965. In chapter 2, I
pointed readers in that direction when summarizing the work of
the Pontifical Council for Promoting Christian Unity.

But in this book I may serve readers better by recovering some memories and spelling out my own personal perspectives on what has been happening. Fruitful dialogue with other Christians and with members of other religions takes place on the human level. Even well-crafted joint statements will not lead anywhere, unless they are grounded in personal exchanges and a loving regard for one another. Hence it seems worthwhile telling the story of my own journey of dialogue with others. It is the only story that I can tell directly and out of my personal experience, since I have never been invited to become a member of any official ecumenical dialogue.

Other Christians

Contacts with other Christians stretch back to my childhood in a small town, Frankston (Victoria, Australia). I grew up in a large house, set on a hill surrounded by twenty-four acres of land and looking across a vast bay to the city of Melbourne and the mountains beyond. My parents were practicing Catholics, who took for granted that their six children would attend Mass every Sunday. A crucifix, papal blessings, and pictures of the Sacred Heart and of the Blessed Virgin Mary hung on the walls of our home. A small supply of water from the shrine to Mary in Lourdes was available. I remember my mother dabbing a little on the scars left by an operation on my father's shoulder. We were tied into the institutional church through Mother's cousin who was a Jesuit priest and some of Father's seven siblings. He had two sisters who were nuns and three brothers who became priests; one of them was a bishop who attended Vatican II (see chapter 1). When Bishop James O'Collins came to stay with us, he carried a battered suitcase containing the vestments, vessels, and missal to celebrate Mass. My brothers and I had to practice serving, and remember an extra washing of the hands and the variations in Latin responses required for a bishop. But among the endless stream of visitors whom my parents invited home were many who were not Roman Catholics.

Yet it was even more the local Peninsula Country Golf Club that fostered contacts with other Christians right from my earliest years. General Harold Grimwade (of the Felton, Grimwade, and

Duerdins drug company, later Drug Houses Australia) served for years as the club president. He became my archetypal general and president. I am sure that years later he made it easier for me to accept General Eisenhower's election as president of the United States and General de Gaulle's emergence as French president. Sir Norman and Dame Mabel Brookes, whom I met as a child, were also members of the club and local residents. A most successful tennis player, Norman had been the first left-hander to be a Wimbledon champion (1907) and helped win the Davis Cup for Australia (1907–11, 1914); years later I was to visit the scene of some of his tennis triumphs at Newport, Rhode Island. Descended from a British officer who had guarded Napoleon until his death on St. Helena, Mabel was a flamboyant, warmhearted person, the leading society hostess of Melbourne, and president of the committee of management for the Queen Victoria Memorial Hospital for fifty years. Like my parents, she showed generous hospitality during the Second World War to many American officers and soldiers. But in her case they included Lyndon Johnson, a future president of the United States, and General Douglas MacArthur, whom she entertained for several months in 1942 when he had his headquarters in Melbourne.[1] I learned the local adaptation of the Boston lines about the Cabots[2] and the Lowells: "Frankston is a pleasant place full of bays and nooks. God knows the Grimwades / And the Grimwades know the Brookes."[3]

Before Settling at the Gregorian

Social contacts with other Christians happened naturally. But praying with them was still forbidden in the Catholic Church, a latecomer to the ecumenical movement in which many members of other churches were far ahead. A significant experience that set me on a genuinely ecumenical path came in the 1950s through a symposium at the University of Melbourne during a week of prayer for Christian unity. A professor of scripture, Davis McCaughey, spoke movingly about the work of a Catholic trailblazer, Abbé Paul Couturier (1881–1953). Through his vast correspondence and tracts on prayer for Christian unity, Couturier had enjoyed contacts with Christians around the world and encouraged innumerable people to pray for "the unity Christ wills, by the means he wills."

Presbyterians from Northern Ireland whose republican views endorsed union with the South and made them strikingly different from many of their coreligionists, Davis and his wife Jean decided to migrate with their children to Melbourne in the early 1950s. Davis became Master of Ormond College, University of Melbourne (1959–79), and a prime mover in bringing together the Methodists, most Congregationalists, and a majority of Presbyterians to establish in 1977 the Uniting Church in Australia. Davis and his friends chose the word *Uniting* (instead of calling the merger "the United Church") since they cherished the hope that this move would one day lead to a wider union—with Anglicans and Catholics. When preparing in the 1960s for the creation of the Uniting Church, Davis and his theological colleagues published their views of what they understood the New Testament to teach about the many-sided nature of the church and its leadership willed by Christ and practiced from the time of the earliest Christian communities. At one point I considered doing my doctoral research on what they had written. Davis became the first president of the Uniting Church (1977–79) and later returned from retirement to serve as governor of the State of Victoria (1986–91)—a choice that met with general public agreement, since his wisdom and integrity were widely recognized. Davis (d. 2005), his wife Jean, and their family always proved inspiring friends. In 1974 I dedicated a book to Davis and Jean "with love and admiration."[4] By that time I had just finished five years teaching in an interdenominational setting which as Master of Ormond College he had helped to construct in Melbourne.

After completing my PhD at the University of Cambridge on four modern approaches to divine revelation (under the supervision of the Anglican Regis Professor of Divinity, Dennis Nineham), from 1969 to 1973, I taught for six months each year as a staff member of the Jesuit Theological College, on Royal Parade in Melbourne. We held classes across Royal Parade in the theological hall of Ormond College, where our library was housed, and we shared other facilities with the Congregationalist, Methodist, and Presbyterian students and staff in the United Faculty of Theology. Eventually the Jesuit Theological College formally joined the UFT, as did the

Anglican group from Trinity College (University of Melbourne). In the early months of 1973, my last term of lecturing in Melbourne, I taught fundamental theology to a class of fifty, which included Anglican, Catholic, Methodist, and Presbyterian students, as well as a Coptic priest, a Greek Orthodox priest, and a Norwegian Lutheran. My course dealt with such basic issues as divine revelation and the human response of faith. There were few points of conflict. The main challenge came from a handful of Protestant students, who felt that even raising questions about God's self-manifestation in Jesus Christ was to put faith in doubt. I enjoyed the ecumenical setting of my theological work in Melbourne, as well as the chance of sometimes joining Davis and his family on Sunday evenings in the Master's Lodge at Ormond College.

During that time between completing my doctorate and being posted full-time to Rome in 1974, I also taught a semester a year for Weston School of Theology in Cambridge (Massachusetts), one of the seven theological faculties or departments that joined together in 1968 to form the Boston Theological Institute. Students at one school could take courses at any of the others, even though they continued to receive their degrees from their own institution. The inauguration of the BTI meant that the Jesuit priests and students of Weston College moved from the town of Weston twelve miles into Cambridge, Massachusetts. There we used the lecture theaters, seminar rooms, chapel, cafeteria, library, and other facilities of Episcopal Theological School (later renamed Episcopal Divinity School), and enjoyed very close relations with ETS and Harvard Divinity School, which was just across the Cambridge Common. Theological education alongside students who belonged to other Christian churches delighted many of the Jesuit seminarians (called scholastics). But it seemed unsettling and even threatening to a few. Some Jesuit faculty members had opposed entering the BTI: "The scholastics will all want to rush off to the Protestant teachers." In fact, a few Jesuit professors of Weston College drew many Protestant and Episcopalian students from the other schools of the BTI, while the Jesuit scholastics often seemed slow to exploit the opportunity to study with the best available professors in various branches of theology. For years the imbalance between cross-registration *into* rather than *out of* Weston College proved flattering and even embarrassing.

I learned much from and made friends with various colleagues in the BTI, for instance, with Harvey Cox, a Baptist theologian at Harvard Divinity School who had become famous through his perceptive study of Christianity and the modern world, *The Secular City* (1965). At the launch of my *Man and His New Hopes* in the fall of 1969 (see chapter 1), Harvey spoke and we were all filmed by a German television team that was making a program on Christian theology in the United States. Harvey contrasted my "Protestant" book with his own "Catholic" *Feast of Fools*, which was to be published a few months later. My book highlighted God's word of promise, while Harvey's drew inspiration from Catholic customs in the Middle Ages to encourage festivity and celebration. One hundred and forty people attended, compliments flew around, and we enjoyed some lively discussion about the scriptures, the resurrection of Christ, and the dangerous implications of a theologian's self-interest. "All of us," Harvey remarked, "take Caesar's money." I went home immensely encouraged, if haunted by one question. A girl left the auditorium, loudly demanding, "What the hell does the resurrection have to do with life anyway?" In later years that question came back to me, every time I wrote articles and books on Christ's resurrection.

During my first semester at Weston School of Theology, the fall of 1968, the warden of (the Anglican) Lincoln Theological College (England), Alan Webster, wrote me a cheering letter about a German Protestant theologian whom I had suggested inviting: "I know you will be delighted that [Jürgen] Moltmann's visit [to Lincoln] was a very great success. He did relatively simple papers—on the theology of revelation—and did them very well indeed. We liked particularly his constant reiteration that one can face the future either with anxiety or hope, and most of us waver between these two." The previous year at the University of Tübingen, I had attended Moltmann's lectures on the theology of hope. We struck up a lasting friendship, and I soon found myself in a position to bring him out to Australia. As a member of the committee planning an ecumenical component for the International Eucharistic Congress held in Melbourne in early 1973, I encouraged inviting

Moltmann, Mother Teresa of Calcutta, Dr. Lukas Vischer (head of the Faith and Order Commission, the theological arm of the World Council of Churches), and others who included Cardinal Johannes Willebrands, then head of the Secretariat for the Promotion of the Unity of Christians (renamed in 1988 the Council for Promoting Christian Unity), and Father Tom Stransky, who with Willebrands had been one of the founding members of the secretariat. Both Willebrands and Stransky were fully and intelligently committed to fostering ecumenical relations. Willebrands always struck me as a bit stolid, while Stransky was constantly sparkling and interesting.

On one memorable evening in the Melbourne Town Hall, Moltmann joined Mother Teresa and spoke to three thousand people on the Christian vocation to spread peace. He teased me afterwards: "Is that what you wanted to do at this Eucharistic Congress? Make a team out of a Catholic saint and a leading Protestant theologian?" On one occasion during the congress I was sitting in the back of a taxi between Moltmann and a European Catholic theologian telling them that I had just been invited to take up a teaching position at the Gregorian University in Rome. The Catholic theologian cut in sharply: "Don't you go to that clerical ghetto!" By way of rebuttal Moltmann shook the lock of dark, silky hair that constantly hung over his forehead, and quoted a German proverb: "Rome is worth a journey (*Rom ist eine Reise wert*)." I am happy to have followed Moltmann's advice, and he was to visit me several times in Rome. But before any of that happened, we were together again, but this time in West Africa.

Dr. Lukas Vischer had invited me to attend the Faith and Order Commission meeting at the University of Ghana before I took up residence in Rome. During two weeks (July 22–August 5, 1974), the commission continued revising its document on baptism, Eucharist, and the ordained ministry (BEM), a seminal statement to be published in 1982, selected topics for new studies, discussed future steps toward church unity, and drew together a study by Christians all over the world on "giving account of the hope that is in us." I enjoyed working with two hundred theologians from nearly fifty countries, wrote reports for journals in Australia, England (*The Tablet*), Ireland, Italy, New Zealand, and the United States (*Theological Studies*), and found that two experiences threw light on my own hopes.

With some members of the commission I visited the dungeons of Cape Coast Castle to the west of Accra. Bats darted over our heads, as the guide took us through those vaulted caverns. In past centuries up to a thousand slaves were held there, before being hurried through three outlets to the beach and the waiting ships. Archaeologists had unearthed beads, pipes, and human bones from the mud-encrusted floors. From one section of the dungeons slaves could hear Christians praying and singing in the chapel directly above them. I climbed up to the main courtyard outside the chapel, silent and appalled. All those slaves crammed together in stench, darkness, and misery seemed to cry out to me, as they waited to continue walking their way of the cross. I went around the castle wall, looked down into a small courtyard, and noticed three prison officers pacing up and down among groups of convicts. From a wall high above, seven vultures scanned the scene. A prisoner glanced up at me and put two fingers in front of this mouth. I understood his gesture, but had no cigarettes to throw down to him. That visit to Cape Coast Castle pushed the question at me: How far was I willing to commit myself in trying to bring peace to suffering men and women? One Sunday I went with Moltmann to a Presbyterian service in Accra. The African congregation thundered out the hymns. From either side we could hear the beat of drums from two "spiritual" churches, where the Christians sang, clapped their hands, and danced. In our service drums were used only at the offertory procession, the whole style was more sedate, but warm happiness hung in the air. My eye drifted beyond the brightly dressed ladies to the back of the congregation. A giant Ghanaian in a vivid green shirt took off his dark glasses and smiled at me. I felt at home with my brothers and sisters. The joyfulness of their faith shouted the message: Keep spreading Christ's good news.

It was just ten years since I first left Australia in June 1964 and visited the Faith and Order secretariat of the World Council of Churches in Geneva. There Lukas Vischer had welcomed me warmly and encouraged me to tackle a doctorate (at the Gregorian University in Rome) on some fundamental theological issues connected with interchurch dialogues and unions: for instance, criteria for using the scriptures to bridge confessional differences. Instead I had gone to the University of Cambridge, written a thesis on God's self-revelation, and traveled incessantly between Australia, Europe, and the United States. By bringing me to Accra, Vischer did more for me than simply mark the beginning and the end of a decade that made up my midlife journey. He confronted me with the suffering and vitality of Africans and African Christianity. That encounter injected joy into my determination to accept my place and work in the church. I would do my best to serve suffering humanity and let Christ's love shine in my world. Those two weeks in Ghana were a last touch in preparing me for Rome and the Gregorian University, where the students come from well over one hundred nations and have made the Gregorian a deeply satisfying international setting for much of my academic life.

Ecumenism at the Gregorian

The Canadian dean of theology, René Latourelle, who had invited me to begin teaching at the Gregorian, appreciated the value of contacts with great outsiders for our students, above all for those doing the two-year, specialized licentiate programs. He secured courses of six weeks or even a whole semester not only from top Catholics but also from leading Anglican, Orthodox, and Protestant theologians. After Latourelle retired as dean, I maintained his practice of enriching our offerings by inviting outside scholars—especially with the help of the McCarthy Family Foundation.

In the spring of 1987 Moltmann came down from Tübingen to teach a course at the Gregorian on the "last things": death, judgment, purgatory, heaven, and hell. But he had already been in Rome a number of times before that. In October 1975 he lectured at an international congress on the theology of the cross, and I persuaded him to give a talk one evening at the North American College in Rome. We had dinner first with two Americans, Archbishop Joseph Bernardin (still at Cincinnati and not yet Cardinal Archbishop of Chicago) and Cardinal Humberto Medeiros of Boston. It happened that the baseball teams of their respective cities were meeting that evening in the World Series. But Moltmann managed to steer the conversation away from sports to the seeming ineffectiveness of so much preaching and what might be done to improve homilies and sermons. It was the first time I had met Bernardin. As I wrote later to a friend, "Bernardin seemed frank, open, and altogether a good thing." After dinner Medeiros came to Moltmann's talk, which was more or less an introduction to his new book on the church. Then we had a chat and a drink until nearly midnight, discussing the Eucharist and intercommunion. Medeiros looked surprised to hear Moltmann's frank endorsement of intercommunion. But he gave Moltmann a warm hug at the end, and invited him to come and stay at his residence in Boston. Moltmann told me afterwards how pleased he was to meet such a human cardinal. I told Moltmann how glad I was to be able to run an informal seminar for a cardinal by enlisting good Protestant support.

In 1991 a Lutheran biblical scholar and retired bishop, Eduard Lohse, came to the Gregorian as a visiting McCarthy Professor. When he was presiding Lutheran bishop in Germany, Lohse led the way in ecumenical affairs and welcomed Pope John Paul II to Germany in 1980. In October 1991 I collected Bishop Lohse and his wife at Fiumicino airport and took them to a private hotel that faces the Piazza Farnese and is run by Rome's most picturesque group of nuns, the Sisters of St. Bridget of Sweden (d. 1373). They still wear a distinctively Scandinavian headgear. My imagination adds a spear in their right hand to complete the Nordic look. When I walked in that day with the Lohses and their luggage, we ran into the Catholic bishop of Stockholm, a German with a name that trips off the tongue, Hubertus Brandenburg. Lohse and Brandenburg fell into each other's arms, the first and only time I have ever seen two German bishops giving each other a hug. Their friendship went back to World War II, when they served together in the German navy.

In his six-week course at the Gregorian, Lohse examined major themes from St. Paul's Letter to the Romans, a choice I had encouraged him to make. Where better to discuss that letter than in Rome itself? In a major public lecture Lohse dealt with Paul's view of the ministry of St. Peter. The huge audience included in the front row a weary Cardinal Joseph Ratzinger who occasionally nodded off. As prefect of the Congregation for the Doctrine of the Faith, the cardinal (who had himself been a visiting professor at the Gregorian in 1972) was the most visible defender of orthodox faith in the Catholic Church. Lohse analyzed passages from the First Letter to the Corinthians and the Letter to the Galatians in which Paul explicitly refers to Peter and his ministry. It was a superb and balanced analysis that kept its distance from the implicit references to Peter that some (self-indulgent) scholars optimistically detect elsewhere in the Pauline correspondence. In the discussion period that followed the lecture, the last question summed up the drift of the lecturer's argument: "Bishop Lohse, your interpretation seems to mean that Paul contributed in a major way to the emerging view of Peter's ministry. Would you call Paul the principal architect of the Petrine office?" Time had run out, and all Lohse could say was to state emphatically, "Yes." His affirmative answer rested on Paul's recognition of Peter as primary witness to the risen Christ (1 Cor 15:5) and on Paul's deference to Peter, despite their clash at Antioch (Gal 2:11–14).

Another delightful visitor was Professor John McIntyre, then Moderator of the Church of Scotland. This outstanding Presbyterian theologian had welcomed John Paul II when the pope visited Edinburgh in 1982. On that occasion they sat stiffly side by side on two dignified chairs especially provided for the occasion. A day or two later a van turned up and two respectable-looking men in overalls carried the chairs away as if they had every right to do so; it was in fact a cool theft, perhaps on contract for some specialist collector. McIntyre came to Rome to return the pope's visit to Edinburgh. On the day he visited the pope, he also came to the Gregorian, attended my seminar for licentiate students, and complained to me about the way students for the ministry become impoverished as communicators of Christ: "We take away their imagination and fill them with concepts." Before and after that session I brought McIntyre everywhere I could in our building, wanting to show him off to anyone we met. Even by Roman standards he looked unusual, wearing black breeches that clung tightly to his stockings and ended well over his silver-buckled shoes. A white-lace jabot covered his throat above the somber jacket. The Roman public is long accustomed to a wide range of clerical dress, both official and disheveled. But McIntyre held their attention that day in his official Moderator's attire, reminiscent of Rembrandt's portrayal of some Dutch Calvinists.

Anglican leaders have been constant visitors to Rome since 1960, when Dr. Geoffrey Fisher visited Pope John XXIII and was the first archbishop of Canterbury to visit a pope since 1397. Archbishop Michael Ramsey set up a representation in the city, a symbol of belief in the ecumenical future. The Anglican Communion is still the only non-Roman Catholic Christian Church to have a permanent office in Rome. Groups of Anglicans (often joined by some others) come regularly to Rome for courses, which often feature one or more local speakers. I have been recruited to speak on the study of theology, teaching about Christ, and "Peter in Rome" (or the ministry of St. Peter and his successors, the bishops of Rome). In spelling out Peter's ministry, I base it primarily, but not exclusively, on his role as witness to the resurrection.

The Anglican Centre is housed in the Doria Palace, where Don Frank and Donna Orietta Doria Pamphilj repeatedly entertained Anglican visitors, high and low. In 1989 they put on a big reception for Dr. Robert Runcie, who had come on an official visit to Rome as archbishop of Canterbury. The visit outraged the Reverend Ian Paisley, a fundamentalist preacher from Northern Ireland. He descended on the city; on the evening of the reception he stood across the Via del Corso from the Palazzo Doria holding up a hostile placard. An enterprising middle-aged guest spotted him on her way into the reception. She darted over the road through the traffic, held out her hand, and said with a smile, "I've always wanted to shake the hand of a totally dedicated bigot." To his credit Paisley laughed. But he had been at his antics since early morning, when he had taken a friend with him to protest at the Holy Communion service that Archbishop Runcie celebrated in the Anglican Church of All Saints close to the Spanish Steps. Worship had hardly begun before the two protesters rose to their feet and denounced Runcie for betraying the martyred archbishop of Canterbury, Thomas Cranmer (1489–1556), and all that the sixteenth-century Reformation stood for. Church wardens ushered Paisley and his friend out. Then Runcie resumed by saying, "Let us now continue with the words of Archbishop Cranmer as found in the Book of Common Prayer."

Bevan Wardrobe was the priest in charge of All Saints when Runcie came. I have ongoing contacts with the incumbents of that church as well as with the American Episcopal Church, St. Paul's Within the Walls. The story goes that when Bevan was short-listed for All Saints, the other prominent name on the list was that of a Reverend Mr. Pope. The appointments committee saw at once that they could not be responsible for nominating a second Pope in Rome; so Bevan got the job.

Rome saw the start of a warm friendship with George Carey. As a parish priest he first came to Rome for a course in 1977, and later attended another course also organized by the Anglican Centre shortly after his consecration in 1987 as bishop of Bath and Wells. I contributed to both courses, and on the second occasion got to know George even more when he stayed on for a few days after the other bishops had left. It seemed only a short time when he was back in Rome in 1992 as archbishop of Canterbury and invited me to take part in a theological conversation about the role of doctrines in the life of Christians. It was the day on which I joined in celebrating Gesine Doria's wedding in the family church, St. Agnes in Piazza Navona. I returned to the Doria Palace for one quick course of a megameal, and then disappeared upstairs to share the conversation with Archbishop Carey in the part of the palace given over to the Anglican Centre. Later there was to be a magic Sunday at Canterbury with George and Eileen Carey when Cardinal Carlo Maria Martini of Milan (who had been rector at the Gregorian 1978–79) came and preached. In the cathedral everything was done with Anglican precision and style, and lunch was a delightful family affair prepared by the Careys' daughter Rachel and her husband, Andy Day. Subsequently George and Eileen spent a memorable week with me at the University of Notre Dame (South Bend, Indiana) where George and I were teaching during the summer program of 1996. We met out in Melbourne (Australia) in mid-1997 when George spoke at an ecumenical service in St. Patrick's Cathedral, which had just been restored and refurbished for the centenary of its opening. Christians from all manner of communities attended and participated with gusto.

There were groups cheerfully meeting there at the bottom of the world, who would still disdain praying together in some parts of Europe. No local Ian Paisley denounced George or any of the other Christian leaders for betraying their faith.

In London I occasionally called on the Careys at Lambeth Palace—for a meal, a cup of coffee, and once for a most cheerful Christmas carol service with those who worked there and their families. A more solemn visit came at Easter 2001 when, on the eve of completing ten years as archbishop of Canterbury, George hosted in the Lambeth Palace Chapel a service of thanksgiving for the lives of Frank and Orietta Doria. His address stressed the Dorias' persistent commitment to ecumenical relations and their generous support of the Anglican Centre in Rome. Frank had died in 1998, and Orietta in November 2000.[5] Less than three months after the memorial service for the Dorias, George and Eileen, together with Rachel and Andy, came on a lightning visit to Rome to celebrate my seventieth birthday. George wrote the foreword to the *Festschrift*[6] and spoke at the presentation. At the end of the proceedings he joined Cardinal Edward Cassidy, then president of the Pontifical Council for Promoting Christian Unity, in giving a concluding blessing to those who attended in our *aula magna*. George, now retired as Lord Carey of Clifton, returned to the Gregorian in the spring of 2004 as the visiting McCarthy Professor on the Gregorian's faculty of theology and lectured on "Unity and Mission: The Task of the Church to Include All and Be One."

Cardinal Cassidy once summed up what many Christians have envisaged for interchurch relations since Vatican II by speaking about "ecumenism of the heart." Friendship, networking, and being constantly available for other Christians count more than dozens of documents and consensus agreements. We need the agreed statements (see chapter 2) and the "silent service" of such scholars as the Anglican Professor Henry Chadwick, who worked for many years on the Anglican-Roman Catholic International Commission to establish the degree of doctrinal convergence on the Eucharist, the ordained ministry, and authority in the church. But without our being or becoming real friends with one another, such statements risk remaining simply pieces of paper. Henry himself has proved a wonderful friend to me and other Catholics.

In the fall of 1991 a committee of Catholics, Episcopalians, and Lutherans invited speakers for an international conference on St. Augustine of Hippo held at the University of Wisconsin, Madison. For my lecture I gathered and evaluated some themes from Augustine's teaching on the resurrection. A bonus from that meeting was the chance of spending time with Henry, who gave a vintage lecture on Augustine that concluded the conference. For me and many others Henry has always epitomized scrupulous scholarship elegantly presented. He gently urged me to begin writing for Oxford University Press. I set to work on a study of Jesus Christ, which appeared in 1995 as *Christology: A Biblical, Historical, and Systematic Study of Jesus Christ*. Before publication, OUP submitted the manuscript to seven different readers. All of them helped to improve the final product, not least the one who sent several pages of extremely negative evaluation. Since then I have published or edited a half-dozen books for OUP. I owe Henry a great debt of gratitude for pushing me in the direction of OUP and for the inspiring example of his own learning and life.

After Vatican II closed in 1965, many dramatic changes and advances have taken place in ecumenical relations. The closing decades of the twentieth century saw the continuing growth of Christianity in Africa and parts of Asia, a sensational spread of Pentecostal churches,[7] and a decline in some mainline Protestant churches. The former attract people by their openness to new impulses from the Holy Spirit and warm sense of community. The latter at times have either seemed tied to dead controversies of the past, or else have allowed the authority of the scriptures to be eroded as they take their moral standards from contemporary society. Since the end of the 1960s the charismatic renewal has brought a kind of "Pentecostalization" to the Catholic Church—due not least to Vatican II's respect for personal charisms or gifts of the Holy Spirit, a sea change in how they were viewed in the Catholic Church. The scriptures have become much more important in the public worship and private lives of Catholics, even if there is still a long way to go toward implementing the Vatican II dream of the church being utterly biblical. My own life has been enriched by friendship with such non-Roman Catholics as George and Eileen Carey, Henry and Peggy Chadwick, Davis and Jean McCaughey, and Jürgen and Elisabeth Moltmann. Feeling myself for years to be the "vicar of Anglicanism" at the Gregorian University, I have been grieved at the way some Anglicans have "let the side down." I think of the deconstructed versions of Christian doctrine that have come from such Anglican bishops as Richard Holloway and John Spong,[8] and of various ethical capitulations to decadent standards in Western culture. I share the grief of Anglican friends over the consecration of an openly gay bishop in New Hampshire and endorse what George Carey wrote in a letter to *The Times* on November 8, 2003: "As the archbishop of Canterbury who presided over the 1998 Lambeth Conference, which declared its mind so decisively on the issue of practicing homosexuality, I can only share the principled distress of the [Anglican] Primates of the Global South and others who have expressed themselves so strongly in recent days. The damage done to ecumenical relations, interfaith dialogue and the mission of the worldwide church is incalculable."

Looking back at what I have tried to do for ecumenical relations since Vatican II, I have few regrets. My major regret is not having joined other Christians in working for the poor and needy. Asian Catholics and other Christians are second to none in their commitment to such common service of those in distress. The remark made by Harvey Cox in the fall of 1969 continues to trouble me: "All of us take Caesar's money." Openness to other Christians can be cozy and comfortable, and be implicitly dictated by the self-interest of theologians. Through common service of our sufferings brothers and sisters everywhere in our world, we have a better chance of growing together as true and honest followers of Christ.

Jews

Almost all Catholics seem to have given up the poisonous idea that Jews are "rejected by God" for having killed Jesus. But many still appear to think or quietly presuppose that Judaism is at best a fossil that has somehow survived against all human possibility, even though Christianity simply superseded Judaism. This was clearly not the view of John Paul II, who early in his pontificate echoed St. Paul (Rom 11:29) by speaking of "the People of God of the Old

Covenant which has never been revoked."[9] That and further teaching by the pope on the Jewish religion fed into a thesis written by a Polish student under my direction.[10] Apart from welcoming Jewish scholars to the Gregorian University, directing that thesis has been probably the most significant thing I have managed to do for Catholic-Jewish relations in Rome itself.

Unlike Australia, England, and the United States, where I enjoyed the company of various Jewish scholars, rabbis, professional people, and the relatives of my eldest niece (who married into a Jewish family), I have come to know few Jews resident in Rome. Jews came to Rome as part of their dispersion around the Middle Eastern and Mediterranean world that seems to have begun even before the Babylonians captured Jerusalem in 587 BC and carried its inhabitants away into exile. One of the few Roman Jews with whom I struck up a close friendship was Giorgio Barzilai. He claimed a family tree stretching back three thousand years and assured me that, despite the slight difference in spelling, he was descended from Barzillai the Gileadite who cared for King David and his troops when they were on the run during the revolt led by David's son, Absalom (2 Sam 17:27–29; 1 Kgs 2:7). In his youth Giorgio had been one of the young men gathered around the atomic physicist Enrico Fermi (1901–54), who settled in the United States before the Second World War. Fermi had gone to Sweden in 1938 to collect his Nobel Prize and did not return to Italy because the new, anti-Semitic laws affected his Jewish wife. Giorgio himself rose to be a professor of electrical engineering at the University of Rome. His father, Salvatore Barzilai, was a notable politician and trial lawyer, and one of the delegates who had created the Treaty of Versailles at the end of World War I. Giorgio enthralled me with his stories of his father's skill in court. In one case Salvatore was prosecuting a murderer: He had propositioned a nun who worked as a nurse in a hospital, and then killed her in a fit of rage when she refused his advances. The defense lawyer had his client admit that he had killed the nun—which in any case was beyond doubt—but allege that he did so because he was outraged *at her propositioning him*. When he rose to address the jury, a normal enough cross section of practicing and nonpracticing Catholics, Salvatore said with righteous anger, "You know that I don't share your religion. But I find this plea an outrageous insult to a woman who dedicated her life to serving the sick and the dying." The killer was convicted.

Over the years my best input into Catholic-Jewish relations has come in the United States: in Burlington (Vermont) and New York. For twenty-five years (1966–90) an energetic Sister of Mercy, Miriam Ward, brought together four or five speakers to present Catholic, Protestant, and Jewish scriptural scholarship for an average audience of well over 150 participants attending the annual Trinity College biblical institute. Like many other lecturers I returned for several summers. The bewitching beauty of Vermont, the vivid interest of the audience, the smooth organization of those weeks, and the chance of spending time with Christian and Jewish scholars make them linger happily in my memory. I remember a particularly pleasant week in 1981 when the other speakers included Theodor Gaster of Columbia University, New York. Then in his late 70s, Gaster had been born in London, where his father was the rabbi for a Spanish and Portuguese congregation. Gaster peppered his lectures with wonderful asides: "We should have taken the scrolls out of the Qumran caves and put the scholars in"; "there were forty Isaiahs and thirty of them lived in Leipzig." (Prior to the Second World War, Leipzig had been a center for biblical studies and some extravagant claims about the authors of the Bible.) When I told Gaster that I had a niece who worked as a New York lawyer, he urged me, "Either get her to leave the city, or pray for her night and day." During that summer week I spent even more time talking with Gaster, after Sister Miriam asked me to take his arm whenever he went out. She did not want a distinguished guest to slip and break a bone on one of the steps or grassy slopes around the campus.

The "summits" I cochaired four times at Easter in New York—on the resurrection (1996), on the Trinity (1998), on the incarnation (2000), and on the redemption (2003)—involved friendly and productive exchanges among twenty or more scholars from various disciplines: biblical studies, the history of theology, philosophy, fundamental and systematic theology, homiletics, literary criticism, and the fine arts. As well as being interdisciplinary, these conferences were also interdenominational, with the participants being not only Anglicans, Catholics, Orthodox, and Protestants but also Jewish. Christian scholars are always helped by the active presence of Jewish colleagues who remind them that Jesus cannot be adequately understood if we leave out the Jewish background from which he came and within which he preached, ministered, and died. Hence my cochair, Stephen Davis of Claremont McKenna College (California), and I invited Alan Segal of Barnard College, New York, to all four summits. For the last summit we also invited a second Jewish scholar, Peter Ochs from the University of Virginia. Segal contributed chapters to the first three books that emerged from these summits and which Oxford University Press published: *The Resurrection* (1997), *The Trinity* (1999), *The Incarnation* (2002). Ochs contributed a chapter to *The Redemption* (Oxford University Press, 2004). John Wilkins, then still editor of *The Tablet*, attended the first summit and wrote later, "I doubt whether in England, despite Christian-Jewish dialogue being well advanced, any Jewish participant could have joined a Christian group with the same ease and assurance as Professor Alan Segal."[11]

Other Religions

In 1965 the Second Vatican Council unpacked and developed what *Lumen Gentium* had said the previous year about Jews and Muslims (nos. 16–17). The Declaration on the Relation of the Church to Non-Christian Religions (*Nostra Aetate*) broke new ground in the history of general councils not only by reflecting very positively on the faith of Jews and Muslims (nos. 3–4) but also by showing appreciation for the spiritual gifts of Hinduism, Buddhism, and "other religions." Their "precepts and doctrines…often reflect a ray of that Truth which enlightens all people" (no. 2).

In the years after the council I tried to improve my knowledge and appreciation of other religions through one visit for lectures to Japan (the summer of 1980) and two more visits to India. My last visit to India (for lectures in 1979 at various centers) also took me to Kerala in the south, where I visited the birthplace of the Hindu thinker Sankara (AD 700–50). The inside walls of a winding staircase in the circular temple carry scenes from the life of this holy philosopher: the power of his prayer saving him from a crocodile; Sankara refusing to follow his mother's wishes and marry; Sankara confusing the old by his youthful wisdom, setting off to find his guru, crossing a river on a pathway of lotus leaves, dividing the water to bring his old mother across, sending her off to heaven, and finally reaching a kind of apotheosis—apparently in Nepal. From the top of the temple we looked across neat rice fields stretching away in the sunset and bordered everywhere by coconut palms. I was surprised to find how deeply I was affected by this visit to India. Back at the Gregorian in Rome, I read with a graduate seminar group the Bhagavad Gita (the philosophical dialogue in the Hindu epic *Mahabharata*) and the Qur'an. The students found the former to open up major divine attributes, and the latter more devout than they had expected. In 1998 I spoke at a symposium cosponsored by Tenri University (Japan) and the Gregorian University. That Japanese university belongs to Tenrikyo, a Shinto sect founded in the nineteenth century and now enjoying several million members. But any small contribution I have been able to make to dialogue with other religions has largely been in what I have written.

When I published *Foundations of Theology* in 1971, I remarked, "History takes time to evaluate the significance of Church Councils and Vatican II will be no exception to this universal law."[12] I made the remark in a chapter entitled "Theology of Revelation out of Vatican II." That chapter, which offered thirteen points for such a theology, limited its dialogue to Western theologians, both Catholics and other Christians. It took me some time to evaluate and interpret the doctrine of God's self-revelation more broadly. Ten years later, when I published *Fundamental Theology*, I received and expressed the council more fully by using *Nostra Aetate* and *Gaudium et Spes* to construct a whole chapter ("Christ and the Non-Christians") that reflected on the revelatory and salvific self-communication of God beyond Christianity.[13] Two years later my *Interpreting Jesus* ended by spelling out why believers should hold Christ to be the source of salvation for the whole world. That chapter drew not only from *Gaudium et Spes* (no. 22) and other relevant Vatican II documents but also from the 1979 encyclical of John Paul II and its reflections on Christ's mysterious and powerful presence everywhere (*Redemptor Hominis*, 11, 13).[14] In the 1990s I first examined what the council taught or at least implied about the revelatory activity of Christ and the Holy Spirit among those who have not explicitly accepted faith in Christ or have never been in a position to do so.[15] Two years later my *Christology* described and explained what mainstream Christian faith holds about Christ as *redeemer* for all men and women of all times and places, as well as facing the question: How can we interpret redemption for those who do not or have not (yet) heard the New Testament message of light and life coming through Christ? I suggested how he is universally present through the Holy Spirit and as Word and Wisdom. Exploiting the rich vein of Wisdom teaching in the scriptures, I proposed that all genuine wisdom shows the saving and revealing presence of Christ.[16] The theme of Christ as the Wisdom of God can, I believe, be wonderfully exploited to elucidate his personal presence and power among all people. So far I have not had the time myself to take up and develop that theme of Christ as universal Wisdom. But I did encourage one doctoral student to prepare the ground for such a way of reading and interpreting the heart of all the religions and cultures of the world.[17]

As I mentioned in chapter 1, from late 1997 the debate about Jacques Dupuis's landmark study, *Toward a Christian Theology of Religious Pluralism*, has made me read and think even more about the activity of the tripersonal God in bringing to all people light and life. The debate led me to publish two articles and a chapter in a book,[18] attempting to clarify better both issues and terminology about Christianity and the religions in the light of the scriptures, the council's documents, and the teaching of John Paul II. I wish here to emphasize only one point about which I wrote, as it still seems to be widely neglected: the way in which the saving *and revealing* activity of God belong inseparably together in constituting the one history of divine self-communication.

To put this in terms of Christ, he is inseparably not only the savior of all people but also the revealer to all people. His being the Light of the world belongs inseparably with his being the Life of the world. Some early Christians from Asia Minor left striking testimony to Christ as the Light and Life of the world by combining on the tombs of their beloved dead two Greek words: *phôs* (light) and *zôê* (life). *Phôs* ran down the inscription and intersected in the letter ômega with *zôê*, which ran across. The central position of ômega reminds us that Christ, who is the Light of the world and the Life of the world, is also the end of all things.[19] Often enough in discussing other religions, writers concern themselves more or less only with Christ's saving role for all, with that "one salvation" that St. Irenaeus highlighted (*Adversus Haereses*, 4.6.7). But the same Irenaeus dealt also with the one revelation offered to all through the Son, who "from the beginning reveals the Father to all" (ibid., 4.20.6–7). Christ is the source and agent of revelation for the whole world, no less than he is the source and agent of salvation for the whole world. He offers the truth to all, so that they may share in the divine life of the Trinity.[20]

Such then are some of my personal memories of and perspectives on post-Vatican II relations with other Christians, Jews, and members of other religions. Scores, probably hundreds, of Catholic theologians have matched and surpassed my efforts and experiences. Yet I hope the Cappadocians would approve of my small but persistent efforts to be led by Jesus Christ and the Holy Spirit in receiving creatively and living out the teaching of the council in the area of what Cardinal Arinze has called "meeting" with all other believers.[21] To complete this chapter let me add a brief summary of some major achievements of John Paul II in applying and developing what the council taught about relations with "the others."

Pope John Paul II

As regards other Christians, perhaps the pope's most earnest outreach was to the Orthodox. He was sensitive to the way Greek and Russian Orthodox have believed, with some justification, that Catholics make the Holy Spirit subsidiary in the Trinity. In the hope of healing the rift, John Paul II reached out in various ways, not least by his 1986 encyclical on the Holy Spirit, *Dominum et Vivificantem* (Lord and Giver of Life). That encyclical letter was nothing less than a heartfelt prayer for the love, unity, and peace that the Holy Spirit wishes to bring to separated Christians and their world. Writing three years before the fall of European Communism and the subsequent break up of Yugoslavia in brutal wars that were fueled in part by religious allegiances, the pope's prophetic prayer, to all human appearances, failed. Like the Catholic Church, many of the Orthodox churches had been victims of Communism, and in the Soviet Union the Orthodox themselves had a part in the persecution of Ukrainian-rite Catholics. In the fall of Communism, John Paul II played a significant role and so helped to liberate the Russian Orthodox Church. He hoped that Catholicism and Orthodoxy would come together to reinforce Europe's Christian heritage and character. But relations with the Orthodox deteriorated after 1989. The pope came from Poland, and the Poles were traditional enemies of Russia. The Orthodox leaders rejected the pope's vision of East and West reunited with him as the Christian world leader. They were angered by what they saw as the imperializing Eastern-rite Catholics who emerged from decades of persecution. Even if Mikhail Gorbachev, the general secretary of the Soviet Communist Party of the USSR (1985–91) and president (1988–91), visited the pope in December 1989, Patriarch Alexis never wanted John Paul II to come on a visit to Moscow.

What live on in my memory are the "first-time" gestures and actions of John Paul II in relations to others. As the first pope to visit Britain, in 1982 he shared an ecumenical service in Canterbury Cathedral with Archbishop Robert Runcie, the head of the Anglican Communion. They pledged together their commitment to Christian faith. In December 1983, on the occasion of the five-hundredth anniversary of Martin Luther's birth, John Paul II preached at the Lutheran church in Rome and became the first pope ever to do so in a Lutheran church. In October 1986 he boldly broke new ground by going off with the Dalai Lama and other heads or representatives of the world's religions to Assisi, where they all prayed for world peace. While returning from a visit to Zaire, Kenya, and some other African nations, John Paul II went home via Morocco. On August 19, 1985, in Casablanca, at the invitation of King Hassan II, he spoke to a crowd of more than 100,000 young Muslims about the religious and moral values common to Christian and Muslim faith. Since the days when Muhammad launched Islam more than 1,300 years ago, no pope has ever been invited by any Muslim leader to do anything like that. In April 1986 John Paul II was welcomed at the Jewish synagogue in Rome, probably being the first pope to visit a synagogue since the early centuries of Christianity. He was certainly the first pope to pray in a mosque, as he did on a 2001 visit to Damascus. More than ninety times he acknowledged the sins of Catholics and begged pardon from Jews, Muslims, Protestants, and Orthodox Christians. He was an outstanding role model in trying to reconcile peoples. He had a vivid faith in the Holy Spirit, present in every human heart and prompting authentic prayer wherever it goes up to God. That brings me to two themes that sum up John Paul II's reception and development of Vatican II teaching on Christianity and "the others."

Like the council (for example, *Ad Gentes*, 1–4), he took a deeply trinitarian view of God's loving activity. In particular, John Paul II attended to the universal action of the Holy Spirit (*Redemptor Hominis*, 6)—something he expressed even more strongly in *Dominum et Vivificantem* (no. 53) and in his 1999 postsynodal apostolic exhortation *Ecclesia in Asia* (nos. 16, 18). He affirmed the active presence of the Spirit of God in the religious life of non-Christians and their religious traditions. As he stated in an address to the members of the Roman Curia on December 22, 1986, "Every authentic prayer is called forth by the Holy Spirit, who is mysteriously present in the heart of every person." To this the pope's 1990 encyclical *Redemptoris Missio* (The Mission of the Redeemer) added the theme of the presence of the Spirit affecting not only individual persons but also the cultures and religious traditions of the world (no. 28).

Besides highlighting the role of the Holy Spirit not only in the life of every human being but also in the world's religions and cultures, the pope encouraged solidarity and cooperation between all religions in their common responsibility for human welfare—a second major contribution to teaching on ecumenical and interfaith dialogue. In a letter dated September 10, 1992, encouraging a day of prayer for world peace, he stressed the need for believers of all kinds to remedy the situation of extreme economic and social differences between rich and poor countries. His 1995 encyclical on the value and inviolability of human life, *Evangelium Vitae*, called for "the concerted efforts" of "all those who believe in the value of life." They must defend and promote together human life as "everyone's task and responsibility," a common service shared by

Christians and "followers of other religions" alike (no. 91). This sense of a common cause for all religious believers, "men and women without distinction" who strive together to build "a civilization of love, founded upon the universal values of peace, justice, solidarity and freedom," introduced the chapter on "the service of human promotion" in *Ecclesia in Asia* (nos. 32–41). True human development and justice in human affairs, particularly for the poor and oppressed, were themes of Vatican II, especially in *Gaudium et Spes*. John Paul II exhorted Catholics to make a common cause here with all believers everywhere.

Note: For some of the points raised and briefly discussed in this chapter, fuller treatment and bibliographies are available in NCE: "Anglican/Roman Catholic International Commission (ARCIC)," vol. 1, 440–42; "Buddhism," vol. 2, 657–74; "Ecumenical Dialogues," vol. 5, 66–70; "Ecumenical Directory," vol. 5, 70–71; "Ecumenical Movement," vol. 5, 71–80; "Faith and Order Commission," vol. 5, 606–8; "Hinduism," vol. 6, 840–53; "Islam," vol. 7, 606-14; "Judaism," vol. 8, 2–14; "Justification," vol. 8, 75–91, esp. 90–91; "Lima Text," vol. 8, 588–90; "Pontifical Council for Interreligious Dialogue," vol. 11, 479–80; "World Council of Churches," vol. 14, 840–43.

7

THEOLOGY FOR THE CHURCH AND THE WORLD

Bishops and theologians sometimes get the impression that their orthodoxy is questioned lightly and that their difficulties and industry are not appreciated. This leads to a loss of trust which only damages the Church.

Archbishop Francis Rush (of Brisbane, Australia),
at the Extraordinary Synod to assess
the work of Vatican II, 1985

Bishops will derive particular benefits from open dialogue and cooperation with theologians.

Pope John Paul II, *Pastores Gregis* (2003), 29

As the heritage of Vatican II comes under scrutiny in 2005, forty years after the council closed, I hope there will be renewed reflection on the role and importance of theologians and their work. What do theologians contribute to the life of the church? How can their work be a resource for the entire church? Through their work in and for the church, what further benefits can theology bring to the wider society of human beings?

Vatican II on Theology

In one way or another all sixteen documents of the Second Vatican Council had something to say about the sources, methods, "audiences," and functions of theology in the life of the church. However, the teaching is by and large gathered together by the

Decree on the Training of Priests (*Optatam Totius*) of October 28, 1965. That document goes beyond "merely" academic teaching and study and attends to the spiritual and pastoral training of future priests. At least ten points figure in the vision of theology proposed by the council.

1. Vatican II endorses the classical understanding of theology as a "sacred science" that draws its essential data from the self-revelation of God (*Optatam Totius*, 15–16) communicated through the history of Israel and reaching its climax with Christ's life, death, and resurrection, along with the coming of the Holy Spirit. Entrusted by Christ and his apostles to the post-New Testament church, this foundational revelation is to be proclaimed, taught, and applied for all subsequent generations until the end of time. While theology needs to be "scientific" in its methods, which means using precise terminology and being clear about procedure, it remains "sacred" in its source: God's self-revelation that climaxed with the mission of the Son and the Holy Spirit. Undoubtedly tensions do arise between this "sacred" source in the divine self-manifestation and "scientific" methods. But such tension never justifies reducing or even eliminating either the sacred or the scientific character of theology.

2. Revelation and salvation through Christ are almost synonymous, since God's self-disclosure aims to redeem us from evil and communicate life. The council sees theology as studying not only "revealed truths" but also "the mysteries of salvation" (*Optatam Totius*, 16). The divine self-revelation and the history of salvation are to be combined as the central "given" for theological teaching and reflection.

3. The scriptures have a central place as "the word of God" coming to us from the apostolic or foundational generation of the church. It was under a special inspiration from the Holy Spirit that the story of God's

revealing and saving activity was recorded and interpreted in the Bible. No other theological sources, not even infallibly true statements from the church's magisterium, have been written under that special guidance of the Spirit. These books have not only human authors but also "God as their author" (*Dei Verbum*, 11). Hence the Bible "should be the soul, as it were, of all theology" (*Optatam Totius*, 16). The scriptures should be both *the* norm and also the primary inspiration for all theological reflection.

Along with the scriptures, the church's living tradition plays an essential role for theological study. At the start of Vatican II a battle royal broke out over the relationship of scripture and tradition. Although the Council of Trent in 1546 had spoken of only one "source" of the gospel, that is to say, of revelation (DzH 1501; ND 210), many Catholic theologians and bishops maintained two sources supplying revealed truth. If some truths were not clearly established from scripture (for example, the assumption into heaven of the Blessed Virgin Mary at the end of her earthly life), tradition provided a more or less independent source for holding such truths. The Constitution on Divine Revelation (*Dei Verbum*) elegantly solved the issue by insisting on "the close connection and communication existing between sacred tradition and sacred scripture. For both of them, flowing from the same divine wellspring, in a certain way merge into a unity and move toward the same goal" (*Dei Verbum*, 9). Since tradition and scripture are thus intimately connected in their past origin, present function, and future goal, it is obvious that, in relying on and drawing from scripture, theologians must also take into account tradition and its constant interpretation and application of the scriptural message—not least, in the teaching and practice of the church fathers (*Dei Verbum*, 24; *Optatam Totius*, 16). In short, theologians are to be guided by the way "Sacred Tradition and Sacred

Scripture form one sacred deposit of the word of God" (*Dei Verbum*, 10).

4. The teaching office of the church or living magisterium has "the task of authentically interpreting the word of God," according to *Dei Verbum*. Nevertheless, the magisterium "is not above the word of God but serves it, teaching only what has been handed on, listening to it devoutly, guarding it scrupulously, and explaining it faithfully by divine commission and with the help of the Holy Spirit." This is a beautiful vision that captures the essential harmony of magisterium, scripture, and tradition: "Sacred Tradition, Sacred Scripture and the Magisterium of the Church...are so linked and joined together that one cannot stand without the others, and that all together and each in its own way, under the action of the one Holy Spirit, contribute effectively to the salvation of souls" (*Dei Verbum*, 10). To that we might add, "and also contribute effectively to the fruitful practice of theology."

5. The service of theology to the church is not, however, limited to the functions fostered and guided by the official teaching office (*Optatam Totius*, 16). Six times this key paragraph of *Optatam Totius* indicates the wider context. Theology exists in and for the living community of the whole church, and as such makes its contribution.

   The council's Constitution on the Church in the Modern World (*Gaudium et Spes*) outlines some broader roles theologians can play for the church. They should engage in "new investigations" demanded by fresh questions coming from "science, history and philosophy." They are "invited to seek for more suitable ways of communicating doctrine" to the people of our time. *Gaudium et Spes* obviously includes theologians among "all the faithful" who "possess a lawful freedom of inquiry and of thought, and the freedom to express their minds humbly and courageously about

those matters in which they enjoy competence"
(*Gaudium et Spes*, 62).

6. Supported by other documents of the council,
Optatam Totius encourages theologians to adopt a
liturgical "style" of theology. Students of dogmatic
theology should be taught to recognize how "the mysteries of salvation" are "always present and operative"
in "the liturgical actions" (*Optatam Totius*, 16).
Theologians should never forget how God's salvific
self-revelation in Christ is now expressed and made
effective through all the liturgy. This liturgical outlook should be promoted not only by professors of
liturgy (*Sacrosanctum Concilium*, 15) but also by other
members of theological faculties: "The teachers of
other disciplines, especially of dogmatic theology,
sacred scripture, and spiritual and pastoral theology
should take care...to expound the mystery of Christ
and the history of salvation in such a way that will
bring out the connection between their subjects and
the liturgy" (ibid., 16).

7. Theological teaching and training is to be ecumenical.
Optatam Totius asks for students of theology to "be led
to a more adequate understanding of the churches and
ecclesial communities separated from the Roman see"
(no. 16). Here this document applies to theology what
the Decree on Ecumenism (*Unitatis Redintegratio*) says
about the common responsibility for Christian unity:
"Concern for restoring Christian unity pertains to the
whole Church, faithful and clergy alike. It extends to
everyone, according to the potential of each, whether
it be exercised in daily Christian living or in *theological*
and historical studies" (*Unitatis Redintegratio*, 5; italics
mine).[1]

8. In a wider sense of ecumenism, *Optatam Totius* recom-
mends also the study of other religions as part of the
syllabus of Catholic theological students: "They
should be introduced to a knowledge of other reli-

gions.... In this way, they can better understand the
elements of goodness and truth which such religions
possess by God's providence, and will learn how to
disprove the errors in them and to share the full light
of truth with those who lack it" (no. 16). The reference to "elements of goodness and truth" matches that
of another conciliar document promulgated on the
same day (October 28, 1965), the Declaration on the
Relationship of the Church to Non-Christian
Religions (*Nostra Aetate*): "The Catholic Church
rejects nothing which is true and holy in these religions" (no. 2).

9. Given what has happened from the time of St. Justin,
a martyr and philosopher of the second century,
Vatican II endorsed the contribution that philosophy
makes to theology. *Optatam Totius* requires the study
of philosophy as an essential part of the program for
priestly formation. It expects "a better integration of
philosophy and theology" (no. 14). Theology draws
concepts, questions, and techniques of analysis from
philosophy. Concepts should be understood here
broadly—to cover not only individual notions but also
terminology and even entire philosophical schemes.
Thus a particular philosophy could offer sacramental
theology not only an account of "symbol" as an isolated concept but also an elaborate terminology and
theory about symbolism.

  Then come the questions that through the ages
philosophers have been asking, reflecting on, and
refining: ultimate questions about the world and
human life, and their origin, nature, and destiny. Faith
and theology are in the business of offering replies.
Revelation answers the questions about God and the
final meaning of life. Thirdly, a philosophically trained
mind has a much better chance of analyzing theological texts, spotting their presuppositions, catching
inconsistencies, seeing vital nuances in meaning (for

example, the difference between *distinguish* and *separate* or between *definitive* and *decisive*), and weighing the strength of their conclusions.[2]

10. Philosophy also plays its part in helping theologians to understand, clarify, and *communicate* more successfully the divine revelation. That is their pastoral task. *Optatam Totius* hopes that students of theology will learn to communicate "eternal truths in a manner appropriate to the people of today" (no. 16). *Gaudium et Spes* has more to say about the role of theologians as communicators. The constitution notes how "from the beginning of her history" the church "has learned to express the message of Christ with the help of ideas and terminology of various peoples, and has tried to *clarify it with the wisdom of philosophers*" (no. 44; italics mine). *Gaudium et Spes* invites theologians to play their part in reformulating and *communicating* more effectively revealed truth to the people of our time (no. 62).

Let me sum up the vision of theology proposed by the council for the good of the whole church and the world at large. Vatican II understands theology to be (1) a sacred science, based on God's self-revelation and (2) on the Christ-centered history of salvation. It should be (3) deeply biblical and founded in tradition (expressed in a vital, early way by the fathers of the church), (4) guided by the magisterium, (5) at the service of the church, (6) constantly linked with worship, (7) ecumenical in its concerns, (8) informed about and respectful toward other religions, (9) aided by philosophy, and (10) able to communicate more successfully the truth of Christ within the church and beyond.

Catholic Theology Since 1965

Since the council closed in 1965, there have been some major changes in Catholic theology.

1. In the last four decades Catholic theology has, to some extent, ceased to be a clerical monopoly. In almost all countries prior to the council, theological colleges and seminaries trained only male students for the ordained ministry, had only male teachers on their staff, and were sometimes situated in the countryside. Now they have opened their doors to others and often enough shifted from the isolated countryside to city settings. In Australia, Brazil, Canada, England, Italy, the United States, and many other countries, religious women, nonordained religious men, laymen, and laywomen are much more involved as students and teachers of theology. The Gregorian University in Rome, for instance, has three women full-time and ten women part-time on its faculty of theology. Around one-third of those enrolled in theology are women. One could multiply such examples almost without end and with more striking examples.

2. The steady progress in biblical studies has made an obvious and positive impact on how theology is taught and studied. Those who teach and write in the area of the doctrine of Christ often draw, more or less appropriately, on New Testament exegetes to present the ministry of Jesus, his preaching of the kingdom, his passion, death, and resurrection. Yet Catholic theology must progress further before we could claim that it has realized the dream of Vatican II that the study of scripture should be "the soul of all theology." Some theologians, for example, continue to gloss over the differences between the more "historical" gospels—Matthew, Mark, and Luke—and the more "theological" Gospel according to John, and even treat John as a straightforward historical source for the words and deeds of Jesus. Others misinterpret St. Paul in such passages as 2 Corinthians 3:12–18 and, above all, in verse 17, which is often unreflectingly taken to identify the risen Christ with the Holy Spirit ("the [risen] Lord is the Spirit"). As verse 17

141

echoes Moses' experience in Exodus 34:34, no reference seems to be made directly to the risen Christ but rather to God identified as "the Spirit" by Paul in his commentary—something expressed well by the Revised English Bible (even if this translation introduces here a striking addition): "the Lord *of whom this passage speaks* is the Spirit" (italics mine). In these and other ways, even leading writers about Christ can leave much to be desired when precisely scrutinized in their use of scriptures.[3] All in all, Catholic theology must progress further before we could claim that it has realized the dream of Vatican II that the study of the sacred scriptures should be "the soul of all theology."

3. Meanwhile, despite the council, neglect of the liturgy continues to impoverish theological reflection on the divine self-revelation and gift of grace. Surprisingly, those who teach courses on such themes as revelation, grace, and the sacraments regularly ignore the rich witness of texts used for centuries in public worship. Day after day, the revelation of God is actualized through all the sacraments and their symbolic actions and not merely through the Liturgy of the Word with which they begin. The appropriation of the new life of grace runs through all the liturgical celebrations; their twofold purpose is that of giving glory to God and of bringing salvation to human beings (*Sacrosanctum Concilium*, 5–10). Neglect of the liturgy continues to impoverish theological reflection on the divine self-revelation and gift of grace.

It is even sadder when those who teach courses on the sacraments draw sparingly on liturgical texts and even disregard such liturgical teaching on the sacraments as the General Instruction of the Roman Missal (5th ed., 2000), the introduction to the 1981 edition of the Lectionary, and the introductions to the rites of Christian Initiation, Penance, the Anointing and Pastoral Care of the Sick, Marriage, and the Ordination of Deacons, Priests, and Bishops. It would be unthinkable for theologians of Eastern Christianity, when expounding the sacraments, to gloss over or even flatly ignore the liturgical texts and teaching.

4. On the ecumenical front, Catholic theology has registered considerable gain. Around the world, Catholics often study and teach theology alongside colleagues of other Christian communities. The patient and fruitful work of many ecumenical dialogues has brought agreements that Catholic professors of theology sometimes incorporate in their work. Thus the 1999 "Joint Declaration on the Doctrine of Justification," which was produced by the international Catholic-Lutheran dialogue and which contains forty-four common statements covering basic truths regarding justification, has enjoyed a wide impact on Catholic theologians who teach courses on grace. Sometimes, however, theological colleagues fail to show much interest in such other common statements as the 1994 declaration about the doctrine of Christ between the Catholic Church and the Assyrian Church of the East. This official text, signed by Pope John Paul II and Mar Dinkha IV, the patriarch of the Assyrian Church of the East, displays an exceptional ecumenical openness and a remarkable sensitivity in reading and receiving the teaching of the First Council of Ephesus (431) and the Council of Chalcedon (451).[4] Much more remains to be done—not least in appropriating the published results of official dialogues.

5. In the wider or interreligious sense of *ecumenical*, Catholic theologians have often entered into serious dialogue with Judaism, Buddhism, Hinduism, Islam, and other major religions. In the Western world contact with Jews and Jewish thought has profoundly affected much teaching and writing by Catholic theologians—not least writing on Christ where most have acknowledged the Jewish matrix of Jesus' life and min-

istry. From the 1980s the term *pluralism* has been used and misused in the area of interreligious dialogue. Unfortunately a few Catholic thinkers have joined "pluralists" like John Hick, who puts Christ more or less on a par with other religious founders (as if he were merely one among many revealers or saviors) and alleges that Christ differs from them only in degree but not in kind. Yet an openness to other religions as "ways" through which God's revelation and salvation reach their adherents[5] does not rule out the universal revelatory and salvific role of the risen Christ and the Holy Spirit. Jacques Dupuis (1923–2004), a veteran Belgian theologian who spent over thirty years in India, has shown in his *Toward a Christian Theology of Religious Pluralism* how we can profess and proclaim faith in Jesus Christ as the one, constitutive redeemer of humankind and at the same time recognize the Spirit at work in the world's cultures and religions. His subsequent book, *Christianity and the Religions: From Confrontation to Dialogue*, expounds the same theme.[6]

Theology in Service of the World

Obviously the more authentically ecumenical and interreligious Catholic theologians become, the more they will contribute to human society beyond the Catholic Church. Dialogue with other Christian communities and with other religions does not exclude proclamation of the full Catholic heritage, nor does such proclamation exclude dialogue. Catholics can both share the wonderful riches of their own living tradition and learn from the lives of those who are led by the Holy Spirit along other "ways." Growth in ecumenical and interreligious knowledge and sensitivity will impact not only on life within the Catholic Church but also on relations with and service of others.

Perhaps it is in the area of morality that Catholic theologians are called most visibly and dramatically to influence the ways in which human society can and should move. A whole range of moral issues has emerged with great urgency in the aftermath of Vatican II. I am thinking here not only of questions of human rights, international economic justice, and world peace, but also of organ transplants, in vitro fertilization, abortion, same-sex unions, environmental degradation, and ecological responsibility. Catholic moral theologians have a special role to play as experts assisting their bishops, not only as teachers who help Catholics to share moral conclusions based on faith and reason but also as spokespersons of Catholic convictions for a wider public in the countries where they live and teach.

When I look around the world at the work done by Catholic theologians in the aftermath of Vatican II, there is much to highlight and praise in Africa, the Americas, Europe, and Oceania. In particular, conditions in Latin America have prompted theologians to denounce injustice and oppression, and to speak for the millions of victimized suffering persons in that continent and, indeed, in the whole world of today. Liberation theology at its best has retrieved the denunciation of social evil typical of the Jewish prophets and draws inspiration from Jesus' solidarity with the marginalized of his day. The alliance between throne, altar, and army that used to be characteristic of countries in Latin America is now widely at an end, and this is partly because of liberation theologians. But in some ways the work done by Asian theologians has been even more outstanding. In their triple dialogue—with the Asian poor, the Asian cultures, and the Asian religions—theologians have contributed well to proclaiming the good news. This triple dialogue brings Catholic theology and witness to bear on the wide society of Asian nations, and illustrates how theology can function not only within the Catholic Church but also for the benefit of society at large.

Conclusion

Let me conclude by applying to theologians Vatican II's description of Christ's redemptive role as priest, prophet, and king/shepherd (*Lumen Gentium*, 10–13), another threefold scheme that has its Old Testament roots and was used sporadically down through the centuries. According to the council, bishops (ibid., 25–27), priests

(*Presbyterorum Ordinis*, 1, 4–6), and all the baptized (*Lumen Gentium*, 34–36) share in this priestly, prophetic, and royal role.

Theologians, so far from being freelance operators, are called to be prophets, kings, and priests at the service of the church and the world. As prophets, theologians proclaim what is true and call to account those who deny it. As kings, they work for justice and peace. As priests, they play their role in animating and enlightening those who worship God, who is truth, goodness, and beauty itself. To the extent that they can help open up the way to the truth, goodness, and beauty of God, theologians will benefit the Catholic Church and through Christ prove a blessing to society at large.

At the close of chapter 3, I drew from the example of a fourth-century Cappadocian family of saints and writers four tests by which to evaluate any reception of Vatican II's teaching: sensitivity to the work of Christ and the Holy Spirit; fidelity to the scriptures; a richer experience of community worship; and generous service of those who suffer. These criteria also serve to assess what theologians do as prophets, kings, and priests. To the extent that their prophetic, kingly, and priestly work truly exemplifies sensitivity to Christ and his Spirit, fidelity to the scriptures, a life of worship, and service for the needy, they are proving a wonderful asset to the whole church and the entire world.

Note: For fuller treatment of some of the points discussed in this chapter see various entries on theology in NCE, vol. 13, 888–927.

8

THE COMING CHURCH

To make the Church the home and the school of communion: that is the great challenge facing us in the millennium which is now beginning.

John Paul II, *Novo Millennio Ineunte*, 43

With renewed hope in the vivifying power of the Spirit we are going to take up once again the position of the Latin American episcopate in Medellín, which adopted a clear and prophetic option expressing preference for, and solidarity with the poor. We do this despite the distortions and interpretations of some, who vitiate the spirit of Medellín, and despite the disregard and even hostility of others.

Conference of Latin American Bishops,
Puebla document (1979), 1134

The Second Vatican Council forced Catholics to think hard and differently about their church. No longer maintaining a vision of the church as a perfect society, a model elaborated by St. Robert Bellarmine (1542–1621) that remained more or less standard among Catholics for well over two hundred years, the bishops at Vatican II acknowledged the need for that "continued reformation to which Christ always calls his Church" (*Unitatis Redintegratio*, 6).

From his election in 1978, John Paul II repeatedly asked Jews, Muslims, Protestants, Orthodox Christians, and other groups to forgive crimes committed against them by Catholics. On the First Sunday of Lent 2000 in St. Peter's Basilica, he underlined the constant need for repentance as an integral part of the church's celebration of the Great Jubilee Year. The confession of sins at the

Eucharist on that Sunday featured seven representatives of the Roman Curia asking pardon for such sins of the present and past as intolerance, anti-Semitism, discrimination against women, and contempt for various cultures and religions.[1] On June 22, 2003, John Paul II visited Banja Luka in northern Bosnia and celebrated Mass near the ruins of a Franciscan convent destroyed in 1995 by Serbian forces, who were taking revenge for the evils perpetrated by Father Vjekoslav Filipovic, a Franciscan expelled from his order during the Second World War. He led a 1942 attack by Croatian fascists who butchered more than two thousand local Serbs, including hundreds of women and children. "From this city, marked by so much suffering and bloodshed," the pope said in his homily, "I ask Almighty God to have mercy on the sins committed against humanity, human dignity and freedom by the Catholic Church." The words of John Paul II showed once again how the self-image of the Church has profoundly changed and is still changing as Catholics continue to assimilate two basic themes from Vatican II: being a holy sign and being at the service of the world.

Holiness and Service

The two constitutions on the church approved by the council understood the church to be the "sacrament" or visible and holy sign of what the invisible Christ does (*Lumen Gentium*), and to be a servant Church of repentant sinners who embrace a ministry of justice and peace for the whole of humanity (*Gaudium et Spes*).[2] *Lumen Gentium* saw the church as the sacrament of what Christ has done and is doing through the Holy Spirit to bring together all human beings into the kingdom of God.

CHRIST AND THE SPIRIT

Christ and the Holy Spirit are at the center of a truly Catholic life. Each believer's personal relationship to Christ, the founder of the church, holds him or her together in the communion that is his body. The Spirit dwells in the church as in a temple. The "mystery" (or inexhaustibly deep and divine truth) of Christ and the Spirit invests the church and allows *Lumen Gentium* to speak of "the mystery of the holy Church" (no. 5). This Christ- and Spirit-oriented vision of the church justifies a choice made by Philip Jenkins (a notable commentator on contemporary Christianity at Pennsylvania State University) for *The Next Christendom: The Coming of Global Christianity.*[3] Four striking images of Christ himself make up the cover of a book concerned with the Catholic Church and other Christian communities. The choice of cover fittingly illustrates the utter centrality of Jesus for those who wish to understand and interpret the church on its pilgrimage into the third millennium.

A contrast between two figures of Vatican II, Pope Paul VI (d. 1978) and Archbishop Marcel Lefebvre (d. 1991), brings out the essential perspective of a Christ-centered version of the church. On a visit to Manila in November 1970, five years after the council closed, the pope vividly expressed his faith in Christ, without whom the conciliar renewal could never be effected: "He is the center of history and of the world; he is the one who knows us and who loves us; he is the companion and friend of our life.... It is he who will come and who one day will be our judge and—we hope—the everlasting fullness of our existence."

Archbishop Lefebvre attended the council, but dissented from much of its teaching and went on to form a dissident group that broke off communion with the Catholic Church in 1988. In support of his position, Lefebvre invoked "the tradition" (understood in the sense of what came from the sixteenth-century Council of Trent) and "the church" (understood in the sense of French Catholics who longed for the restoration of the monarchy), and avoided appealing to the gospels or invoking Jesus himself and the guidance of the Holy Spirit. Thus in an interview published by *Newsweek* for December 19, 1977, Lefebvre spoke thirteen times about the "church," three times about tradition(s), and twice about "God," but uttered not a word about Jesus and the gospels and other New Testament scriptures. One did not find the archbishop asking, "Am I and my followers proving faithful to Jesus in what we are doing? Are we truly open to the guidance of the Holy Spirit? Where should prayerful pondering of the scriptures take us?" The questions we continually revisit that guided the Cappadocians in their creative assimilation of the

First Council of Nicaea (see chapter 3) failed to shape the discernment and actions of Lefebvre and his group. In support of the 1570 Tridentine Mass, they pressed the third question we gleaned from the Cappadocians ("Does this help us to worship better?"), but without understanding worship in the early Christian sense of *leitourgia*, a worship that spilled over into a *diakonia* or service of those brothers and sisters of Christ who desperately need help.

A Christ-centered life entails constantly mulling over the scriptures. The closing chapter of *Dei Verbum*, "Sacred Scripture in the Life of the Church" (nos. 21–26), dreamed of the church living the Bible at every level of its existence. The council exhorted "all the Christian faithful to learn 'the surpassing knowledge of Jesus Christ' (Phil 3:8) by frequent reading of the divine scriptures" (ibid., 25). The Decree on the Apostolate of Lay People declared: "The fruitfulness of the apostolate of lay people depends on their living union with Christ" (*Apostolicam Actuositatem*, 4). Those preparing for the ministerial priesthood in the church should "learn to live in familiar and constant companionship with the Father, through Jesus Christ, his Son, in the Holy Spirit." They "should be taught to look for Christ in many places" and, especially, "in faithful meditation on the word of God" (*Optatam Totius*, 8). A prayerful knowledge of all the scriptures fosters a personal relationship with Christ. As a twelfth-century Augustinian canon of Paris, Hugh of Saint Victor, wrote, "All divine scripture speaks of Christ and finds its fulfilment in Christ, because it forms only one book, the book of life which is Christ."[4] *Dei Verbum* put the same point negatively, when it quoted St. Jerome: "Ignorance of the scriptures is ignorance of Christ" (no. 25). A biblically oriented life will be a Christ-centered life, which is fed through the word of God, long ago written under the inspiration of the Holy Spirit, "the same Spirit" who now guides the reading and interpretation of the scriptures (*Dei Verbum*, 12). Like the Eucharist with its remembrance of Christ (*anamnesis*) and invocation of the Holy Spirit (*epiclesis*), steady contact with the scriptures makes one's life Christ-centered and blessed by the Spirit.

Vatican II's Dogmatic Constitution on the Church associates the mission of the Spirit very closely with the communion of the baptized in quest of holiness. *Lumen Gentium* has a remarkable section on "the call of the whole Church to holiness" or the ways of heroic holiness open to everyone (nos. 39–42). It recalls how Christ wishes all members of the church to be sanctified, to grow in the perfection of love, and to manifest unceasingly holiness "through those fruits of grace that the Spirit produces in the faithful" (no. 39). Through the power of the Spirit, the visible holiness of the church works as a "sacrament" to reveal Christ who, albeit invisibly, is powerfully present and effectively there for all humanity.

THE RICH AND THE POOR

When delivering its account of the socioeconomic life of the world, *Gaudium et Spes* shows how the bishops were keenly aware of "the immense economic inequalities which now exist" (no. 66). Forty years later these inequalities have increased and not decreased. Never has the world been so unequal. *Gaudium et Spes* highlighted the contrast between luxury and misery: "While an enormous mass of people still lack the absolute necessities of life, some, even in less advanced countries, live sumptuously or squander wealth" (no. 63). By the late 1990s, in a world of just over six billion people, over one billion were living in absolute poverty and surviving on a dollar a day or less. The income gap between the top fifth and the lowest fifth of the world's people has been getting wider: 30 to 1 in 1960, 60 to 1 in 1990, and 74 to 1 in 1997.

In a dramatic sermon St. Gregory of Nyssa—to go back to our Cappadocian models from the fourth century—expanded on the parable of the rich man and Lazarus (Luke 16:19–31) to picture what was happening inside the palace (with its "unbridled banquets" and "frenzy of pleasures") and outside. Inside are the "gourmands" who "squander their goods on enormous houses and superfluous ornaments" and enjoy "wine bowls, tripods, jars, ewers, platters, all sorts of cups, the clowns,…chanters, poets, male and female musicians, dancers, and all of the equipment of debauchery." Outside "a myriad of Lazaruses sit at the gate, some dragging themselves along painfully, some with their eyes gouged out, others with amputated feet, some quite literally creep, mutilated in all their members. They cry out and are not heard over the flutes' whistling, loud songs, and the cackling of bawling laughter." Gregory developed further the story line of the parable: "If they [the Lazaruses] beg more loudly at the door, the porter of the barbarous master bounds out like a brute and drives them away with strokes of a stick, setting the dogs on them and lashing their ulcers with whipcord." The Lazaruses, "the beloved of Christ," move away, "without having gained one mouthful of bread and meat, but satiated with insults and blows. And in the den of Mammon, some vomit up their meal like an overflowing vessel; others sleep on the table, their wine cups besides them." Gregory summed up his contemporary application of Christ's parable about the rich man feasting with his family and friends while the hungry and ulcerous Lazarus begs at his door: "Twofold is the sin that reigns in this house of shame: one is the excess of the drunkards, the other the hunger of the poor who have been driven away."[5]

The scene pictured by Jesus and, in even more vivid detail, by Gregory of Nyssa has repeated itself endlessly through the centuries, down to the present. In June 2001 on the island of Sardinia, a corporate titan threw a two million dollar party for his wife's fortieth birthday. Men wearing only shorts cavorted with women in see-through gowns; a replica of Michelangelo's *David* urinated vodka; and the protruding portions of a birthday cake were shaped like a woman's breasts.[6] Such lavish and execrable displays of wealthy executives keep alive the truth of Jesus' parable, with which the Second Vatican Council and Pope John Paul II have confronted Catholics and all those ready to hear their message.

Recalling the picture of "the rich man who ignored Lazarus, the poor man," *Gaudium et Spes* insisted on "the inescapable duty to make ourselves the neighbor" to everyone in distress. In drastic detail the council lists various sufferings that afflict millions of human beings and which Catholics and others should do their best to alleviate (no. 27). In his first encyclical, *Redemptor Hominis* of 1979, John Paul II drew attention to the tragic difference between "the rich, highly developed societies" and the "broad sectors" of other societies who "suffer from hunger, with many people dying each day of starvation and malnutrition." "This pattern," he added, represents a "gigantic development of the parable in the Bible of the rich banqueter and the poor man Lazarus" (no. 16). In a

November 1995 meeting on the occasion of thirty years since the publication of *Gaudium et Spes*, the pope emphasized the continuing relevance of this constitution and, in particular, quoted its painful observation about the savage contrast between rich and poor: "In no other age has humankind enjoyed such an abundance of wealth, resources and economic well-being; and yet a huge proportion of the people of the world is plagued by hunger and extreme need" (no. 4).[7]

Over and over again *Gaudium et Spes* pointed to Jesus as *the* unique answer to the world's questions (especially in nos. 22, 32, and 45). Through their faith in Christ, his followers are summoned to promote justice and peace and serve all people, especially those crucified by poverty and oppression. This carefully crafted document highlighted the crying need to end wars, strengthen family life, and promote much wider justice in the socioeconomic order. Forty years later those needs remain as urgent as ever. Christians (and others) are now much more aware of a further mission, their mission to an earth that suffers. Reckless exploitation of oil and other mineral resources, the greed of ranchers and timber companies who clear forests, and the consequent erosion of arable soil and loss of water supplies have produced widespread and perhaps irreversible degradation of the environment.[8] At the start of the third millennium, drought, drought-related famines, global warming, the loss of ozone protection, and other phenomena make the question very real: Will we survive our abuse of the planetary ecosystem? In the face of the massive needs of the whole planet, the call to mission and service issued by *Gaudium et Spes* has a new and urgent focus.

In view of Vatican II's basic message about the call to holiness and mission of all the baptized, there is a strong case for carrying further some paths of renewal clearly initiated by the council and for creatively going beyond them. I will dwell more on the church within (*ad intra*) than on the Church in its relations to others (*ad extra*). It will be a flourishing of the church *ad intra*, however, which will empower its mission *ad extra*.

The extent to which some or even many of the proposals that follow are ever going to be implemented depends, at least partly, on the policies and practice of the pope and the Roman Curia and that willingness to listen sketched by John Paul II in a 2001 letter *Novo*

Millennio Ineunte (no. 45). The challenge here was illustrated when Cardinal Stephen Kim Son-Hwan of Seoul recalled difficulties that arose with the Roman Curia when, in the aftermath of Pope Paul VI's 1970 visit to Manila, the presidents of eleven Asian bishops' conferences met to form an umbrella organization to unite all the bishops of Asia—in what was to emerge as the Federation of Asian Bishops' Conferences (FABC). Paul VI "was supportive," Kim remarked. "However, not everyone in the Vatican was so pleased.... It was a matter of control. Rome did not want to lose control."[9] In the event, the FABC began its meetings in 1974, and they have proved an inspiring exercise of an episcopal collegiality attentive to local situations and not opposed to papal primacy. That example brings me to the crucial doctrine of collegiality or the shared responsibility of all the bishops for the church around the world.

Collegiality

By the mid-twentieth century, at least among many Catholics of the Roman rite, bishops had come to be regarded as primarily employees of the pope. Since he appointed them, they were understood to be officials simply working for him, almost on the model of subordinates to a papal CEO. The local church or diocese was misconstrued as a merely administrative subdivision of the whole church run by the pope as a kind of "universal bishop" or even absolute sovereign. At the First Vatican Council (1869–70) some bishops had expressed the fear that the doctrine of the primacy of papal jurisdiction could be taken to imply that the world is one huge diocese, with the pope as its bishop. That would reduce the bishops to being papal assistants, officials of a centralized authority who did not exercise their episcopal mission in their own right. But in a precise way the universal jurisdiction of the pope was expressed by Vatican I and interpreted by Pius IX. After the council he came out in support of the German bishops, who had insisted, "It is in virtue of the same divine institution upon which the papacy rests that the episcopate also exists. It too has its rights and duties, because of the ordinances of God himself, and the Pope has neither the right nor the power to change them."[10]

Nevertheless, popular perception often misunderstood bishops to be merely administrators for the pope.

Vatican II reasserted the collegial authority of the bishops, who in communion with the pope and united among themselves share responsibility for the shepherding of the universal church (*Lumen Gentium*, 22). While primarily exercised by all the bishops meeting in a general council, collegiality also applies, analogously, to national episcopal conferences and to other groups and situations: for instance, to the coresponsibility of the laypeople, religious, and priests who constitute parishes. How well or badly has collegiality functioned, for example, in the primary case of the worldwide episcopate? Chapter 2 of this book summarized the postconciliar work of three organs of episcopal collegiality: the synods of bishops in Rome, the national episcopal conferences, and such international bodies as CELAM and the FABC. Neither the synods nor the bishops' conferences show collegiality to be already functioning fully.

Over and over again, and not least when they gathered in late 2001 for the Tenth Ordinary General Assembly of the Synod of Bishops (on "The Bishop, Servant of the Gospel of Jesus Christ for the Hope of the World"), bishops questioned the existing structures of these synods. As merely consultative bodies, the bishops at the synods have less power than the offices of the Roman Curia. Furthermore, the impact of the bishops chosen and sent by the episcopal conferences around the world is muted by the presence (critics would say, imposition) of delegates and others appointed by Rome. Thus the participants at the synod in 2001 included not only two hundred bishops representing the episcopal conferences but also thirty-two delegates nominated by the pope, along with sixteen experts and twenty-three observers. At this and earlier synods some of these "extra" members, according to the elected representatives, have repeatedly dampened down proceedings and helped to "tame" the final propositions presented by the synod to the pope as material for use in a postsynodal document to be published by him.

As we saw in chapter 2, the 1998 "motu proprio" of John Paul II, *Apostolos Suos*, limited the power of episcopal conferences—above all in matters of doctrine, where the bishops must agree unanimously; otherwise, Rome must approve the teaching. Even so, where transparency operates in the way matters are discussed and decisions made, the conferences function well and show how the whole is greater than the sum of the parts. Christ and his Spirit assist individual bishops in carrying out their mission, but bishops do not hang up their teaching function with their hats when attending meetings with their colleagues. Indeed, one can expect more help and effective exercise of collegial responsibility where fifty or more bishops are gathered together in the name of Christ. But the work of conferences can be sadly impaired when a small minority of bishops (or even one bishop) with private (or even quite secret) relations with the Roman Curia can block initiatives of the whole conference.

Subsidiarity

Closely connected with the function of collegiality is the principle of subsidiarity, something strongly endorsed by Cardinal Stephen Fumio Hamao in December 2003: "I am convinced that the local churches should have more decision-making power, applying to them the principle of subsidiarity."[11] In essence, the principle teaches that decisions and activities that naturally belong to a lower level should not be taken to a higher level. This means, for instance, that central organs of a state should not intervene unnecessarily with local authorities. In expounding the limited duty of public authority to intervene in social and economic affairs, Pope Pius XI spoke of subsidiarity (*Quadragesimo Anno*, 79), and the principle was later approved and further applied by Pope John XXIII (for example, in the latter's *Mater et Magistra*, 53, 80). The Second Vatican Council appealed to the principle of subsidiarity in dealing with international cooperation in economic matters (*Gaudium et Spes*, 85–86) and when indicating the limits of the state responsibility in education (*Gravissimum Educationis*, 3, 6).

On February 2, 1946, when addressing a consistory at which he created thirty-two new cardinals, Pius XII stated that subsidiarity should be applied not only to social and economic affairs but also to the internal life of the church. He showed how different the church was from the centralization of totalitarian dictatorships that had crucified Europe in the first half of the twentieth century. The

Synod of Bishops in 1967 voted to make subsidiarity one of the ten guiding principles for the revision of canon law, and the 1969 Synod voted to apply subsidiarity to the functioning of episcopal conferences. Hence subsidiarity shaped the reform of the Code of Canon Law (promulgated in 1983).[12] Subsidiarity, or not taking to a higher level matters that can and should be dealt with at a lower, local level, clearly constitutes a healthy principle for our lives together, both in human society at large and in the Catholic Church in particular. Indeed, as the preface to the 1983 Code of Canon Law stated when enumerating the ten principles that guided its composition, the principle of subsidiarity must be more widely applied in the church, since "the office of the bishops with its attached powers is a reality of divine law."[13]

Cardinal Hamao's plea for subsidiarity was based on the dignity of all the faithful in the local churches and the special powers received by their leaders when they are ordained bishops and take charge of particular dioceses. He knew how participants at the 1998 Synod for Asia invoked subsidiarity in defense of the proper rights of local churches, and how they found their efforts frustrated.[14] At the 2001 Synod, despite many bishops giving firm support for the principle, opponents of subsidiarity ensured that it was labeled "ambiguous" within the life of the church and in the exercise of episcopal authority (*Pastores Gregis*, postsynodal apostolic exhortation by John Paul II, 56).[15] Yet his pastoral experience in Asia and, especially, in Japan convinces Cardinal Hamao that the practice of subsidiarity, or what often amounts to the same thing, decentralization and more autonomy for the local churches and their episcopal conferences, is essential for the successful mission and full life of those churches.

In an interview published by the London *Tablet* on November 8, 2003, the archbishop of Tegucigalpa in Honduras, Cardinal Oscar Andres Rodriguez de Maradiaga, firmly agreed with the need for the practice of subsidiarity in the life of the church. His experience (1995–99) as president of CELAM, Latin America's council of twenty-two bishops' conferences, confirmed his convictions about the right and need for CELAM to adopt its own policies and produce its own documents.

In his apostolic letter of January 2001, *Novo Millennio Ineunte*, John Paul II wrote: "Much has been done since the Second Vatican Council for the reform of the Roman Curia, the organization of Synods and the functioning of Episcopal Conferences. But there is certainly much more to be done" (no. 44). Two years later in *Pastores Gregis* (no. 59) he reiterated this point, using the very same words. The synods and episcopal conferences need to be more effective. That progress will come, Cardinal Fumio Hamao maintained, only if "the Roman Curia listens more and shows greater respect for the local churches." He added, "The Roman Curia is used to instruct, teach and correct," instead of being more inclined "to listen, help and encourage." In terms of the language of the Book of Revelation, the cardinal wanted the central authorities, who after all are separated from direct engagement with Catholics around the world, to hear what the Spirit (or Christ himself) is saying to the local churches (Rev 2:7, 11, 17, 29; 3:6, 13, 22)—a listening process that the Cappadocians, with their sensitivity to Christ and the Holy Spirit, would have heartily endorsed. Rather than mistrusting the persons "on the spot," the officials of the Roman Curia should be attentive to and supportive of initiatives emerging in local situations. That could bring about something highlighted in *Pastores Gregis* (nos. 55–65), a healthier communion of the local bishops and churches with the bishop of Rome.

Collegiality and Parishes

I mentioned above the collegial functioning of parishes. How would collegiality and its spirit affect the traditional institution of the parish, where Catholics live out their faith with their families and among their neighbors? The parish remains the primary place where the ministers of the Catholic Church communicate to laypeople a sense of fellowship, supply at times necessary material support, and provide spiritual comfort and even the chance of lives being transformed through conversion. In the Western world and elsewhere, when their needs, both spiritual and material, and the hunger in their hearts for healing and deeper religious experience are not being satisfied in the parish, Catholics have departed, not least to sects of various kinds. In the Western world where lay ecclesial ministers now outnumber ordained priests in the parish ministry, there may be a new chance for the whole parish to assume responsibility in a collegial way for what the parish is doing and where it is going. How might such a fresh vision engage the entire parish? It would be a parish that develops leadership among young adults, practices broad hospitality especially toward the needy, engages in a social ministry of charity and justice, and—in the case of multicultural situations—enables each ethnic group to feel at home and to have their needs met.

Perhaps most of all, parishes and their pastors should develop small groups, where people can pray together, share with each other their journey of faith, and come to a deeper relationship with God and each other. For decades, in the form of "base communities," such grassroots communities revitalized Catholic life in Latin America and elsewhere by studying the scriptures together, using their personal gifts in the service of others, and becoming involved in common social and political action. By the late 1970s there were around eighty thousand such communities in Brazil alone.[16] However it happens, whatever name the groups bear, whether they read the scriptures, watch relevant videos, or do other things together, and wherever they meet (in homes, schools, parish halls, or pubs), their collegial sharing will help them to meet Jesus and receive help from his Spirit. The collegial coresponsibility of such groups will let parishes flourish as microcosms of the universal church by being rich in gifts, diverse in culture, and united with Christ on mission.

Lay Ministry

Each parish draws life and strength not only from the pastor but also from laymen and laywomen. Their Magna Carta is a 1988 apostolic exhortation of John Paul II, *Christifideles Laici*. Building on Vatican II's prophetic vision of the laity, this document summarized the work of the 1987 Synod of Bishops in Rome on the "Vocation and Mission of Lay People in the Church and in the World Twenty Years after the Second Vatican Council." Understanding the church to be communion or *koinonia*, the pope developed the theme of "organic" communion, characterized by "diversity and complementarity of vocations and states of life, of ministries, of charisms and responsibilities." As in "a living and functioning body," every faithful layperson belongs fully to the church, shares in the priestly, prophetic, and kingly mission of Christ, and "offers a totally unique contribution on behalf of the whole body." The "ministries" and "roles" of laymen and lay-women are dynamically nourished by the Eucharist, and find their foundation in the sacraments of baptism and confirmation, and for many of them in the sacrament of matrimony (nos. 9, 14, 20, 23; ND 894–96; 1448). What *Christifideles Laici* says applies to *all* "the lay faithful," and not merely to those who belong to parish councils, to the pastoral councils of dioceses, or to lay groups and associations. The exhortation pays some attention to such lay movements (nos. 29–30, and briefly in nos. 2 and 62), but without suggesting they are the only way for laypersons.

Some of these movements predate Vatican II and others have emerged after the council. The Society of St. Vincent de Paul was founded in Paris in 1833; it has grown around the world and continues its program of common prayer and work to help the homeless, hungry, and unemployed. In 1912 Joseph (later Cardinal) Cardijn (1882–1967) started the *Jeunesse Ouvrière Chrétienne* (Jocists) or Young Christian Workers, a movement aimed to imbue the work environment with Christian values and make it a place for evangelization. In 1921 Frank Duff (1889–1980) founded the Legion of Mary in Dublin. A lay association, it advances the spiritual and Catholic life of its members through prayer and apostolic work. The Cursillo ("little course") Movement began in Spain in 1948 and through weekends of intense experience in Christian community, followed up by later reunions, trains Catholic laity to spread the good news everywhere. Started in Chicago in 1947, the Catholic Family Movement brought married couples regularly together and also helped to create "Marriage Encounter," which through weekends together gives couples the opportunity to rediscover and enhance their original vision of love. Founded in the slums of Madrid in 1962, the year Vatican II opened, the Neocatechumenal Way aims to help people to discover or rediscover what faith and baptism entail by replicating the early Christian catechumenal pattern. Laypersons and even families, formed through this reinitiation into their Christian life, go out as itinerant missionaries to all parts of the globe. The Neocatechumenal Way now includes priests who work for dioceses around the world. The Community of the Beatitudes, which was founded in France in 1974 and has spread to Africa, Asia, and elsewhere, is likewise "mixed": It comprises priests, religious with vows, married couples, and single laypersons. In 1971 another "mixed" movement, *Chemin Neuf* (the New Way), was founded in Lyons, and seems to be flourishing even more.

Many ancient religious orders and later institutes long ago gave rise to lay movements that followed the basic spirituality of those in consecrated life. Thus laypeople who wished to be closely associated with older orders such as the Carmelites, Dominicans, and Jesuits could join "third orders" or, in the case of the Jesuits, the Sodalities of Our Lady (now called "Christian Life Communities"). The Third Order of St. Francis (now called "Third Order, Secular") is open to men and women, married or single, as well as to diocesan bishops, priests, and deacons who are not members of religious institutes. It is organized into local, self-governing fraternities who live by the gospel of Jesus, promote family life, work for peace, justice, and the care of the poor, and cherish and protect all creation.

In 1968 a group of high school students in Rome started the San Egidio movement, a lay association that encourages its members to reach out to the world from a base of prayer. It supports starving children and other people in desperate need, including those who suffer from AIDS, and promotes international and interreligious peace. The movement helped to broker peace in Mozambique in 1992 and has involved itself in numerous peace initiatives around the world.

Some of these lay movements, like the Jocists and the Legion of Mary, flourished and spread to several continents, but have now waned. Others, like the Society of St. Vincent de Paul, are proving stronger than ever. All of the movements listed above are international. But some lay associations are very local, like the John Carroll Society. Founded in 1951 and named after the first Catholic bishop in the United States, it includes laymen and laywomen drawn from all areas of professional and business life in the area of Washington,

D.C. It aims to promote spiritual, intellectual, and social fellowship among its members, and to be at the service of the cardinal archbishop of Washington.

All the baptized enjoy a fundamental equality, share responsibility for the church, and are more and more being employed by their local bishop in the service of the whole diocese. As John Paul II put matters in his 1999 postsynodal apostolic exhortation, *Ecclesia in America*, baptism confers on all who receive it "a dignity which includes the imitation and following of Christ, communion with one another, and the missionary mandate" to bring "their brothers and sisters to encounter the living Jesus Christ." Any renewal in Catholic life will be impossible without "the active presence of the laity...they are largely responsible for the future of the Church" (no. 44).

Vatican II started with no laypersons as participants. Before the third session began in 1964, a number of laypeople, including fifteen women (eight women religious and seven laywomen), were invited to take part in the council as auditors.[17] Since the council closed in 1965, lay and religious women are becoming more prominent in the Catholic Church. They had long served as part-time or full-time catechists, and in some countries made up the vast majority of the catechists. Women now teach in theological colleges, university faculties, and seminaries. Some laywomen are chancellors of dioceses and judges in marriage tribunals; many administer parishes for which no ordained priests are available. Not a few serve their bishops on commissions for justice and peace that sprang up in many Catholic dioceses after the council, and some have paid with their lives for protecting the dignity and rights of their brothers and sisters. It seems important to recall here at least one name out of that army of heroic laypeople who, often in situations of extreme danger, have continued to serve the church and the world by defending human rights, assisting refugees, and sharing their faith in Christ through teaching catechism. In August 1981, Rosa Judith Cisneros was shot dead one morning on her way to the office for justice and peace in San Salvador. Cisneros is only one of those thousands of modern "martyrs" of charity, followers of Christ who heroically set themselves to serve and teach others unselfishly. Many bishops, priests, and religious have suffered imprisonment, torture, and even death.

But far more laymen and laywomen have faced danger, violence, and martyrdom when living out their "following of Christ" and "missionary mandate" for their local church and bishop.

Deacons and Priests

Laypersons are, to quote again John Paul II's words, "largely responsible for the future of the Church." But what of the ordained ministry in North America, Latin America, the Pacific islands, and other parts of the world? For a long time in many Latin American countries, the Catholic faithful have lacked a sufficient number of priests and can enjoy the celebration of the Eucharist only every few months, if that.[18] The departure from the active ministry of thousands of priests and a serious decline in priestly vocations have meant that many parishes in North America and elsewhere have become priestless. By October 2003, there were 2,500 parishes in the United States that did not have a resident priest. Many such parishes have been entrusted to the pastoral care of women religious, some to permanent deacons, and a few to laypersons. Often called pastoral administrators, these leaders offer, in place of the celebration of the Eucharist, a communion service in which hymns, prayers, readings from the scriptures, and a homily precede the distribution of communion. They visit the sick and prisoners, sometimes bury the dead, run religious education, and preside over parish councils. This situation raises two questions: Should the women parish administrators be ordained permanent deacons? Should male permanent deacons, many of whom are married, be ordained priests?

The Second Vatican Council taught that "forms of social or cultural discrimination in basic personal rights on the grounds of sex, race, color, social conditions, language and religion must be curbed and eradicated as incompatible with God's design" (*Gaudium et Spes*, 29). Are we witnessing such a discrimination on the grounds of sex between male and female parish administrators in priestless parishes? They carry out similar functions, but, because of a difference in sex, the former are ordained deacons and the latter are not. One would expect the same sacrament for the same (parish) ministry.

The sacramental character of the diaconate was not, however, totally clear before Vatican II, or at least not totally clear to many Catholics. Since many, if not all, of the functions of a deacon could be exercised by a layperson, how could one claim that these functions or "powers" originated in a sacramental ordination? The council clarified the unity of the sacrament of orders, a unity found in three different grades: bishop, priest, and deacon. These three ordained ministries are exercised "in the person of Christ the Head" (the 1983 Code of Canon Law, 1008). A few years later the 1992 *Catechism of the Catholic Church* drew on *Lumen Gentium* (nos. 29, 41) and *Christus Dominus* (no. 115) to make it clear that, while there is one ordained ministry, two grades (bishop and priest) entailed priestly participation, whereas the grade of deacon is a grade of "service." Vatican II, when recognizing the unity of the sacrament of orders, also taught that, unlike bishops and priests, deacons are ordained "not for priesthood but for service" (*Lumen Gentium*, 29).

In the churches of the Christian East there was a long tradition of ordaining women deacons, and even as recently as the 1950s the Greek Orthodox Church ordained women deacons for monasteries. Within the Catholic Church the question of women deacons has been officially studied for years, in particular by the International Theological Commission. In late 2002 it produced *Le Diaconat: Évolution et perspectives*, and concluded by leaving open the question of ordaining women to the diaconate.[19] Phyllis Zagano and others have documented the case for women being once again ordained to the diaconate.[20] In an address on October 5, 1957, Pope Pius XII declared that the time was not yet ripe for restoring the permanent diaconate for men. But less than ten years later, the bishops at Vatican II believed that pastoral and missionary needs meant that the time was ripe, and they voted to reestablish such a diaconate (*Lumen Gentium*, 29). One major reason for doing so was the fact that in Latin America, Africa, Asia, and elsewhere many laymen were already performing the tasks of deacons but without being ordained to that ministry.[21] That is precisely the situation nowadays with female parish administrators; it is hardly convincing to block their ordination to the permanent diaconate by invoking the principle of "unripe time." If the time is ripe for them to work as deacons, the time is also ripe for them to be ordained deacons.

This would be to ratify sacramentally who they really are and what they are doing as "permanent official leaders of a parish which is without a priest."[22] Along with the parish administrators, one should include as well women, both lay and religious, who already parallel much of the work of male deacons by their ministry as chaplains in hospitals, prisons, and schools, and who might also be considered for ordination to the diaconate.

Some obviously fear that ordaining women deacons would prove "the thin edge of the wedge," and would open the way to women priests or at least encourage false hopes about such a step. Maybe. Yet, like appeals to the principle of "unripe time," fears about "the thin edge of the wedge" have been used to block appropriate changes in the church and civil society. Such fears should be taken into account but cannot be allowed to decide an issue. In the case under discussion here, it seems right to ratify sacramentally what thousands of women are already doing in practice. One needs to ponder carefully the two major conclusions reached by the International Theological Commission in its study of the diaconate: "The deaconesses mentioned in the tradition of the ancient church—as evidenced by the rite of institution and the functions they exercised—were not purely and simply equivalent to the deacons." That implies recognizing some (substantial?) equivalence, even if it was not "purely and simply" a perfect equivalence. The other major conclusion is: "The unity of the sacrament of Holy Orders, in the clear distinction between the ministries of the Bishop and the Priests on the one hand and the Diaconal ministry on the other, is strongly underlined by ecclesial tradition, especially in the teaching of the magisterum."[23] But does one stress "the unity" more than "the clear distinction" or vice versa? If one stressed more "the clear distinction," it would be easier to decide for the ordination of women as deacons.

Any decision to ordain Catholic women to the diaconate would, however, leave unresolved the problem posed by (a) the chronic lack of priests in many countries, and (b) the declining number of priests in other countries which until recently had a sufficient number of priests to staff the parishes. But the celebration of the Eucharist is the heart of the life of the Catholic Church. The church is where the Eucharist is, and the Eucharist forms the church. Far too many Catholics in the Roman rite are unable, Sunday by Sunday, to share in the Eucharist, find in it the center of their existence, and draw from it the strength they need for their lives.[24]

Officially, since the Second Lateran Council (1139), celibacy has been obligatory for priests ordained in the Roman rite. There were and are undoubtedly very good religious reasons for such a renunciation of marriage. But one cannot push these reasons too far, even to the point of claiming that celibacy is an integral part of priestly identity. That would be to ignore the married clergy of the Eastern Catholic churches (and of the Orthodox churches). The primary issue here is not the nature of any "match" between presbyterate and celibacy, but the crisis of so many priestless parishes.

A very serious priest shortage threatens the eucharistic life of the church. The local community has a right to the regular celebration of the Eucharist and not merely to the distribution of holy communion, with the possibility of sharing in Mass limited to only a few occasions during the year. In "Pastoral Ministries and Community Leadership," Karl Rahner wrote: "Provision for sufficiently large numbers of pastoral clergy is an obligation imposed on the Church as a matter of divine law, an obligation that takes precedence in a case of conflict over the Church's legitimate desire for a celibate pastoral clergy."[25] Walter (later Cardinal) Kasper agreed with Rahner's recognizing the Eucharist as a higher value than celibacy. He disallowed giving precedence to "a great good such as celibacy—while endangering a higher one, namely the availability of priests to build up the body of Christ as presidents of the Eucharist."[26] If a sufficient number of priests is not available to provide parishes with the Eucharist, the conditions for admission to the priesthood should be changed. Right now in many countries a longstanding lack of priests is producing a loss of even vestigial Catholic identity, a flight to other Christian communities, or else simply religious indifference. Change is demanded by the clear teaching of Vatican II about the celebration of the Eucharist being "the summit toward which the activity of the Church is directed" and "the fount from which all her power flows" (*Sacrosanctum Concilium*, 10). Elsewhere the council put the same teaching negatively: "No Christian community is built up which does not grow from and hinge on the celebration of the most holy Eucharist" (*Presbyterorum Ordinis*, 6).

In such countries as Australia, England, Germany, and the United States, a number of married men who were previously ministers in other Christian churches and then entered the Catholic Church have been ordained to the priesthood and continue in the ministry. They have certainly helped to provide the Eucharist for communities that would otherwise have remained priestless. But to meet the challenge we need the farsighted policy of ordaining to the priesthood married men, who in many cases are already exercising pastoral leadership as catechists, pastoral administrators, or permanent deacons. Male catechists have long played an integral part in the development of Catholic Christianity in many African and other countries. In its Decree on the Church's Missionary Activity, the Second Vatican Council paid its tribute to "that army of catechists" to whom "missionary work among the nations is so indebted" (*Ad Gentes*, 17). Since the council an army of permanent deacons has sprung up; they could be considered for priestly ordination. In 2002, to name one diocese on the East Coast of the United States and one on the West, the Archdiocese of New York had 346 permanent deacons and the Diocese of Sacramento had 115. In 1998 there were 25,122 permanent deacons in the Catholic Church, with 50.9 percent of them in North America and 31.3 percent in Europe. Many bishops at Vatican II expected that some catechists in Africa, Latin America, and elsewhere would be ordained permanent deacons. But by 1998 more than four-fifths (82.2 percent) of such deacons were exercising their ministry elsewhere: in North America and Europe.

The story of the Catholic Church yields more than one example of opportunities lost through forgetting that the Eucharist is more important than celibacy. Along the west coast of Africa, Portuguese missionaries introduced Christianity even before Columbus reached the Americas. In the realm of Kongo, a king was baptized in 1491 and many other Africans followed his example. But by refusing to ordain married Africans to the ministerial priesthood and to approve local liturgies, Catholic authorities lost an extraordinary chance in the story of African Christianity. After a promising start, from the end of the seventeenth century the Kongolese church went into a long period of decline.[27]

Other Dreams

One could press on sketching dreams and hopes for ways in which the church could meet challenges and seize opportunities in this new millennium. Let me mention three. First, it seems pressingly important to have many more women assisting the pope by working in the Roman Curia in positions of real power and influence. Given the fact that women make up the majority of those who follow religious life, it seems extraordinary that only one nun enjoys a leadership role in the Congregation for Institutes of Consecrated Life and for Societies of Apostolic Life. Then, why not have a married woman heading the Pontifical Council for the Family? Or, for that matter, a married couple doing so? Likewise it would seem not only appropriate but also very helpful to have one or more women with an excellent background in health care leading the Pontifical Council for the Pastoral Care of the Health Care Apostolate. In a lecture given in London on December 18, 2003, Cherie Booth, the Catholic wife of the British prime minister, Tony Blair, remarked: "There is little reason why half of all Vatican curial positions could not be filled by women."[28]

My second dream focuses on inculturation, the need to translate ways of expressing and living Christian faith into local thought patterns and traditions. Inculturation is much deeper than just music, drums, and clapping of hands, even though it can call for such liturgical adaptations. Here a dictum from the early centuries of the church that St. Thomas Aquinas endorsed enjoys its importance: "Every truth, no matter by whom it is said, comes from the Holy Spirit (*omne verum a quocumque dicatur a Spiritu Sancto est*)."[29] Since goodness and beauty belong necessarily with truth and since one cannot imagine the Holy Spirit inspiring truth but being unconcerned about goodness and beauty, one could legitimately expand the dictum and declare: "All truth, goodness, and beauty, no matter by whom they are expressed, come from the Holy Spirit." In broader terms, wherever there is truth, goodness, and beauty in a culture, there is the Holy Spirit. Hence the process of inculturation goes beyond familiarity with local terms and concepts and beyond a creativity in adapting religious and liturgical language to local settings. The process calls for a deep sensitivity to the powerful presence of the Spirit who develops everything that is true, good, and beautiful in a given culture. Such elements appear with a certain intensity on the occasion, for instance, of births, marriages, and deaths.

In *Gaudium et Spes*, when dealing with "what the Church can receive from the world," the bishops at Vatican II spoke of "the riches hidden in various cultures" (no. 44). These are riches of truth, goodness, and beauty inspired by the Holy Spirit that, with the help of the same Spirit, can be discerned and appropriated. My dream of inculturation does not simply ask a human question: To what extent must Africans reject their culture(s) to become Catholics? My dream raises a question that St. Basil and the other Cappadocians would have liked: What does an openness to the work of the Holy Spirit in *this* culture lead us to discern and decide? In seventeenth-century China, Catholic missionaries showed a remarkable cultural openness that promised to convert the whole nation to the Christian faith. One of the great might-have-beens in world history came to a stop when the Vatican forbade religious services in Chinese, suppressed recent Bible translations, and reduced the Catholic Church to a small, persecuted body.[30]

One could name further dreams for the church: for instance, a reform in the selection of bishops, a greater representation of the local churches at the papal elections, and a more effective presence of Catholics and other Christians in the world of mass communications. But the third dream with which I want to conclude is a broad one, a dream Vatican II took over from Pope John XXIII, who expressed it in the words of St. Augustine: "Let there be unity in what is necessary, freedom in which is doubtful, and charity in everything (*Sit in necessariis unitas, in dubiis libertas, in omnibus caritas*)" (*Gaudium et Spes*, 92). Sadly in some parts of the Western world we have to endure much polarization and distrust not only in the world but also within the church. I dream of a church and a world in which the Father, Son, and Holy Spirit will liberate the whole human family from all forms of fear and greed and draw them into the eternal mystery of love. Without such love, any reforms in the Catholic Church would remain at best mere cosmetic decorations. By sharing ever so much more in the ecstasy of love that is the life of the tripersonal God, the church will be enabled to bring to the whole world that justice and peace which it so urgently needs.

Note: For many of the points briefly discussed in this chapter, fuller treatment and bibliographies are available in the NCE. See "Basic Christian Communities," vol. 2, 135; "Cardijn, Joseph," vol. 3, 102–3; "Catechist," vol. 3, 248–49; "Chinese Rites Controversy," vol. 3, 513–17; "Christian Family Movement," vol. 3, 536; "Deacon," vol. 4, 550–54; "Cursillo Movement," vol. 4, 443–44; "Deaconess," vol. 4, 554–55; "Franciscans, Third Order Secular," vol. 5, 909; "Jocism," vol. 7, 889; "Lefebvre, Marcel," vol. 8, 446–49; "Legion of Mary," vol. 8, 453–54; "Marriage Encounter," vol. 9, 205–6; "Missionaries of Charity," vol. 9, 731; "Mother Teresa of Calcutta," vol. 10, 15–16; "St. Vincent de Paul, Society of," vol. 12, 591–94.

9

EPILOGUE

For a long time to come it will be granted to new generations to draw on the riches which this Council of the
twentieth century has blessed us with.
John Paul II, Spiritual Testament, March 17, 2000

One generation has passed and the second is well established, since
the Second Vatican Council ended in 1965. In the context of a
church that has seen two millennia pass, forty years is not a long
time. The teaching of the council is still being received as it is
tested in the lives of believers. Undoubtedly there were abuses after
Vatican II. These happen after every council. But there can be no
turning back. This book will have achieved its purpose if it gives
young adults, born after Vatican II, a better idea of the pressing
needs that drove Pope John to call the council. He wanted to
update the Catholic Church, renew it spiritually, heal the divisions
within Christendom, and encourage Catholics to reach out to all
people and promote justice and peace throughout the whole world.

As someone who spans three generations, I have written this
book at the time of the fortieth anniversary of the closing of the
council. I experienced Vatican II as an injection of new life. I have
tried to convey the excitement of that time, which made me frequently remember the promise: "See, I am making all things new"
(Rev 21:5). I have tried to remind the older generation and convey
to the younger what was achieved, just how important it was and
remains, and to urge that full use be made of this heritage.

In the third millennium the human family finds its future existence under threat. More than ever it needs the message of Christ
who is the Light of the whole world. He is the full and final key to
what human life is ultimately about, the One who brings life in

abundance (*Gaudium et Spes*, 22). The council issued no specific document about Jesus Christ. But his presence pervades all sixteen documents. The Constitution on the Church in the Modern World never loses sight of the Son of God who truly became "one of us," and "worked with human hands, thought with a human mind, and loved with a human heart" (*Gaudium et Spes*, 22). The Constitution on Divine Revelation ends with a hymn to the scriptures through which Christ is experienced and the Eucharist through which he becomes most closely present (*Dei Verbum*, 21–26). The Constitution on the Sacred Liturgy proclaims that sharing in the Mass, the supreme "activity" of the whole church, sets the faithful "aflame with Christ's love" (*Sacrosanctum Concilium*, 10).

The place of Christ in the living legacy of Vatican prompted the words of Archbishop Frank Rush, president of the Australian Bishops' Conference, at the extraordinary synod of 1985 that was called to review the work of the council twenty years after its end. "The Church," he said, "needs to search for and shape an answer to the only ultimate question: 'Who is Christ for the world of today?'" In the last analysis, what the council sought was nothing less than to equip believers for furthering among the human family a life-transforming experience of Jesus. One might sum up its deepest message by applying some words of a former general of the Jesuit Order, the saintly Pedro Arrupe (1907–91): "Fall in love with Jesus, stay in love with Jesus, and that will decide everything."

In his homily at the inaugural Mass of April 24, 2005, Benedict XVI insisted that the church is "young" and "alive," because "Christ is alive." It is his "love that redeems us." It was in terms of Christ that the new pope took up his ministry as successor of Peter: "If we let Christ into lives, we lose nothing, nothing, absolutely nothing of what makes life free, beautiful and great." Benedict XVI ended his homily with words that echoed John Paul II and serve to sum up the central message of Vatican II: "Open wide the doors to Christ, and you will find true life."

APPENDIXES:
SOME POSTCONCILIAR TEXTS

For the appendixes on the reception of Vatican II, I have selected four postconciliar documents from the years 1975 to 2002: one from a priest who served as secretary to an archbishop and as an interpreter at the 1974 Synod, one from an archbishop at the Extraordinary Synod of 1985, one from a national conference of bishops preparing for the 1998 Asian Synod, and one from a layperson (2002). I wish to thank the editor of the London *Tablet*, the editor of *Vidyajyoti*, the managing editor of Orbis Books, the late Jacques Dupuis, John Marshall, and Ormond Rush (the nephew of the late Archbishop Frank Rush) for allowing me to reproduce these texts. Let me now do so in chronological order.

Appendix A: "The Synod of Bishops 1974," by Jacques Dupuis, SJ[1]

In the still short history of the new synodal institution, the 1974 Synod of Bishops in Rome is an important landmark. This is due not merely to the importance of the theme, "The Evangelization of the Modern World," which, among the various topics suggested by the episcopal conferences, was selected by Pope Paul VI. Nor is it simply because, on the recommendation made by the Council of the Synod and ratified by the Pope—a recommendation partly prompted by the vastness of the subject—three full years were for the first time devoted to the preparation of the synodal work. The real significance of the 1974 Synod is rather to be found in what happened during its celebration: that is, however paradoxical this may sound, both in what did take place and in what failed to take place. The event, taken in its totality, is indeed complex; and it is not surprising that, both during the Synod and soon after it, the press drew of it very divergent or even contradictory pictures. The daily releases made to the press in five different languages, however substantial they were, left the journalists, whose number was the greatest ever recorded at a Church event of this type, somewhat dissatisfied; they wished [that] facilities had been provided for them to follow the proceedings themselves on TV sets from the press-conference rooms. It is not likely, however, that such an innovation would have lifted all ambiguities. For, to an extent, there were ambiguities in the assembly itself: the Synod was marked with noticeable ups and downs, the mood shifting to and fro from optimism to pessimism; there were moments of relaxed hilarity and others of high tension; not even to the Synod Fathers themselves was all that was happening equally clear or, as regards the last stage of the proceedings, made known in all clarity. This complex situation makes it difficult even for an eye-witness to correctly evaluate the Synod, let alone give a complete account. The pages which follow attempt to provide an objective appraisal of the Synod's work. They wish to highlight its positive aspects without, however, dissimulating the negative side of the picture; to bring out both the real achievements and the partial failures; in one word, to draw up the balance sheet. Such an evaluation requires that the genesis of the Synod be first explained, from the period of its preparation down to the various stages of its celebration.

I. THE PREPARATION OF THE SYNOD

As is well known, all the local churches were invited to take an active part in the preparation of the Synod, all national episcopal conferences being requested to forward, to the Permanent Secretariat of the Synod in Rome the findings of their deliberations. These findings were to serve a double purpose: together they would secure the necessary background for the preparation by the Synod Secretariat of the Synodal Working Paper *(Instrumentum Laboris)*; on a continental basis they would provide the material for the five reports *(Relationes)*—one for each, continent—the reading of which at the beginning of the proceedings was meant to acquaint the Synodal Fathers with an overall picture of the problems posed in the various parts of the world to the Church's mission of evangelization.

This preparation at the grass-roots level of the local churches is worth recalling here to put on record the remarkable interest with which the Church in India responded to the invitation. It was to be expected that the topic of "Evangelization" would appeal to her in a special manner. Whatever the reason, much time and energy were spent, at various levels and by all the sections of the Church Community, on pondering the subject in depth. Providentially the International Theological Conference on Evangelization, held at Nagpur in 1971—before the topic was assigned to the forthcoming Synod—had provided the Church's reflection with a solid theological foundation. Providentially too, the National Consultation on the same topic, originally scheduled to take place in Madras soon after Nagpur, had to be postponed with the happy result that, when it took place at Patna in 1973, it made manifest on the national level the active involvement which the entire Church community was actually taking in the preparation of the Synod. This appears all the more clearly if one keeps in mind that local seminars had been held in no less than sixty dioceses prior to the Patna Consultation. One may further recall that theological faculties and seminaries had been requested to study special issues and to forward their observations to the CBCI (Catholic Bishops' Conference of India) Standing Committee. It may truly be said that these combined and prolonged efforts prepared the ground for the CBCI Plenary Meeting which took place in Calcutta in January 1974. This meeting, which in turn was primarily devoted to "Evangelization," resulted in the "Communication" sent by the Indian Bishops to the Synod Secretariat in Rome. The text does honor to the Church in India and it is gratifying to note that its publication aroused considerable interest and attention abroad. In the mind of persons who had access to the documents sent by the various episcopal conferences, the Indian document ranked among those which contributed the most valuable reflections to the preparation of the work of the Synod. Mention must also be made of the official statement issued by the First Plenary Assembly of the FABC (Federation of Asian Bishops'

Conferences) held at Taipei, Taiwan, in April 1974. This document too showed a high standard of self-examination on the burning topic of evangelization in modern Asia; it was much in the vein of the communication sent by the Indian hierarchy.

My intention in calling to mind the genuine and energetic interest displayed by the Church in India in preparing the Synod is not to boast of our own achievements. Yet that interest seemed to contrast rather sharply with the apparent apathy which prevailed in some Western countries towards the forthcoming Synod even a few months before its celebration. This contrast itself calls for reflection. While the Church in India had perhaps for the first time deployed all its energy in making an original and substantial contribution to an important Church event, it could hardly be said that a similar interest had been shown in some Western countries from which we have been accustomed to expect the most valuable contributions to events of this kind. The present writer observed with astonishment that, even a few weeks before the Synod was to open in Rome, many priests in Belgium were unaware of the topic proposed for its consideration. Seeking to be enlightened by professors of theological faculties about the reasons for this apparent lack of interest, I derived the impression that a certain skepticism had set in with regard to the synodal institution itself. Was there much to be expected, and was it worthwhile getting truly involved? In spite of the positive contribution it had made to the Church's stand on issues of justice in the world, the 1971 Synod of Bishops had left people disappointed because it failed to face realistically the burning issues concerning the exercise of the priestly ministry in the modern world and could not advance beyond the Vatican II theology of the ministry, which after less than ten years had to an extent already become obsolete. Who then was right as regards the prospects opened by the new Synod, the disillusioned or the hopeful? Only the event would tell.

The Council of the Synod worked for three years with Bishop Wladyslaw Rubin as its general secretary. Its regular sessions led to the circulation in 1973 of guidelines for the reflection of the churches. This document, addressed to the episcopal conferences, was destined to elicit from them a preliminary communication of their experiences. The guidelines met, however, with much criticism. Their approach to evangelization appeared too narrow and their way of posing the questions too formal and aprioristic. The document represented the home-work of a team of theologians, mostly Roman and exclusively Western, little in touch with the concrete problems posed to the Church's evangelizing mission, especially in non-Christian countries and in the Third World. The suggestion, made by some members of the Council of the Synod that the team of experts preparing the last draft of the Working Paper should be enlarged so as to include Asian and other theologians, was not followed. The final preparatory session of the Synod Council did, however, take a decision which was to prove of supreme importance. The first stage of the Synod's work would consist in a communication of pastoral experiences between the representatives of all the local churches; only after this mutual exchange of experiences would the doctrinal issues and theological themes involved be proposed to the consideration of the Fathers. The method was thus inverted from deductive to inductive. The procedure was to follow what Vatican II had done with a considerable measure of success in the Pastoral Constitution *Gaudium et Spes*, by first looking at the reality of the modern world in order to reflect on the Church's task within this world. Here it meant facing with open minds contemporary misgivings and questions with regard to the manner in which the Church is promoting the values of the Gospel and profiting from experiences in various parts of the world, so as to bring those values home to people in a more tangible manner and devise means by which the Church in the discharge of her evangelizing mission may best meet the demands made on her by the modern world. This new perspective brought about an immediate result. The last draft of the Working Paper, circulated to the members of the Synod for their perusal before the session started, was divided into two parts: an introduction to the "mutual communication of experiences" and "some connected theological themes." The content of the Working Paper still remained open to criticism on many counts, but its shortcomings had now to a large extent become immaterial. It was but a preparatory instrument the content of which would to a large extent be disregarded in the actual synodal proceedings. Meanwhile—and this is what mattered—the perspective had been altered and the program of work had been so arranged as to lead from experience to reflection. At that stage it could already be guessed that the success of the Synod would depend on whether and to what extent this new orientation would be consistently followed.

II. THE CELEBRATION OF THE SYNOD

Preludes

On September 27, 1974 the Synod began, as was fitting, with a Eucharist celebrated in the Sistine Chapel. The Mass of the Holy Spirit was presided over by the Pope and concelebrated with him by cardinals representing the various continents. The short homily delivered by the Pope consisted in a prayer addressed to Christ the Lord of the Church.[2] It was a new and striking proof of the deep Christocentrism for which Paul VI has been known, ever since he opened the second session of Vatican II and invited the Council Fathers to seek the only raison d'être of the Church in Christ himself—a theme to which he consistently returned at the Council's third session, in the Encyclical Letter Ecclesiam Suam, and on many later occasions. This prayer to Christ was a tangible sign of the Pope's deep awareness that the Church was entering into an important event.

In the first Plenary Assembly the Pope delivered his opening address; this was followed by a report by the General Secretary of the activities of the Secretariat during the three years of preparation, and by a "Panorama," read by Archbishop (later Cardinal) Aloisio Lorscheider, of the life of the Church during the same period. Only the Pope's speech needs to be commented upon. It was an open speech in which the green light was given to frank exchange and to honest search. Outlining the program of the Synod, the Pope remarked that reflection on evangelization must take into account the socio-cultural conditions of the times, that we must allow our response to the Christian message and our Christian identity to be put to the test by the questions of the world. Recalling the Church's mandate to evangelize, he took note of the burning issues raised for the universality of her mission by the problems of ecumenism and by her encounter with non-Christian religions. He further noted that, its specifically religious finality notwithstanding, evangelization cannot be separated from human progress; rather, both are complementary and tend together to the same end, which is man's salvation.

While the proven values of tradition must be preserved, an honest search for effective evangelization requires openness of mind to fresh experiences. Having thus set the stage for the work of the Synod, the Pope would thereafter assiduously attend its general assemblies as an attentive but silent listener. The proceedings which followed were divided into three periods: the communication of pastoral experiences; the reflection on connected theological themes; the preparation of conclusions.

First Stage: Communication of Experiences

This took place first on a continental basis through the reading of five reports. These reports were destined to acquaint the Synodal Fathers directly with important themes that emerged from the communications sent to Rome by the episcopal conferences, national or multi-national, of each continent. They were presented in rapid succession in one general assembly by Bishop James Sangu for Africa, by Bishop (later Cardinal) Eduardo Pironio for Latin America, by Archbishop (later Cardinal) Joseph Bernardin for North America, Australia and Oceania, by Cardinal Joseph Cordeiro for Asia, and by Archbishop (later Cardinal) Roger Etchegaray for Europe. They gave a first glimpse of the different situations obtaining in various parts of the world and, correspondingly, of the diversity of challenges posed to the Church's evangelizing mission. From these continental panoramas concerns emerged which were shared by the Church everywhere. But, more significantly perhaps, it was clear that some issues acutely felt in two or more continents had much less bearing on others. Instances were: the issue of secularism and atheism in the post-Christian world of Europe and North America; the problems of development and human liberation common to South America, Asia and Africa; the concern for genuine indigenization of the Church equally felt in Asia and Africa. The speeches of the Synodal Fathers which followed confirmed this general diagnosis and added precise details.

It is neither possible nor necessary to sum up the rich material contained in those many speeches. Besides placing on record the straightforwardness and freedom with which the Fathers spoke and the positive approach with which the vast majority tackled the problems, it is enough to say that the speeches filled out the general picture drawn here above. If we consider the concerns more specifically expressed from different quarters, it may be said, at the risk of some simplification, that their distribution followed very much the model of the three worlds. The First World stressed the modern phenomenon of secularization—often considered positively as *praeparatio evangelica* (preparation for the Gospel). The Second World insisted on human rights and on the Church's freedom to evangelize. The Third World was unanimous in bringing out forcefully the themes of the local or particular church, and of human development and liberation, with, however, distinct accentuations and nuances according to continents. Thus, while the Africans stressed the "authenticity" of the local church and the indigenization this required—a concern shared by the Asians—the Asians added to this concern a further dimension: the authenticity of the Church in their countries depended to a great extent on her ability to take deep roots in their rich cultural heritage and to enter into a meaningful dialogue with other living religious traditions. The South Americans brought to bear on the theme of the local church the positive experiences they have made in recent years with "basic communities"; at the same time they insisted that "popular religiosity," even though it needs to be purified of spurious elements and to be given a more substantial foundation, continues to have a role to play in the life of the local church. Nuances were also noticeable in the way in which the Third World approached the issues of development and liberation. South Americans, for instance, voiced, more than Africans and Asians, the Church's duty to take a clear stand with regard to the badly required structural reforms of society.

By this point the impression had already been created that the 1974 Synod was to be the Synod of the Third World. For the first time, perhaps, the Third World was taking the lead and making its voice heard in a truly articulate manner. The future of the Church might well lie in those areas where she was faced with most of the great new challenges of today. It is to the credit of the bishop-representatives of the First World, and especially of the great figures among them who had played a leading role during the Second Vatican Council, that, having sensed this, they not only listened to what the Third World had to say but also gave it their support. This was to become even more evident at a later stage.

Others thought that this would be the Synod of Africa. This was not without foundation, in the sense that the Africans were unanimous in their concerted efforts to insist on the need for "African authenticity" in the Church. Among Asians, on the contrary, although the vast majority reflected the thinking of the Taipei Assembly with regard to such issues as indigenization and dialogue, there were, nevertheless, some discordant voices. Yet it was also clear that the Asian thinking on those issues was based on deeper theological reflections than was the African model—a difference which the situation proper to the churches in Asia would suffice to explain. However this may be, the significant factor at that point was that attention was clearly focused on the reality of the particular church. The Synod, it was thought, would, mostly owing to the contribution of the Third World, be the Synod of the local church.

However stimulating many of the interventions of the Fathers had been, they remained speeches silently listened to by the assembly and in that sense monologues. Real communication of experiences and cross-fertilization of ideas demanded dialogue in discussion-groups. The workshop method—to which greater emphasis was given than in 1971—was to prove very rewarding. To launch it, however, it was necessary that a preliminary synthesis be made which, taking into account all that had already been said, would sum up the main trends and point out the areas calling for discussion. This synthesis was prepared by Father Duraisamy Simon Amalorpavadass, special secretary for the first part.[3] Starting from the great realities which shape the modern world, he analyzed, in its positive and negative elements, the image which the Church projects in the midst of these realities; he described the various dimensions imposed on the Church's mission by the same realities, and outlined the specific demands made by them on the various sections of the Christian community and on special groups. He pointed out the phenomena, both inside and outside the Church, which in the present situation appear most conducive or most detrimental to the Church's discharge of her evangelizing mission, and ended with a list of questions calling for discussion. The headings under which the questions were grouped indicate the themes that were now emerging: interior life; the local church; basic communities; popular religiosity; pastoral care of non-practicing Catholics; dialogue; human liberation; special groups of people; human rights. This document which thereafter would be referred to as the "Red Book" was presented to the assembly in only summary fashion by Cardinal Cordeiro. It was a telling witness to the work already done by the Synod and a spring-board for a more searching examination in the workshops of the issues now clearly defined.

The group-discussions, divided on a language basis, were, in the mind of those who took part in them, the most rewarding experience of the Synod. Views were exchanged in all frankness, without false prudence or inhibition. No fear of being misunderstood prevented bishops from bringing into the open realities which a searching self-examination required to be presented. The reports of the twelve workshops which were later read in a full assembly are a telling witness to the openness of the discussions. They showed, moreover, a striking convergence of opinion between the different language-groups, especially the French (3), the English (3), and the Spanish (3) groups. I mention here only the more important items which recurred frequently and on which a broad consensus of opinion could be anticipated. Prominence was being given to the action of the Holy Spirit: not only was the Spirit considered the source of the Church's evangelizing function but the Spirit's operative influence was understood to extend beyond the boundaries of the Church to all men and women and to the entire world. It was the Spirit who was calling the Church and all her members to a deep conversion to God and to a renewal in her life of prayer and contemplation.

The mystery of the local church was stressed and the various levels of her realization, national and diocesan, attended to. The basic communities were seen as a new and promising form of the presence of the Church to the world in particular milieus; they constituted Church-cells to be nurtured and developed in openness to and union with the broader communities. Various factors were stressed which would help to foster the life, harmonious growth and true identity of the particular churches. It was desired that the legitimate autonomy of those churches be more clearly recognized; this recognition should be put into practice by a more liberal decentralization; allowance should be made for pluriformity with regard to law, worship, pastoral methods, and doctrinal guidance in theology. Human development and liberation were consistently viewed along the lines of the 1971 Synod document, *Justice in the World*, which had considered action on behalf of justice and participation in the transformation of the world as "a constitutive dimension of the teaching of the Gospel"; an advance on what had been said at the previous Synod could be hoped for. The youth whose estrangement from the Church often springs from noble motives called for a self-examination that could not be evaded.

Oddly enough, the reports were jejune on two important issues: only one French group had touched on the problems of ecumenism, in spite of some very pointed interventions made on the subject in the assembly; again, only one French report had seriously tackled the questions raised by the encounter with other religious traditions, in spite of the forceful manner with which the interventions of Asian bishops had brought this issue to the attention of the assembly. These two items were treated in a very positive manner in the reports from the two French groups, but regrettably roused little interest in the other workshops. This double lacuna was pointed out by several Fathers when, after the readings of the reports, they were invited to comment and to make the observations they thought necessary; the wish was expressed that more attention be given to these topics in the second stage of the Synod's work.

As the first stage came to a close, there reigned in the assembly a sense of satisfaction. Something had been accomplished. Not only had mutual exchange resulted in mutual enrichment, but also, more importantly, from the communication of pastoral experiences there had already emerged a theological reflection, based on reality, positive in approach and rich in content. There was every hope that the work well begun would be well continued.

Second Stage: Reflection on Connected Theological Themes

The procedure assigned to the second part of the Synod's work was the same as for the first part: introductory report; speeches by members of the Synod; summing up by the secretary for the second part; group-discussions; reports of the group-discussions, and subsequent observations on the same by the Synod Fathers. This similarity dispenses us from entering into details as regards procedure. What matters is to show whether and in what manner continuity was secured between the first and second part, whether and to what extent the second stage took up and deepened the questions from the point where the first had already led them.

The introductory report aimed at clarifying the theological themes connected with the pastoral experiences was presented by Cardinal Karol Wojtyla. It must be admitted that the Cardinal's task was no easy one: a doctrinal report prepared before the Synod could not in anticipation take into account all the riches brought forward by the communication of experiences, much less the theological orientation which this exchange was already impressing on the Synod's work. To an extent, therefore, the report presented by Cardinal Wojtyla came as an anti-climax. The fear that the proceedings might suffer a set-back was increased by the lack of theological vision of this document and the aprioristic manner in which it proposed the doctrinal themes. These shortcomings did not escape the notice of the assembly. They were pointed out with all clarity by Archbishop Angelo Fernandes in the general press conference which immediately followed the reading of the report. (Such general press conferences by some chosen members of the Synod were officially organized at regular intervals by the Synod's Secretariat.) After a summary presentation of the report had been given to the press by Cardinal Wojtyla, the Archbishop, addressing himself directly to the Working Paper—the theology of which was reflected in the report itself—was glad to point out some positive doctrinal elements, but he regretted the inability of the Working Paper to reflect the theology already embedded in the shared experiences [of the Synod Fathers]. He further noted that the very structure of the document hardly appeared adequate for eliciting that sort of theology. He went on to indicate some of its weak points as follows:

> The Vatican II theology of the Church as the primordial sacrament is obscured and reduced to preaching and the administration of the sacraments. The Church as sign and symbol of the intimate union of man with God and

of the unity of the human race does not stand out to advantage. The old ecclesiology rears its head again.

It is small wonder then that the notion of evangelization is largely restricted to the preaching of the Word, witnessing by life, and the administration of the sacraments. One of the points that came through quite clearly on the floor of the house was the necessity of integrating inter-religious dialogue into the very notion of evangelization.

As for the link between human development, liberation and evangelization, here again, over-emphasis on the eschatological dimension of salvation precludes the widespread human thrust for fullness of life here and now from finding its rightful place within the overall economy of salvation.

By the same token, the concept of conversion remains ambiguous. It seems to limit the notion to conversion to the Church rather than place the emphasis on conversion to God for all men alike, Christian and otherwise, and that too as a never-ending process. Thus the document appears to be unduly centered on the Church rather than on him who is the Gospel, Jesus Christ the Lord.

What is just as distressing is the almost complete neglect of the ecumenical dimension. The statements in the Synod have shown, however, the growing awareness of the presence of the mystery of the Church also in the other ecclesial communions.

Perhaps the most fatal omission is the absence of the theology of the local church which in point of fact has become the focal point of the voice of the witnessing Church in the Synod.

In the process, striking concepts that are emerging in a rather pronounced fashion in the Synod, like pluriformity in the Church, diversification of ministries and charisms and the place of basic communities, have all fallen by the wayside.

I am fully aware that the Working Paper does not pretend to be exhaustive in its choice of themes.

However, one cannot but wonder whether such a document would stimulate bishops into grappling with those crucial questions which many contemporaries direct to the Church and failure to deal with which would leave them even more unconcerned than they already are with the message of the Gospel.

Hopefully, the Fathers of the Synod will go beyond the Working Paper to a broader and really challenging perspective and thus, with a sense of mission, reach out to the multitudes that, consciously or unconsciously, are waiting to encounter the Lord.[4]

The Fathers of the Synod did go beyond both the Working Paper and the Wojtyla report to that broader vision. Many of the speeches which followed had the same punch as those of the first part. Issues raised remained to an extent distributed along the same continental lines as in the first part. But, due to the cross-fertilization that had resulted from the workshops, some themes spread to a larger spectrum. The local church, its existence at the service of the world in a particular human environment, the practical autonomy which the discharge of her mission required, and the various forms of pluralism involved were recurring themes. The Church universal was conceived as the mystery of communion which binds together the various particular churches—a communion over which the successor of Peter presides as "the principle of unity and the bond of charity." The Church was viewed not through a pyramidal, class-structured model, but as the *laos* (people) endowed with various charisms, all for the common good. The Spirit whose resurgence in the life of the Church was pointed out was calling all her members, bishops included, to renewal and conversion.

Evangelization was conceived in the broadest manner as coinciding with the overall mission of the Church, of which work for human liberation and dialogue with all men were integral parts. There was talk about "macro-evangelization," the Church being called upon to collaborate with all men of good will for the promotion of human values. The "others" were unwittingly co-evangelizers with us; by the same token we too remained to be evangelized together with them. All this belonged to the signs of the times. The "reciprocal indwelling" of Church and world called the Church to open herself to a truly "ecstatic" existence. Not all that was said can or need be mentioned; the fact is that many speeches, in spite of some tiresome repetitions, contained much valuable material in line with the first part of the Synod, and in fact hardly distinguishable from it.

The arduous task of summarizing, in view of the group discussions, all that had been brought forward at this second stage fell on Fr Domenico Grasso, S.J., special secretary for the second part and professor at the Gregorian University (Rome). His synthesis of the Wojtyla report and the speeches, a synthesis called the "Blue Book," was presented to the assembly by Cardinal Wojtyla. It was a disappointing document which did less than full justice to all that had come from the floor. Issues were raised in the form of thesis and antithesis, including in some points a twist towards a view that corresponded less to the mind of the Synod Fathers. Underlying this document was an ecclesiology lacking in breadth and vision. To give but two examples: whatever could be said as regard the work of human liberation and dialogue with other religions and ideologies, evangelization in the proper sense as distinct from "pre-evangelization" and the Christian animation of worldly affairs, was understood to refer to the preaching of the Gospel, the testimony of life, and the administration of the sacraments. Because of the organic manner in which, by the will of Christ, the Church exercises her function, evangelization, even though being the work of the whole Church, was said to pertain primarily to the hierarchy (bishops helped by priests, and deacons), the Roman Pontiff being the "supreme evangelizer." The ecumenical issues were conspicuously absent from the summary—in spite of the inspiring plea for unity for the sake of evangelization, which Dr Philip Potter (General Secretary of the World Council of Churches 1972–84) had made in his address to the Fathers. The list of questions prepared for the workshops partly redeemed this omission, the Fathers being asked to discuss if and to what extent common sharing by the various Christian confessions in "evangelization proper" could be admitted. The questions listed under the heading "The Church as Universal Sacrament of Salvation in the Work of Evangelization" were posed in a way that centered too narrowly on the Christian and the Catholic community. Thus the following questions were raised:

"Must we say that the end of evangelization is the spread (*dilatatio*) of the Catholic Church?" "In what sense can we still"—to which, while reading, Cardinal Wojtyla added "and must we?"—"speak of the absolute necessity of the Church for the salvation of the human race?"

The shortcomings of the questionnaire notwithstanding, the discussions in the workshops remained broad-based, positive in approach and fruitful in concrete proposals, as is borne out by the twelve group-reports which were later read in full assembly. These reports linked up with those of the first part in tone and content. The role of the Holy Spirit in the Church's evangelizing action, as well as the Spirit's operative presence in various features and aspirations characteristic of the present world, was being more and more accentuated; this topic had more than any other caught the attention of the workshops. Next in order of priorities came the role of human promotion in evangelization; the Church as universal sacrament of salvation, where emphasis was once again placed on the local church, with all that her harmonious growth implied, and on the commitment of all her members to her mission. The direct preaching of the Gospel, though also stressed, received less attention, owing obviously to the sense of urgency felt in many discussion-groups to come to grips with the more delicate and pressing issues. Dialogue with other religions was touched upon, but somewhat sporadically, mostly because of the dispersion into different workshops of the Asian bishops who had made this topic one of their primary concerns. Ecumenism still remained a Cinderella, touched upon only by one English group, though with a positive approach. The observations made on the reports, after these were read in the assembly, made little impact. At the close of the second stage, the Synod had in hand an impressive amount of rich material. It remained to be seen how it would succeed in putting this to use.

Third Stage: Preparation of Conclusions

To handle this immense amount of material and work out the conclusions, a preliminary meeting of the drafting Committee was now called. Members of this committee included: the three Cardinal President-delegates (Franz König, Juan Landázuri

Ricketts, Paul Zoungrana), the six reporters (five for the first part, one for the second part), the General Secretary and the two special secretaries, thirteen appointed "helpers" to the secretaries (among whom very few were theologians), and the secretaries of the twelve workshops—a total of thirty-seven persons. What happened at that meeting was never fully disclosed to the house, though Cardinal Wojtyla did give some indications of it in a debate that took place later in the assembly. For whatever reasons, the two special secretaries were requested to submit, each separately, a complete draft for the conclusions. Besides imposing on them a task which, single-handed, one man could hardly cope with in a short time, this appeared to be a glaring fault in method.[5] Two drafts were thus presented by the two special secretaries and examined by a smaller group. The two texts, which were not made public, were very divergent in approach and content. They reflected two opposite theological outlooks: one starting from reality and leading from reflection to concrete proposals; the other based on theological principles and failing to reach tangible suggestions. The conflict was one of method: inductive versus deductive. The smaller group (the exact composition of which was not disclosed) rejected both drafts and entrusted Mons. Albert Descamps with the apparently hopeless task of preparing a new draft which would synthesize both. As later explained to the assembly by Cardinal Wojtyla, the idea was to keep the dynamic perspective of one text while integrating the doctrine of the other. Uneasiness began to be felt when the delay caused the postponement of general assemblies, and rumors began to spread. In this atmosphere the reports of the activities of the Sacred Congregations and Secretariats (Congregations for Evangelization and for Divine Worship; Secretariats for Christian Unity, for non-Christians, and for non-Believers), presented to the assembly by the Cardinal prefects, as well as of the activities of Vatican Commissions (Reform of Canon Law; Women in Society and in the Church), aroused little interest and response. The minds of the Fathers were elsewhere.

The new draft of the final conclusions was presented to the assembly by Cardinal Wojtyla. It was a hybrid document, which lacked a unified structure and in some parts of which the amalgamation of divergent sources was clearly noticeable. An analysis of the text showed that the doctrine was almost entirely borrowed from the draft prepared by the special secretary for the second part. The "dynamism" of the draft prepared by the secretary for the first part (with the exception of its preamble and conclusion), its theology, and the concrete proposals it contained were lost. The author of the new draft had made a clear option. To mention what, among other losses, appeared the most damaging one, the local church was, oddly enough, treated in the third part among various "groups of Christians" which today are putting questions to the Church (other groups mentioned under the same heading being non-practicing Christians, youth, etc.). In the light of what had been said at the Synod, one would have expected the local church to be considered as being, under the influence of *the* Holy Spirit, the agent of evangelization.

It is no wonder that, when a preliminary vote was taken on the substance of the document before it could be submitted to amendments, parts II, III and IV were rejected. Part I which was passed had also to be subsequently abandoned because, separated from the rest, it had no consistency of its own. No doubt can be entertained as to the interpretation to be given to the Fathers' disapproval of the text. Cardinal François Marty explained the episode clearly at the plenary assembly of the French bishops which took place soon after the Synod (Lourdes, November 9–15, 1974), adding moreover some details about the circumstances:

> On Tuesday October 22, during nearly two hours Cardinal Wojtyla read out to us the 35 pages of a long text. We were surprised at what was being presented to us as the result of our work. For lack of method the proposed document had become a [piece of] good homework in pastoral theology. It failed to re-capture the testimonies and questions, the searchings and propositions—often very rich—which had characterized the work of the past three weeks.
>
> This is why with a few cardinals we thought it our duty to make a pressing appeal to Cardinal König, president of the session. The serious set-backs that would result if this text were to be presented as the conclusion

of the Synod were without delay brought to the attention of the Holy Father. A vote took place thereafter; out of four parts submitted to the approval of the bishops the last three were rejected.[6]

What was to be the next step? Opening the morning session on the following day, the president-delegates made the following proposal to the assembly: since, for lack of time, it now seemed impossible to compose another elaborate document, a commission could be appointed to prepare a short "message" addressed to the whole Church; for the rest, the entire documentation of the Synod would be presented to the Pope by the Synod Secretariat. When this proposal was opened to discussion, real dialogue took place for the first time in the full assembly—in the absence of the Pope, who, as on every Wednesday, was prevented by the public audience from attending the proceedings. It was during this debate that Cardinal Wojtyla gave the explanations mentioned above. The exchange of views was so frank and lively that in his intervention Dom Helder Camara called it "the most beautiful moment of the Synod." It is impossible to record all that was said; it is enough to mention the main trends. Cardinal Marty spoke first: "the world is waiting for a substantial text, not merely for an edifying message; it is to be regretted that the first two drafts were not communicated to the Fathers for their consideration; an effort should still be made to write a brief but substantial document which would reflect the riches embedded in the Synod's discussions on vital issues." In the same vein, Cardinal Joseph Malula, pointing out what had been the highlights of the Synod's work and the great hopes it had aroused, requested that the draft prepared by the secretary for the first part be presented to the Fathers for their approval. Bishop Brian Ashby suggested that, if this was not possible, the "Red Book" prepared by the same secretary could be put to the vote. Bishop Jean Guy Rakotondravahatra did not hide his opinion that the impasse of the previous day had proved the failure of the Synod. This opinion was, however, countered by many in whose view the riches of the exchanges made and of the documentation gathered forbade a purely negative diagnosis. Yet the question remained: what use should now be made of this rich material in order that it be not lost? Some thought that, since the Synod was but a consultative body meant to give advice, no final text was required; the Synod would have fulfilled its function if the entire documentation was presented to the Pope who, moreover, could decide whether or not to publish it in its entirety (Cardinal Stefan Wyszynski, Bishop [later Cardinal] Moreira Neves Lucas). Others suggested submitting to the Pope a list of issues that had captured the Synod's attention as priority concerns (Cardinal Gabriel-Marie Garrone). Yet others were of opinion that the entire documentation would provide the Pope with ample material for an Encyclical Letter on evangelization and that, if such a letter were written, the Pope's voice would have more weight with the Christian people than the voice of the Synod (Cardinal Gordon Gray, Archbishops Thomas Cahill and Vicente Faustino Zazpe).

But a greater number of speeches favored the opinion that a document should be issued by the Synod itself. However brief, this document should be substantial and include the main proposals and recommendations made by the assembly on vital issues (Cardinal Antonio Poma, Bishops Ramón Torrella Cascante, Sergio Contreras Navia and Roger Emile Aubry, Archbishop [later Cardinal] Hyacinthe Thiandoum). "We need something in our hands when we go home" (Bishop Derek Worlock); "our people expect something concrete from us" (Archbishop Ricardo Durand Flórez); "the world shares this expectation" (Bishops Emmanuel Constant and Vincent Mensah). Such a document would, however, have to be submitted to the approval of the assembly (Bishop Rosendo Huesca Pacheco), even though its publication was to be left to the Pope's discretion (Archbishop Maxim Hermaniuk). The suggestion that a post-synodal commission be appointed to work out the propositions, though favored by some, was strongly rejected by others: such a commission would run the risk of not representing adequately the mind of the Synod (Cardinal Malula). The president-delegates summed up the lively discussion as follows: all seemed to agree that the Synod should issue a final message; almost all seemed, moreover, to favor indicating the main thematic orientations of the Synod and handing over to the Pope its entire documentation. A positive vote having been taken on these three proposals, it was announced that the drafting of the message would be entrusted to the six reporters, while the secretaries of the workshops would take the responsibility for preparing the list of themes.

During the debate much was said about the method of the Synod's work. Many Fathers attributed the failure to produce a final document to defects of procedure. Fr Pedro Arrupe, S.J., pleaded strongly for another debate in which the structures and method of work would be subjected to scrutiny "in order that the aim of the Synod and its very institution be not endangered." The suggestion made by the Jesuit General having been taken up by many Fathers, another debate took place. Besides examining, as had been planned, the question of the frequency of the Synod, its method of work was opened to discussion. The question of frequency was easily settled and the Fathers ratified by vote the decision—which had been taken by the Pope for the present Synod—of a triennial celebration. With regard to method, many suggestions were made. Let me mention only the more characteristic ones. The pre-synodal work should be strengthened in such a way that the reports could reach the episcopal conferences in advance, and clear points for discussion could be included in the Working Paper. The Council of the Secretariat should remain in office during the Synod itself and act as a steering committee. Pastoral experiences and theological themes should not be separated, the latter having to emerge from the former. Theologians should be associated with the Synod's work, especially in the group-discussions. Speeches should be reduced in number and discussion in the assembly emphasized. The reports of workshops should be submitted to a real debate. The preparation of conclusions should be taken up at an early stage by the drafting committee. Moreover, even though the Synod is only a consultative body, being neither a parliament nor a mini-Council, the adoption of strict parliamentary rules used in international meetings would help to determine clearly the collegial advice it meant to give to the Pope.

Before these debates took place, the president-delegate had announced that, at the request of some cardinals (among who were Cardinals John Krol, Stefan Wyszynski and Josyf Slipyj), a special commission had been formed to prepare a draft for a statement on human rights. This commission having done its work swiftly, the draft was proposed to the Fathers for their approval even before the assembly had yet been able to decide what course of action to adopt with regard to the main synodal document. When the draft of this document was read to the assembly and presented for immediate voting, the Fathers were told that the Pope had already given it his own approval. Thus to the text distributed to the assembly, "Human Rights and Reconciliation," a preliminary sentence had to be added: "The Holy Father, in union with the Bishops assembled at the Synod for the study of Evangelization, issues the following message." In these conditions which left no room for discussion, the text was almost unanimously passed and immediately made public. Its content was beyond reproach. Yet, although a concrete sign of solidarity with the churches under oppressive regimes was highly commendable, it seemed odd that the first text published by the Synod was devoted to an issue somewhat peripheral to its main thrust.

The other documents—the Synod's Message addressed to the Church and the list of themes to be submitted to the Pope—went through a double editing before final approval. A vote on the substance of each text was taken after the reading of the first drafts; the result being positive, a discussion on amendments followed. As suggestions for improving the message were many, the president-delegate requested that all *modi* be proposed in writing. Since the text had already been approved in substance, only those amendments would be considered which did not affect ideas but only style and precision. For the list of themes, it was now insisted that it should be conceived strictly as a list of questions raised and studied, without any indication of a position taken by the Synod. All affirmative propositions should, accordingly, be avoided in the final edition. Suggested additions to the list could, however, be made if any important item had been overlooked by the editors; non-Christian religions was one of those oversights.

When the second and final draft of both documents was brought to the house, the president-delegate explained that out of more than 200 *modi* proposed for the Message, only those had been taken into account which fell under the category of style and precision. Additions had been made to the list of questions discussed. The two documents, now called "Declaration of the Synodal Fathers" and "Elenchus of Questions Given Special Consideration in the Synod," were voted upon and approved. When on the next day the result of the vote was announced, the president-delegates told the assembly that to the list of questions approved by the Fathers they had, on their own, taken the initiative of adding the question of "religious liberty." Neither of the two documents requires searching analysis. The Declaration, though intending to "explain the basic convictions and the main orientations" of the Synod, does so in such a subdued and innocuous manner that the thrust of the Synod's work fails to come through effectively. The elenchus of questions would have served as a good working paper at the beginning of the Synod; coming at the end, it rather witnessed to its lack of conclusiveness.

The Last General Assembly

The concluding speech of Pope Paul VI, which closed the Synod on October 26, was awaited with interest but not without apprehension. Given the complexity of the events over the last month of which he had been an assiduous but silent witness, what would be the Holy Father's assessment of the Synod's work? What direction would his own conclusions take? The Pope spoke frankly and openly. He observed that "the width and complexity of the theme (of evangelization) did not allow it to be dealt with exhaustively in a short time. Nor did they allow the hoped for conclusions to be arrived at in their fulness." Nevertheless, the Pope's evaluation was a favorable one: "this has been clearly a positive experience." The reasons for a positive assessment were explained: first, the bishops had shown their deep awareness of their urgent duty to carry out the apostolic mandate; "a consensus of opinions had generally been shown on many points of great importance" which were enumerated. Moreover, the frank recognition of "the difficulty of expressing in an immediate document all the aspects and obligations of evangelization" was by itself a positive factor. The Synod had sought to listen to the voice of the Holy Spirit, had been alerted to many healthy currents of thought, and had reaffirmed the primary duty of communicating to humankind the joyful message of Christ. "In a word, this Synod has been for all of us a call to greater responsibility in the discharge of our duties and obligations." The Pope admitted that there had been deficiencies in the method of work, and graciously indicated that the suggestions made for improving it would be willingly considered.

Next, he noted that among the many points considered by the Synod some required a "more accurate explanation": "not all the elements emerging from the discussions are to be retained"; "some, especially among those that have come out of the workshops, must be better defined, nuanced, completed and subjected to further study." He mentioned some about which he "could not remain silent." "First of all, the relationship between the particular churches and the Apostolic See": the Successor of Peter being "the ordinary pastor of the Church in her unity and entirety," "his interventions cannot be reduced only to extraordinary circumstances"; Vatican II has affirmed that "he has full, supreme and universal power in the Church and can always exercise this power freely" (*Lumen Gentium*, 22). Secondly, "it would be dangerous to speak of the need for diversified theologies according to continents and cultures; for either the content of faith is Catholic or it vanishes." Moreover, human liberation "is not to be excessively emphasized on a temporal level to the detriment of the essential meaning" of evangelization. Again, the "ecclesial life [of small communities] in the organic unity of the single Body of Christ" requires that they remain subject to legitimate ecclesiastical authority. These were the "more important points" on which the Pope said he does not "allow false directions to be followed." Were he to allow this, he would be negligent in his "fundamental office of confirming his brothers."

The cautions were clear. Were they an indication that in the Pope's mind the Synod, especially the workshops, had taken false directions on those points? Were they a disavowal of tendencies expressed, for instance, on liberation or small communities? Some of the cautions were in fact too clear-cut, to the extent of appearing one-sided. Were they fully consistent with other pronouncements made by the Pope himself on the same topics on other occasions? Some observations are worth making here with regard to the local church and theological pluralism.

Earlier in his speech, among points of great importance on which consensus had contributed to the positive results of the Synod, the Pope had mentioned the fact that evangelizing "pertains to the local churches, in communion with the universal Church." The universal power of the Pope and his right to exercise it had not been challenged in any workshop report. The point raised was the way in which this power should be exercised, and the opportuneness for the central authority to dictate detailed legislation on secondary matters for which the local hierarchies often are the better judges. The target of misgivings was not the Pope himself, but rather the Roman Congregations. What was desired in order that the churches might find their true identity and enjoy their "legitimate autonomy" was a more sincere application of the principles of subsidiarity and decentralization, in conformity with the Decree *Christus Dominus* of Vatican II and along the lines already previously followed to a certain extent by the Apostolic Letter *Pastorale Munus* (1963). Practical suggestions made to this end included greater liberty for episcopal conferences with regard to liturgy, theological investigation, discipline, ministries, and eventually the choice of bishops, according to norms to be determined by the Pope himself. That many bishops, even otherwise very reserved, felt strongly on this point is an undeniable fact. It is no less certain that their claims and demands were founded on the centralizing tendency of the Sacred Congregations that has been reinforced in the last few years and of which many examples, sometimes trivial, were given.

The Pope's negative verdict on diversified theologies was disturbing for more than one reason. It seemed to imply that theological pluralism necessarily endangers the unity of faith, the content of which "either is Catholic or vanishes." The distinction between the content of faith and its theological elaboration, for which the recent Declaration *Mysterium Ecclesiae* (1973) of the Sacred Congregation for the Doctrine of the Faith had paved the way in a new manner, seemed overlooked. More puzzling still was the fact that the Pope's reservations did not seem to tally with what, six days earlier (October 20), he had said in his address to the Synod Fathers during the reception organized at the Urbanianum (Pontifical Urban University). On that occasion the Pope, alluding to the work of the Synod, had seemed to rejoice at "the undisputed identity of the faith which in apostolic and missionary language gives rise to and invents flexible forms, truly incarnated in the most diverse ethnic and historical realities."[7]

Perhaps theological "forms" were not directly in the Pope's mind when he spoke those words. But in the Apostolic Exhortation *Paterna cum benevolentia* (on reconciliation in the Church), which, soon after the close of the Synod, he addressed to the Church in immediate preparation for the celebration in Rome of the Holy Year, the Pope's considerations on theological pluralism seemed to cancel the reservations expressed in the concluding speech at the Synod. The Pope expressed himself as follows:

> We recognize that pluralism of research and thought, which in various ways investigates and expounds dogma but without causing its identical objective meaning to disintegrate, has a legitimate right of citizenship in the Church, as a natural component part of her catholicity, and as a sign of the cultural richness and personal commitment of all who belong to her…. Indeed we admit that a certain theological pluralism finds its roots in the mystery of Christ, the inscrutable richness whereof (cf. Eph 3:8) transcends the capacities of expression of all ages and cultures. Thus the doctrine of faith which necessarily derives from that mystery—since in the order of salvation "the mystery of God is none other than Christ"—calls for constant fresh research.[8]

In the same document the Pope went on to stress the need for every expression of faith to be true to the revealed message, to remain in touch with tradition, and to be subject to the Church's teaching authority. The theological pluralism advocated at the Synod meant to respect those criteria, and did not seem in any way different from what, as the Pope himself recognized, has legitimate right of citizenship in the Church. The reservations on theological pluralism made in his closing speech of the Synod thus remain puzzling, and raise disturbing questions as to the influences which may have entered into its composition. This and other factors mentioned above explain why the Pope's address left the Synod Fathers disquieted and disturbed.

III. SOME CONCLUSIONS

Ambiguities continue to hover over the 1974 Synod. It was made up of lights and shadows, of hopes and disappointments. All these elements must be taken into account in facing the question: was the Synod a failure or a success? Its positive and negative aspects must be sorted out. The Holy Father pointed out a number of positive elements. The Fathers of the Synod themselves thought that in more than one way this Synod was the best among those so far celebrated: the lively communication of experiences, the frank discussion and fraternal exchange of the workshops had been an exciting experience; from those discussions an impressive amount of material had emerged, conducive to a deeper understanding of the Church's mission and rich in pastoral applications. The sad part is that all these riches had not found expression in a final document, thus running the risk of being lost. It is true that documents are not what primarily matters, and that unless put into practice they remain ineffective; it is also true that some points needed refinement and further studies. Yet, the lack of a substantial text conveying the main thrust of the Synod makes one feel that a great opportunity has been lost for exposing the Church to a broadened understanding of her mission and for explaining to the world how she situates herself today in the overall picture of human realities. To have put such a document in the hands of the Holy Father, while leaving to his judgment the decision whether or not to publish it, would have given to the Synod a sense of achievement of which it was in fact deprived. To suppose that the elements for a document of this sort were available does not imply that a complete consensus of opinions was reached on all the important issues. To give but one example: while most bishops favored decentralization, those belonging to countries under oppressive regimes were inclined to look upon the strength of a central power as a security factor for their existence and survival. What I want to say here is that some basic tendencies emerged with sufficient clarity, even though applications might have had to depend on concrete circumstances.

Why then did the hoped-for text fail to materialize? Was it merely due to the deficient methods used during the Synod's proceedings? It seems undeniable that another factor came into play, namely a certain divergence of views between the Roman Curia and the world episcopate. Interventions by Cardinal Prefects of Roman Congregations more than once revealed that, in the tension between the universal and the particular, the central administration naturally tends to take the view-point opposite to that of the periphery. As the problems are being approached by the two sides from opposite directions, the wave-length on which they speak and the language they use differ. The Synod did not altogether resolve that tension; to overcome it through real dialogue between the central administration and the local episcopates might well be the important role it will have to play in the future.

But, in spite of its inconclusiveness, the 1974 Synod remains an important and perhaps decisive event. However paradoxical this may sound, it may even be said that its inability to produce substantial conclusions is the most telling witness to the impact it has made. For the fact must be properly interpreted: the divergence between the two preliminary drafts of conclusions was one of theological method, inductive and deductive; the disavowal of the third draft, the substance of which continued to make deductions from a priori principles without reaching down to reality, meant the rejection of a certain manner of reflection. A worn out theological approach had failed and had been rejected. Hopefully the accident may not be repeated on later occasions. Equally revealing of the importance of this Synod is the fact that it started as the Synod of the Third World and of the local church, and that it continued to be so to the end. The voice of the Third World came through with a powerful message which hopefully will continue to be heard; the theme of the local church occupied the central place in the debates, and theological reflection is bound to focus on it in the years to come.

A question-mark, however, still remains as regards the way in which the synodal institution is destined to evolve. Principles governing its nature are clear, but their practical implementation is a delicate operation. For, on the one hand, the Synod is neither a parliament nor a mini-Council, but only an advisory and consultative body. On the other hand, its advisory function is a true exercise in collegiality and a genuine expression of the co-responsibility of the world episcopate with the Pope. As such it must find adequate means for conveying its advice effectively. That these means have not yet been fully discovered should surprise no one who keeps in mind that an institution less than ten years old is a very young institution in the Church's life and that only practice makes perfect.

[Note: This article was published in *Vidyajyoti: Journal of Theological Reflection* 39 (1975), 146–69. When Pope Paul VI issued in December 1975 his postsynodal apostolic exhortation *Evangelii Nuntiandi*, Dupuis published a commentary on the document in *Vidyajyoti* 40 (1976), 218–30. After summarizing accurately and fully the pope's exhortation, in a few final pages (ibid., 228–30) Dupuis showed why he judged that this document did not reflect the open attitude of the synod on a number of important issues: evangelization; particular churches and small communities; indigenous liturgy, catechesis and theology; and non-Christian religions. On the last point Dupuis urged that these religions should be seen not "merely as expressions of human aspirations towards God but [also] as embodying for their followers a first, though incomplete, approach of God to human beings" (p. 230)—a view that Dupuis was to develop at length in his *Toward a Christian Theology of Religious Pluralism* (Maryknoll, NY: Orbis, 1997) and that was to trigger a protracted inquiry into this book by the Congregation for the Doctrine of the Faith. With Dupuis's permission, I have polished slightly his 1975 article reproduced above, but without making any changes of content. The article was reprinted in *Doctrine and Life* 25 (1975), 323–48. On the 1974 Synod see the full chronicle by G. Caprile, *Il Sinodo dei Vescovi. Terza Assemblea Generale* (27 settembre–26 ottobre 1974) (Rome: *Civiltà Cattolica*, 1975). G. O'C.]

Appendix B: Speech of Archbishop Francis Rush at the 1985 Extraordinary Synod of Bishops

[To review the work of Vatican II twenty years after it closed in December 1965, Pope John Paul II called a special meeting of the Bishops' Synod. On November 27, Archbishop Rush addressed the general assembly as president of the Australian Bishops' Conference.]

Most Holy Father and my Brothers and Sisters in Christ, I speak for the Bishops of Australia when I thank God for the Second Vatican Council. I speak with gratitude for the considerable renewal the Council has already achieved, and with unbounded hope that the Holy Spirit will guide this Synod as He undoubtedly guided the Council. If there have been failures, they have not been the fault of the Council. They have emanated from neglect of the Council or from misinterpretation of its spirit and teachings. On behalf of the Bishops of Australia, I should like to underline two concerns. One has to do with the implementation of a major theme of *Lumen Gentium*, the other with the implementation of *Gaudium et Spes*.

Our first concern has to do with that aspect of *Lumen Gentium* which is addressed by the third of our distinguished Relator's four "Argumenta Specialia." [The Church as Communion was the third in Cardinal Godfried Danneels's list of four special themes.] The question of Collegiality and the relationship of the Local Church to the Universal Church is a major internal question, which is causing sufficient anxiety and wasting enough energy to distract the Church from what should be its major concerns. From the first moment of his pontificate the Holy Father stressed the importance of Collegiality. His very first encyclical [*Redemptor Hominis* of 1979] spoke of it at length [no. 5]. Diversity among the Local Churches and the principle of subsidiarity argue that local solutions should be found for local problems, as long as these solutions do not jeopardize the unity of the Local Churches with and under the Holy Father. Bishops and theologians sometimes get the impression that their orthodoxy is questioned lightly and that their difficulties and industry are not appreciated. This leads to a loss of trust which only damages the Church. We welcome the emphasis given by the esteemed Relator to the relationship between the Universal Church and the Particular Churches. We see the need for an even more refined theology [of] and more effective use of Episcopal Conferences.

Our second concern has to do with *Gaudium et Spes*. In *Catechesi Tradendae* [an apostolic exhortation of 1979] the Holy Father wrote of the secularization of our society. He described ours as a world which largely ignores God. It is a world in which too often there is "indifferentism" or even contempt for religion as if it were incompatible with scientific progress (no. 57). Secularisation, in the West and increasingly in every part of the world, is one significant phenomenon at the basis of most of the problems confronting the Church since the Second Vatican Council. Personal [salvation] and global salvation are being sought outside the Church, or along ways only loosely related to the Church, which rightly calls herself the "sacrament of salvation." *Gaudium et Spes* ushered in a transformation in our attitudes to the world. However, its message, or the best of our thinking based on it, has not succeeded in giving enough men and women a sufficiently clear and inspiring vision of the Church's role in the world of our time. Too many people, even among Catholics, find the Church peripheral to their concerns. It has been said but it cannot be exaggerated: the task of translating the Council's theology of the Church into action has only begun. The great merit of the Synod will be the encouragement it gives to those who are anxious to complete the task. Our efforts will be strengthened enormously if they are linked with the preparation of our Local Churches for the 1987 Synod on the Laity.

The Conference of Australian Bishops will be glad to learn that "Quaenam est missio ecclesiae pro mundo huius temporis? (What is the mission of the Church for the world of today?)" has been submitted to our consideration by the Relator as one of the four "Argumenta Specialia" [the fourth in Cardinal Danneels's list of special themes]. Page 12 of the *Relatio* describes vividly how the world's problems have worsened in the twenty years since the Council. It names three kinds of societies [rich countries, developing countries, and countries where the church is persecuted], each with its own special problems. For each the Church needs to search for and shape an answer to the only ultimate question: "Quis est Christus pro mundo huius temporis? (Who is Christ for the world of today?)."

[For a full account of the 1985 Synod, see G. Caprile, *Il Sinodo dei Vescovi. Seconda Assemblea Generale Straordinaria (24 novembre–8 dicembre 1985)* (Rome: Civiltà Cattolica, 1986).]

Appendix C: The Catholic Bishops' Conference of Japan: Response to the *Lineamenta*[1]

THE PROCESS OF PREPARATION OF THE RESPONSE

1. *Three Months Were Needed for Translation.* Upon receipt of the English and French translations of the *Lineamenta* published in Rome on September 3, 1996, we began at once to have it translated into Japanese. This took about three months. Copies of the translation were distributed to each diocese on December 17, 1996. In each diocese, the bishop took the lead in common study sessions and made it the subject of prayer.

2. *Discussion at Two Plenary Assemblies.* After the bishops of each diocese received the Japanese translation of the *Lineamenta*, they studied them together with the priests of their dioceses for about two months and tried to formulate an answer to the questions of the *Lineamenta*. However, though they had asked their priests for an answer to the questions of the *Lineamenta*, the reaction was that it was not possible to answer those questions. At the discussion at the Extraordinary Plenary Assembly (February 18–21, 1997) on how to prepare the official response, as we shall note below, many opinions were expressed on the questions themselves as well as about requests to be made at the synod itself.

(A) Opinions of the bishops concerning the questions of the *Lineamenta* themselves: Since the questions of the *Lineamenta* were composed in the context of Western Christianity, they are not suitable. Among the questions are some concerning whether the work of evangelization is going well or not. But what is the standard of evaluation? If it is the number of baptisms, etc., it is very dangerous. From the way the questions are proposed, one feels that the holding of the Synod is like an occasion for the central office to evaluate the performance of the branch offices. That kind of synod would not be worthwhile for the Church in Asia. The judgement should not be made from a European framework, but must be seen on the spiritual level of the people who live in Asia.

(B) Hopes for the synod: If the synod is to be carried out for the Church in Asia, it must have an approach different from those for other continents. The same approach as [is used] in the West will not be successful. The most important thing is the inculturation of our thinking. As the Holy Father says, our objective must be a "New Evangelization." In other words, a new zeal that is different from that we have had until now, new expressions (and a completely different method of communication), new methods (an approach different from the traditional one). If we are to have a synod for Asia, in order that the method and process may be different from that for a synod for the West or for Africa, the priorities of the Church of Asia must be presented clearly before composing the *Instrumentum Laboris* [that is, the working paper].

Accordingly, the Japanese Bishops' Conference decided that they would prepare their own questions for the Japanese Church and ask the opinions of the major seminaries, theology faculties, and the various religious congregations. Four months later, at the Ordinary Plenary Assembly (June 16–21, 1997), they considered more than 325 replies that had been submitted by the bishops themselves, the major seminaries, the theology faculties, religious congregations, individual priests and religious, councils of the laity, etc., and composed the Official Response of the Japanese Church, which is given below.

REQUESTS OF THE JAPANESE CHURCH
TO THE SYNODAL SECRETARIAT

I. Proposals Concerning Methodology

1. Consideration of Asian Countries without a Common Language

Among all the countries of Asia, there is not one that has as its native tongue any of those languages ordinarily used by the Holy See (Italian, English, French, German, Spanish). Countries such as India and Philippines, which have many different languages, use English as a kind of common language. However, among the almost forty nations which are to take part in the Special Assembly for Asia of the Synod of Bishops, they are exceptions. To fail to take this fact into account and to hold the Special Assembly according to the same schedule and methodology as those of Europe and

America, etc., is ill advised. It is necessary to provide a period of preparation of at least six months from the date of the publication of the *Instrumentum Laboris* until the synod itself. (We should like to point out that it took three months from the publication of the *Lineamenta* to its translation into Japanese and distribution to the bishops.) The bishops of Japan consider it most important to translate the *Instrumentum Laboris*, study it carefully, and prepare themselves in prayer.

For the same reason we request that, together with determining English and French as the languages to be used at the synod, provision be made for simultaneous translation from English and French to Japanese, and other languages as requested by other episcopal conferences.

2. Use of a Methodology Suited to Asian Spirituality

Unlike Europe and Africa, the differences among the various nations of Asia are so fundamental that a basically different methodology from that used in the synods held up to now is called for. Using the methodology of the West "as is" for the Special Assembly for Asia will not be successful. Some sessions and activities should be included to work toward a united image and a new paradigm to include the varying realities and cultures of Asia, its different mentalities and spiritual traditions.

The issues to be discussed during the Synod should be decided right after the bishops have convened. This is to assure that there is ample time for mature deliberation in order to arrive at the final recommendations. The decision concerning the global direction of the Synod should not be made by the Roman Secretariat, but should be left to the bishops from Asia. The choice of the chairpersons of the committees and small groups which are to direct the work of the synod should also be left to the bishops from Asia. They should follow their own sense of the process and the special needs of the assembly. The bishops taking part in the Synod should be permitted to consult and ask for the comments of experts concerning the different matters treated during the sessions. These experts should be persons recommended by the bishops themselves for their knowledge of the Church, the world, and especially the realities of Asia.

3. Use Should Be Made of the Fruits of the Federation of Asian Bishops' Conferences; Focus Should Be Limited from the Beginning

For more than twenty-five years, the Federation of Asian Bishops' Conferences (FABC) has been involved with the reality of the Church in our countries and has made important statements. We propose that the fruit of the work of the FABC should be made good use of at the Synod. For example, we propose that the practice of having a representative of the Church of each country give a report (which usually takes two weeks) be discontinued, and that a representative of the two blocks, namely, the FABC and the Middle East, first give a report on their history and current problems and thus give focus to the issues to be taken up by the Special Assembly for Asia of the Synod of Bishops.[2] In this way, the very wide-ranging and many-faceted reality of the living Church in Asia will be presented, the main points of the presentation will become clear, and there will be time at the end to make a concrete plan.

4. Dividing into Groups

At the synods up to the present, groups were formed according to the languages of the West (Italian, English, French, German, Spanish, etc.). However, we request that for this Special Assembly for Asia the groups be divided not according to language, but according to themes or religious cultures (Islamic Culture, Hindu Culture, Hinayana Buddhist Culture, Mahayana Buddhist Culture, Confucian Culture, etc.).

5. Participation of Various Observers

One common anti-evangelical problem among the countries of Asia is discrimination against and oppression of women. In order that we can grasp and judge this reality, we request the participation of women observers well acquainted with this problem. The Major Superiors' Association of Religious Women of Japan is prepared to send a religious woman qualified for this task. With few exceptions, the Catholic Church in almost all the countries of Asia is [in the] minority. In order to grasp and judge this situation, we request that representatives of the traditional religions and experts in dialogue with other religions be invited to participate as observers.

6. To Revitalize the Catholic Church of Asia

The Catholic Church in Asia, at the dawn of the third millennium, has to continue the work of evangelization in the midst of many other religions. Making the most of this fact, we hope that the synod will be one that will encourage the work of evangelization that we are carrying on. The Church in Asia has many tasks and problems, but we hope that, rather than stressing the negative side, this synod will be one that will encourage us to continue our efforts against heavy odds. We do not hope for a synod aiming at discovering how the Asian Church can be propped up by the Western Church, but one where the bishops of Asia can have an honest exchange and learn how they can support and encourage one another. In other words, we wish to participate in the spirit of people really involved with one another, not seeking how "they can have life more abundantly," as if we were speaking of some third persons, but how "we together can have life more abundantly."

7. Focus on Relationship with Other Asian Religions

In Asia, in addition to Christianity and Judaism, there are also Hinduism, Islam, Buddhism, and other great religions. Moreover, there are animistic religions, which believe in the existence of spirits (and popular religions, cosmic religions, etc.), which have a wide influence. A culture that has developed under the influence of these various religions is a fundamentally different reality. Thus, should not the Special General Assembly for Asia consider, not the global connection of Christianity with all the problems of Asia, but the relationship of Christianity with each religion and each culture? Unless we do so, we may end up only with abstract discussions and without anything concrete or useful that the Church of Asia can do for an effective service to the Kingdom of God.

II. Considerations for Composing the Instrumentum Laboris

1. *Christology.* One finds in the *Lineamenta* a certain defensiveness and apologetic attitude. This makes its presentations of certain other theological positions clearly unfair and inadequate. This is especially clear in the section on Christology. This does not help the faith of Asian Christians. What is necessary is an open and spiritual Christology rooted in real life and alert to the problems of

modern people. We should try to discover what kind of Jesus will be a light to the peoples of Asia. In other words, as the Fathers of the early Church did with Greco-Roman culture, we must make a more profound study of the fundamentals of the religiosity of our peoples, and from this point of view try to discover how Jesus Christ is answering their needs.

Jesus Christ is the Way, the Truth, and the Life, but in Asia, before stressing that Jesus Christ is the Truth, we must search much more deeply into how he is the Way and the Life. If we stress too much that "Jesus Christ is the One and Only Saviour," we can have no dialogue, common living, or solidarity with other religions. The Church, learning from the kenosis of Jesus Christ, should be humble and open its heart to other religions to deepen its understanding of the Mystery of Christ.

2. *Ecclesiology.* The image of the Church presented in the *Lineamenta* is not as rich or deep as that of Vatican II. In particular, the images of "the Church as people of God" and "the Church as servant" are not stressed. These two images have special meaning for the Church in Asia, which in order to serve God's kingdom lives in a minority position with and for others. Their absence would be unfortunate for the Synod. The central issues of "Service" and "Dialogue" developed by the FABC are two very important points for the Catholic Church in Asia, which are not sufficiently stressed in the *Lineamenta.*

3. *Soteriology.* The theme of "Mission of Love and Service" proposed by the Catholic Church in Asia must be one that responds to the real thirst of the people of Asia. That is to say, it must make clear, in a way the people can understand, the content of the salvation that Jesus brings.

Again, in order to proclaim to the people of Asia the universal message of salvation, we must study how to express this message.

4. *Missiology.* In the *Lineamenta*, without attempting to explain what the term can or should mean, the word "Proclamation" is stressed and used over and over again. Considering the Asian context, not enough attention is given to the necessity of "Dialogue." In the context of evangelization in Asia, "compassion with the suffering" has been identified time after time at the General Assemblies of the FABC as a most important element. In missionary work

among those of other religions, what is more important than convincing words is the attitude of standing by the side of the weak and powerless and showing them compassion. In the *Lineamenta* a great deal is made, as in traditional scholastic theology, of "distinctions" and "differences." However, in the tradition of the Far East, it is characteristic to search for creative harmony rather than distinctions. In the documents published by the FABC over the past twenty-five years, there have been many examples of this "Asianness." Isn't it important for the Asian Synod to discuss how we are to accept the truths to be found in Hinduism, Islam, Buddhism, etc., how we are to evaluate them, and how we are to work together?

The questions at the end of the *Lineamenta* ask for an evaluation of our missionary activity. However, when we treat a situation in Asia where it is difficult to increase the number of baptisms, a "success orientation" of "trying for better results" can only discourage the missionary. We need a vision of evangelization that gives joy and a sense of purpose to a Christian living as one of a minority in the midst of many traditional religions. An evaluation based not on the number of baptisms but rather from the point of view of "How faithful have we been to our mission of evangelization?" is necessary.

5. *Other Points.* The theology on which the *Lineamenta* is based is the theology of the Christian West, and appears to the eyes of non-Christians as overly self-complacent and introverted. Based on this kind of theology, we cannot approach the unsettled Asia of today. In the *Lineamenta* there is a lack of understanding of the Asian culture, especially the Asian culture of today, which is a mixture of traditional Asian culture and an Americanized modern culture. Moreover, it does not appear that we can be satisfied with modern Western theology, either, especially if we consider that we can never say that the redemption of Christ and the work of the Holy Spirit are absent even in non-Christian cultures.

The historical analysis of the Church gives the impression of being centered in India. There is a great lack in the treatment in the *Lineamenta* of the problems of the Churches in the Siberian area of the former Soviet Union, those of the Churches of the Middle and Near East, those presently faced by the Church in China, the difficult situation of the Socialist nations of the Indochinese peninsula, and the pain of separation between the Republic of Korea and the Democratic People's Republic of Korea, etc.

Appendix D: "My Voyage of Discovery," by John Marshall

My appointment to the Pontifical Commission on Population, Family and Birth set up by Pope John XXIII in 1963 was for me a voyage of discovery. At the outset, like so many of my colleagues on the commission, I accepted the traditional teaching that contraception is intrinsically evil. But the inexorable unfolding of the scientific evidence and theological argument showed me otherwise, and gradually I came to believe that the traditional ban on artificial birth control could not be upheld. Unlike some of my colleagues, it was no "Road to Damascus" experience of blinding revelation that made me change my opinion in this way. Rather, it was as though the traditional teaching was contained in a corroding cistern; one leak in the argument was plugged only for another to develop, until it became obvious to most of us that nothing but a new cistern would suffice.

The Second Vatican Council was in session. Its theological commission was engaged in a bitterly fought battle between those who wished to restate the traditional view that procreation is the primary end of marriage, love being only secondary, and those who wished to do away with such a hierarchy of ends. A compromise was [to be] reached in paragraph 50 of the Council's Pastoral Constitution on the Church in the Modern World, *Gaudium et Spes*, where it is stated that the whole meaning of family life is to enlarge God's family "while not making the other purposes of matrimony of less account."

As this battle continued, Pope John XXIII suddenly announced that the question of birth control was to be removed from the Council's agenda and given to a special body which came to be known as the birth control commission. Action was needed because international agencies, such as the United Nations and the World Health Organization, had decided to become involved in a major way with the population question, which until that time had been avoided out of deference to Roman Catholic sensitivities. One task of the birth control commission [was] to advise the Holy See on how it should respond. There was some criticism of the decision to remove the question from the Council, the highest teaching authority in the Church. But many welcomed the move, since the birth control commission contained both laity and clergy, and hence was felt to be better equipped to deal with the subject than a solely clerical group.

The original commission consisted of three priests and three laymen (of which I was one) with backgrounds in sociology, economics, medicine and international diplomacy. My qualification was that as medical adviser to Britain's Catholic Marriage Advisory Council, I had carried out and published extensive research into natural family planning. We first met in a hotel in the woods outside Louvain in Belgium and quickly identified two tasks: thoroughly to assess the growing body of demographic, economic, sociological and psychological evidence related to population growth; and to prepare a clear explanation of the Church's teaching on birth control. It was hoped that the latter would at least gain respect for the Church's position. These tasks required wider skills than we possessed and so we recommended enlargement of our numbers. Pope John accepted the recommendation and added demographers and theologians, among others, bringing the total to eighteen.

The enlarged commission met at Domus Mariae in Rome in 1964 and soon reached what proved to be the first turning point in its existence. Canon Pierre de Locht, who had done much work with family movements in Belgium, made a powerful presentation. In essence he said that the Church's view of marriage had been distorted by the teaching that procreation is the primary end of marriage and sexual intercourse; this did not accord either with the scientific evidence or with the experience of married couples. The need was to start again from scratch. The Redemptorist theologian, Fr Bernard Häring, said, "But you are raising questions of fundamental [moral] theology," to which de Locht replied, "Yes, I suppose I am." (It must be remembered that up to this point the remit [terms of reference] of the commission was to prepare a coherent account of the traditional teaching.) It was decided that we should take a break to allow time for private reflection and discussion. When we resumed, we concluded that unless we addressed fundamental questions, a coherent presentation of the teaching on contraception could not be achieved.

The Swiss Dominican, Henri de Riedmatten, secretary-general to the commission, presented an interim report to Pope Paul VI, who, on succeeding Pope John, had confirmed the existence of the commission and its work. The outcome was awaited with some trepidation, but Pope Paul's response was the discussion should continue in a serious and responsible fashion, wherever it led. At the same time he again enlarged the commission to some 64 members to include different cultures—the original members were all Europeans—cardinals and bishops, theologians, scientists and, most important, married people.

We met in 1965 at the Spanish College, Rome. Among many significant contributions was the dossier presented by the American couple, Pat and Patsy Crowley: the women among us were playing a significant part. The Crowleys had conducted a survey among members of the Christian Family Movement in the United States which revealed something of the suffering experienced by married people in trying to observe the Church's ban on contraception. Attempts were made by some observers to dismiss this evidence by nostrums such as, "The Church is not a democracy," or "Morality is not determined by surveys." This was to miss the point, for the survey had been carried out among loyal Catholics who were often the backbone of their parishes; the previously hidden evidence of the damaging effect of the teaching on marriage could no longer be ignored. Instead of operating with intellectual constructs divorced from reality, the theology of marriage had to reflect living experience. This was not situation ethics; it was ethics grounded in reality.

During this session it was decided that the theologians should meet by themselves as a group, maintaining the interdisciplinary nature of the commission's work by having Donald Barrett, professor of sociology at Notre Dame University, in attendance. The aim was to examine the history and theological basis of the teaching on birth control in depth. This the theologians did over a period of two weeks, most reaching the conclusion that the intrinsic evil of contraception could not be demonstrated and should not be sustained; a minority agreed that the intrinsic evil of contraception could not be demonstrated, but thought the teaching should nevertheless be sustained because of the authority the Church had invested in it.

This was the second turning point in the life of the commission. The conclusions of the theologians were thoroughly debated in plenary session, and most members of the commission agreed with the majority view. It was a time of great crisis. The debates were always scholarly, calm and courteous, but many commission members had invested greatly in the traditional teaching and they could not conceal their personal anguish.

Everyone was conscious of the tremendous significance of the conclusion of the majority. It was as though infallibility was being challenged. In fact it was not. The mistake had been to adopt a description of a natural phenomenon, sexual intercourse, as primarily procreative which did not accord with the scientific evidence (the majority of acts of intercourse do not have procreative potential) nor with the experience of couples. The Church is not infallible about natural phenomena. I was scandalized by the view of the minority that, although the validity of the teaching could not be demonstrated, it should be sustained because otherwise the authority of the Church and its authority as an infallible guide would be threatened. I thought it was wrong to put authority before truth. My final decision was much influenced by revolt against such an argument for maintaining the status quo.

The third and final turning point in the life of the commission was the presentation of the conclusions to a session of all the member bishops. Karol Wojtyla, later Pope John Paul II, had been named as one of them but he never once attended because, it was said, the Polish authorities would not give him a visa. In keeping with the interdisciplinary nature of the commission, individual bishops had taken part in specialist groups throughout and were seemingly in accord with the development. But how would the bishops as a body react? In the event, the majority agreed with the majority conclusion.

Three years after the first meeting of the original six, in 1966, a final report was presented to Paul VI. This has never been published officially, but an authentic account appeared in *The Tablet* [in several installments, starting on April 22, 1967] and in *The National Catholic Reporter* of Kansas City [for April 15, 1967].

The commission had now concluded its work and was disbanded. There followed 18 months of silence during which the Congregation for the Doctrine of the Faith (CDF) was feverishly active. Because the commission had been established to advise the Holy See on its stance in relation to the international organizations, its verdict should have been the responsibility of the Secretary of State, not the CDF. Cardinal [Alfredo] Ottaviani, prefect of the CDF, was a member of the commission but said little; he was no doubt biding his time, as experienced bureaucrats do. The CDF set up a highly secret group, composed entirely of hand-picked clergy, to produce a new report. This was reportedly so conservative that even the CDF found it unacceptable. So a second group, again entirely clergy, was convened and reported in due course, with what influence is unclear; the belief is that a draft of the 1968 encyclical *Humanae Vitae* was prepared for Paul VI by the French Jesuit, Gustave Martelet. As we know, the encyclical, though eloquent on the role of love in marriage, rejected our commission's line, and upheld the traditional teaching that contraception is intrinsically wrong.

What might have happened if the question of contraception had not been removed from the Council? It is unlikely that the theological commission, composed as it was of clergy, would have been able to conduct a similarly wide-ranging, in-depth review. They might not have been able to get further than revising the previous doctrine that procreation was the primary end of marriage. On the other hand, if the conclusions had been those of the Council, they could not have been strangled at birth by the CDF.

Yet there has been change. During the long wait for the encyclical, Cardinal [John Carmel] Heenan [Archbishop of Westminster], with great prescience, said to me, "It does not matter now what the Pope says. It is too late. The people have made up their minds." Cardinal Heenan was a member of the commission and insisted throughout that both sides of the argument be presented fairly and squarely. I have no doubt that initially he accepted the traditional teaching, but in the final session he voted with the majority to change it.

Catholics as a whole did not accept the encyclical's teaching, and this non-acceptance differed from times past when someone who disagreed might argue: "I know the Church says this is wrong, but what else can I do in the circumstances? The Lord will understand." Now, however, the judgment of many was: "The teaching reaffirmed in *Humanae Vitae* is wrong. I cannot accept it as the word of God." To have the Pope saying that contraception is intrinsically evil and his followers saying it is not, and acting accordingly, greatly weakens the witness of the Church in every field. It is ironic to recall that Paul VI was so powerfully motivated by a concern to uphold the Church's authority. Instead, it seems to me, he showed that the Church needs to re-evaluate the origin and nature and exercise of its authority on moral questions.

The story of the birth control commission and its aftermath illustrates the achievements and the shortcomings of the Second Vatican Council. There remains much unfinished business.

[John Marshall is emeritus professor of neurology at the University of London. He published this article in *The Tablet* for November 23, 2002, 8–9. For further details see Robert Blair Kaiser, *The Encyclical That Never Was. The Story of the Pontifical Commission on Population, Family and Birth* (London: Sheed & Ward, 1987). G. O'C.]

NOTES

1. How Vatican II Changed My Church

1. Rahner's thought is reflected in "Concupiscence," an article Pedro wrote for the 1967 edition of the *New Catholic Encyclopedia* (hereafter NCE), an article that was reproduced in the 2003 edition. That entry and some related pieces led Pedro to enjoy in certain quarters the nickname of "concupiscence Kenny."

2. See "Morality, Systems of," NCE, vol. 9, 876–80; "Probabilism," vol. 11, 727.

3. I cannot resist telling another Myles Lovell story. After twelve years of tough priestly service in Guyana, he was taking a sabbatical in Rome around 1977, when the Jesuit general asked him to help re-open a seminary in Wau, deep in the south of the war-torn Sudan. I visited Myles, noticed on his wall a large map of the Sudan with a piece of string connecting Khartoum and Wau, and asked, "What's that about?" "Supply routes," Myles informed me.

4. For the Roman rite the vernacular was officially introduced on November 27, 1964, the First Sunday of Advent.

5. The prayer ran: "Thanks be to thee, my Lord Jesus Christ, for all the benefits which thou hast given me—for all the pains and insults thou hast borne for me. O most merciful Redeemer, Friend and Brother, may I know thee more clearly, love thee more dearly, and follow thee more nearly."

6. The exorcism at baptism was still, however, said in Latin. "Does the devil not understand German?" I asked the parish priest.

7. *Theology and Revelation* (Cork: Mercier Press, 1968). This book was also published in French, Italian, and Korean. A dedicated ecumenist, Yarnold was an English Jesuit based at Campion Hall in Oxford.

8. "Spes Quaerens Intellectum," *Interpretation* 22 (1968), 36–52; "The Principle and Theology of Hope," *Scottish Journal of Theology* 21 (1968), 129–44.

9. *Man and His New Hopes* (New York: Herder and Herder, 1969). This book was also published in Spanish.

10. Ibid., 118, 128.

11. *The Theology of Secularity* (Cork: Mercier Press, 1974).

12. Ibid., 84.

13. *Foundations of Theology* (Chicago: Loyola University Press, 1971).

14. *Problems and Perspectives of Fundamental Theology* (New York: Paulist Press, 1982). This book had first been published in Italian (1980), and was also published in French, German, Portuguese, and Spanish.

15. *Fundamental Theology* (Ramsey, NJ: Paulist Press, 1981; new ed. 1986). This book was also published in Italian, Korean, and Portuguese.

16. *Vatican II: Assessments and Perspectives*, 3 vols. (Mahwah, NJ: Paulist Press, 1988). This work was first published in Italian (1987) and was also published in French and Spanish.

17. *Dictionary of Fundamental Theology* (New York: Crossroad, 1993). This dictionary was first published in Italian (1990) and was also published in French, Portuguese, and Spanish.

18. *Retrieving Fundamental Theology* (Mahwah, NJ: Paulist Press, 1993). This book was also published in Italian.

19. *Christology* (Oxford: Oxford University Press, 1995; rev. ed. 2004). This book was also published in Italian.

20. Other theses that I directed on the teaching of Vatican II included: Peter Matheson, "The Notion of Truth in *Gaudium et Spes* (1982); Carmen Aparicio Valls, "Revelation in *Gaudium et Spes*" (1996); Raul Biord Castillo, "The Resurrection of Christ as the Fullness of Revelation according to *Dei Verbum*" (1997).

21. J. Ratzinger, *Eschatology: Death and Eternal Life* (Washington, DC: Catholic University of America Press, 1988). The German original appeared in 1977.

22. J. Dupuis, *Toward a Christian Theology of Religious Pluralism* (Maryknoll, NY: Orbis, 1997). This book was also published in French, Italian, Portuguese, and Spanish. I wrote an obituary of Dupuis for the London *Tablet* of January 8, 2005, 36.

23. J. Dupuis, *Christianity and the Religions: From Confrontation to Dialogue* (Maryknoll, NY: Orbis, 2002). This book was also published in French, Italian, Polish, Portuguese, and Spanish. On the many issues raised by this book and its predecessor, see O'Collins, "Christ and the Religions," *Gregorianum* 84 (2003), 347–62; id., "Jacques Dupuis' Contributions to Interreligious Dialogue," *Theological Studies* 64 (2003), 388–97; and the Festschrift honoring Dupuis on his eightieth birthday:

D. Kendall and G. O'Collins, eds., *In Many and Diverse Ways* (Maryknoll, NY: Orbis, 2003). For some details of the CDF's investigation of Dupuis, his suffering, and my involvement in his defense, see O'Collins, ibid., 18–29.

24. See the declaration *Dominus Iesus* from the CDF in 2000, no. 7.

25. See G. O'Collins, *A Month with Jesus* (Denville, NJ: Dimension Books, 1978).

26. We will see more of the way Paul VI centered on Christ in chapter 8 below and in the document from Jacques Dupuis included in an appendix to this book.

27. Archbishop Rush's speech is found as the second document in an appendix to this book.

28. For instance, *All Things New: The Promise of Advent, Christmas and the New Year* (Mahwah, NJ: Paulist Press, 1998); *Experiencing Jesus* (London: SPCK, 1994); *Finding Jesus* (New York: Paulist Press, 1983); *Following the Way: Jesus Our Spiritual Director* (London: HarperCollins, 1999); *What Are They Saying About Jesus?* (New York: Paulist Press, 1977; 2nd ed. 1983).

2. Facilitators or Gatekeepers?

1. After several separations, amalgamations, and renamings, which included the end of the Congregation of Rites that had existed since 1588, the one office of the Holy See now responsible for the liturgy is the Congregation for Divine Worship and the Discipline of the Sacraments.

2. This was firmly verified for me when I directed an excellent license (that is, master's) dissertation by Antonio Olmi on four documents of the Theological Commission concerned with the doctrine of Christ (published in 1980, 1982, 1986, and 1994). After finding almost no secondary literature on those documents, Olmi checked with the secretary of the commission and discovered nothing further. By and large, the commission's documents have not been widely discussed and evaluated. Olmi's dissertation was published as a monographic number of *Sacra Doctrina* 45/5 (September/October, 2000).

3. Although it did not trigger a wide and enthusiastic reception, the 2001 document of the Biblical Commission, "The Jewish People and Their Sacred Scriptures in the Christian Bible," was also a valuable and challenging study.

4. Örsy's article, originally published in German, was fully translated into English for *Doctrine and Life* 48 (1998), 453–66, and appeared in

summary form in the London *Tablet* for January 16, 1999. The CDF itself may have realized that its procedures leave something to be desired from the point of view of justice. Up to 2002 in its "historical notes" for the CDF, the *Annuario Pontificio* carried the observation that "in all the proceedings there is granted the widest possible right of defense (*in tutti i procedimenti è concessa la più ampia facoltà di difesa*)." But this sentence disappeared in the same section of the *Annuario Pontificio* for 2003 (1697).

5. The 120 were made up of 87 Chinese and 33 foreign missionaries; they included laypersons, priests, seminarians, women religious, and six bishops. The majority died in the 1900 Boxer Uprising.

6. See P. Endean, *Karl Rahner and Ignatian Spirituality* (Oxford: Oxford University Press, 2001).

7. See A. Flannery, ed., *Vatican Council II: The Conciliar and Post Conciliar Documents* (Northport, NY: Costello, 1988); id., ed., *More Post Conciliar Documents* (Northport, NY: Costello, 1998).

8. The order follows the information provided by the 8th Forum on Bilateral Dialogues, Faith and Order Paper 190 (Geneva: WCC Publications, 2002), 75–77. The Centro Pro Unione, run by the Franciscan Friars of the Atonement in Rome, issues extensive bibliographies of interchurch and interconfessional theological dialogues in its semiannual bulletins.

9. Thomas Stransky, who joined Cardinal Bea in founding the Secretariat for Promoting Christian Unity, explains why the Catholic Church has not become a member of the WCC: "World Council of Churches," in R. P. McBrien, ed., *The HarperCollins Encyclopedia of Catholicism* (San Francisco: HarperSanFrancisco, 1995), 1339–40.

10. On this declaration see G. O'Collins and D. Kendall, "Overcoming Christological Differences," *Heythrop Journal* 37 (1996), 382–90.

11. *"Gaudium et Spes": Thirty Years Later* (Vatican City: Libreria Editrice Vaticana, 1996).

12. See M. A. Fahey, "Reflections on the Synod of America," *Theological Studies* 59 (1998), 486–504.

13. Peter C. Phan edited an outstanding study of the Asian Synod, *The Asian Synod Texts and Commentaries* (Maryknoll, NY: Orbis, 2002). This joint work reproduces J. M. Prior's very perceptive analysis of *Ecclesia in Asia*, 236–48. On the Asian Synod see also T. C. Fox, *Pentecost in Asia: A New Way of Being Church* (Maryknoll, NY: Orbis, 2002), 149–90.

14. In *Pentecost in Asia* (189), Tom Fox points to similar statistics in *Ecclesia in Asia:* In the footnotes John Paul II is quoted sixty-eight times and Vatican II only fifteen times.

15. See P. C. Phan, "Reception of Vatican II in Asia: Historical and Theological Analysis," *Gregorianum* 83 (2002), 269–85; J. Yun-ka Tan, "Theologizing at the Service of Life: The Contextual Theological Methodology of the Federation of Asian Bishops' Conferences (FABC)," ibid. 81 (2000), 541–75. In *Pentecost in Asia* Tom Fox provides extensive information and comment on the origins and work of the FABC. See also G. B. Rosales and C. G. Arevalo, eds., *For All the Peoples of Asia. Federation of Asian Bishops' Conferences: Documents from 1970 to 1991* (Maryknoll, NY: Orbis, 1992); F.-J. Eilers, ed., *For All the Peoples of Asia: Federation of Asian Bishops' Conferences: Documents from 1992 to 1996* (Quezon City: Claretian Publications, 1997). For background material see S. W. Sundquist, ed., *A Dictionary of Asian Christianity* (Grand Rapids, MI: Eerdmans, 2002).

3. Receiving a Council with Creative Fidelity

1. See J. T. Lienhard, "*Ousia* and *Hypostasis:* The Cappadocian Settlement and the Theology of '*One Hypostasis,*'" in S. Davis, D. Kendall, and G. O'Collins, eds., *The Trinity* (Oxford: Oxford University Press, 1999), 99–121.

2. N. P. Tanner, ed., *Decrees of the Ecumenical Councils*, vol. 1 (London: Sheed and Ward, 1990), 28.

3. Ibid.

4. The full form of the axiom is "*legem credendi lex statuat supplicandi* (let the law of prayer establish the law of belief)."

5. Repeatedly we find the Cappadocians grappling with texts that Arians, for instance, invoked to establish the inferiority of the Son, or with texts that seemed incompatible. Thus Basil in his *Contra Eunomium* (1.24–25) labored over the apparently discordant texts from St. John's Gospel: "The Father and I are one" (John 10:30) and "the Father is greater than I" (John 14:28).

6. See S. R. Holman, *The Hungry Are Dying: Beggars and Bishops in Roman Cappadocia* (New York: Oxford University Press, 2001), 48–49.

7. For three such sermons, hitherto untranslated into English, one by Basil and two by Gregory of Nyssa, see Holman, *The Hungry Are Dying*, 183–206.

4. Liturgical Progress

1. Some local churches, while belonging to the Roman rite, did not necessarily use Latin for the liturgy. Right down to Vatican II, many Croatian parishes maintained Old Slavonic as their liturgical language; they had resisted or ignored attempts after the Council of Trent (1545–63) to have Latin adopted everywhere in the Roman rite.

2. As filmmakers know very well, visual images can carry a wealth of meaning and do so in only a few seconds.

3. In fact, traditionally the *epiclesis* prior to the institution narrative was one of the moments when bells were rung.

4. In the Eucharistic Prayers, the first *epiclesis*, or invocation of the Holy Spirit, asks that the Spirit descend upon the gifts to change them into the body and blood of Christ.

5. See *Catechism of the Catholic Church*, 1066–67.

6. See P. Steinfels, *A People Adrift* (New York: Simon & Schuster, 2002), 165–202; D. C. Smolarski, *How Not to Say Mass: A Guidebook on Liturgical Principles and the Roman Missal* (Mahwah, NJ: Paulist Press, rev. ed., 2003).

7. Nowadays taking a whole day to prepare the Sunday homily seems frankly impossible in the life of most parish clergy. One should also add that good homilies will draw not only on the immediate preparation but also on wide reading and insights gained from days of "in-service" training.

8. In November 2003 I read of a parish featuring a "stop-and-go" Mass, in which the pastor paused to explain the different parts of the liturgy as they occurred. Obviously there is a need for instructions that explain each step of the Mass, but to do this during the liturgy itself seems like offering a "stop-and-destroy" Mass.

9. Dancing during the liturgy has its place in Catholic Christianity. In Spain the feasts of the Immaculate Conception and Corpus Christi involved dancing. Even today young boys in peasant garb dance in the Seville cathedral before the Blessed Sacrament, and accompany their dance with castanets. See T. A. Kane, "Dance, Liturgical," in P. Bradshaw, ed., *The New Westminster Dictionary of Liturgy and Worship* (Louisville, KY: Westminster John Knox Press, 2002), 150–51.

10. See Brother Roger of Taizé, in W. Madges and M. J. Daley, *Vatican II: Forty Personal Stories* (Mystic, CT: Twenty-Third Publications, 2003), 151–53.

11. On these matters see D. R. Hoge et al., *Young Adult Catholics: Religion in a Culture of Choice* (Notre Dame, IN: University of Notre Dame Press, 2001).

12. Basil Pennington, "Liturgical Moments," in *Vatican II: Forty Personal Stories*, 66.

13. See the London *Tablet* for November 1, 2003, 23; on earlier difficulties see R. J. Clifford, "The Rocky Road to a New Lectionary," *America* (August 16, 1997), 18–22.

14. See the letter in the London *Tablet* for November 15, 2003, by John McIntyre, a former rector of the Scots College in Rome.

15. On liturgical language that communicates and is inclusive, see P. Steinfels, *A People Adrift*, 285–92.

16. See the letter in the London *Tablet* for December 20/27, 2003, by Tom McIntyre, who expressed his appreciation for Tolkien as follows: "Tolkien…wrote English as good and clear as any in the current liturgy—elevated where appropriate, natural in rhythm, paratactic, rhetorically restrained, strong in monosyllables, rich and precise in vocabulary."

17. Here is the translation of these verses from the King James Bible: "But Jonah rose up to flee unto Tarshish from the presence of the Lord, and went down to Joppa, and he found a ship going to Tarshish: so he paid the fare thereof, and went down into it, to go with them unto Tarshish from the presence of the Lord. But the Lord sent out a great wind into the sea, and there was a mighty tempest in the sea, so that the ship was like to be broken. Then the mariners were afraid, and cried every man unto his god, and cast forth the wares that were in the ship into the sea, to lighten it of them." Tolkien also knew the Douai Version of the Old Testament (first published in 1609 and thus two years before the King James Bible); its rendering of the three verses anticipated the translation found in the latter: "And Jonas *rose up to flee* into Tharsis from the face of the Lord, and he *went down* to Joppa, and *found a ship going to* Tharsis; and *he paid the fare thereof, and went down into it, to go with them* to Tharsis from the face of the Lord. *But the Lord sent* out *a great wind into the sea;* and a great *tempest* was raised *in the sea,* and *the ship* was in danger *to be broken.* And *the mariners were afraid,* and the men *cried* to their *god;* and they *cast forth the wares that were in the ship, to lighten it of them*" (italics added to show where the King James Bible matches the Douai Version).

18. In Australia an interdenominational hymnbook, *Australian Hymn Book*, was published in 1977. This came to be widely used also outside Australia under the title *With One Voice*.

19. One could add the names of many other such composers as Sydney Carter, Bob Dufford, Bernadette Farrell, John Foley, Richard

Gillard, Marty Haugen, Bob Hurd, William Jabusch, Michael Joncas, Carey Landry, James MacMillan, Tim Manion, Marianne Misetich, Gregory Murray, Roc O'Connor, Alexander Peloquin, Richard Proulx, Dan Schutte, John Tavener, Suzanne Toolan, and Christopher Walker. The list could be extended almost endlessly, especially if one included the names of non-English composers.

20. See Congregation for Divine Worship and the Discipline of the Sacraments, *Directory on Popular Piety and the Liturgy* (Vatican City: Libreria Editrice Vaticana, 2002).

21. Latino households know how to make a kitchen a place both of hospitality and of the divine presence. My own mother made our kitchen teach her children a constant lesson against racism by keeping on a prominent shelf a statue of Martin de Porres (1579–1639), a black saint in a white Dominican habit.

22. See K. A. Codd, "On the Way to Compostela," *America* (December 15, 2003), 8–11.

23. Presumably the reading of the scriptures was left optional, so that "hearing" an individual's confession could be done quickly and other penitents would not have to wait too long.

24. See J. A. Favazza, "Ambiguous Forgiveness: The Uncertain Renewal of the Sacrament of Reconciliation since the Second Vatican Council," in M. Lamberigts and L. Kenis, eds., *Vatican II and Its Legacy* (Leuven: Leuven University Press, 2002), 395–409.

5. Receiving the Council's Moral Teaching

1. W. C. Spohn, *What Are They Saying About Scripture and Ethics?* (Mahwah, NJ: Paulist Press, 2nd ed., 1995), 39.

2. On developments in Catholic moral theology, see J. Mahoney, *The Making of Moral Theology: A Study of the Roman Catholic Tradition* (Oxford: Clarendon Press, 1989).

3. The constitution wrote of "the exalted dignity of the human person" with his/her "universal and inviolable" rights and duties. These rights comprise "everything" necessary for leading a truly human life (no. 26).

4. *Gaudium et Spes* described "the common good" as "the sum of those conditions of social life which allow social groups and their individual members relatively thorough and ready access to their own fulfillment." To achieve this, "the social order" must be "founded on truth, built on justice, and animated by love" (no. 26). See D. Hollenbach, *The*

Common Good and Christian Ethics (New York: Cambridge University Press, 2002); see also an excellent review of this book, P. Weithman, "Hollenbach on the Common Good," *Horizons* 30 (2003), 319–24. Considerations about the common good obviously should affect such matters as the use of health-care resources; see A. Fisher and L. Gormally, *Healthcare Allocation: An Ethical Framework for Public Policy* (London: The Linacre Centre, 2001).

5. See both my *Fundamental Theology* (Mahwah, NJ: Paulist Press, 2nd ed., 1986), 43–45, and *Retrieving Fundamental Theology* (Mahwah, NJ: Paulist Press, 1993), 115–16.

6. The natural law witnesses to universal moral standards and that appropriate conduct that furthers human flourishing and authentic personhood.

7. This universal, divine law provides a common basis for Christians to join others in searching together for true solutions to the numerous moral problems of life. The council saw this cooperation as flowing from the Christian conscience: "In fidelity to conscience Christians are joined with other human beings in the search for truth and for true solutions to the numerous moral problems, which arise both in the life of individuals and in social relationships" (*Gaudium et Spes*, 16). By proposing such a common search for truth, this statement was naturally disputed by those who believed that the church already had the truth and that its task was to communicate this truth to others and not make common cause with them in the search for truth.

8. On redemption through love, see G. O'Collins and D. Kendall, *The Bible for Theology* (Mahwah, NJ: Paulist Press, 1997), 53–73.

9. On the basis of recommendations from the Synod of European Bishops (1999), John Paul II issued the exhortation *Ecclesia in Europa* in 2003; see chapter 2 above.

10. On justice for the world's poor, see George Carey, *Know the Truth: A Memoir* (London: HarperCollins, 2004), 420–37.

11. The report estimated that in the fertile Congo 75 percent of its population were undernourished in the 1999–2001 period; in Afghanistan and Burundi, 70 percent of the people were undernourished.

12. Agricultural subsidies to large agribusiness entities in developed countries also destroy markets for struggling farmers in developing nations.

13. But they do raise such questions. Granted that genetically modified corn, rice, soya beans, and sweet potatoes are more resistant to pests and weeds, possess a higher nutritional value, and enjoy a higher yield, nevertheless, are the medical and ecological risks only minimal?

Obviously such products offer huge agricultural companies a chance to expand their overseas markets. But, in the face of very varied societies and cultures around the globe, do such genetically modified plants have the potential for alleviating world hunger?

14. See, for example, J. Barrow and F. Tipler, *The Anthropic Cosmological Principle* (Oxford: Oxford University Press, 1986) and C. de Duve, *Vital Dust* (New York: Basic Books, 1995).

15. See Nick Bostrum, *Anthropic Bias: Observation Selection Effects in Science and Philosophy* (New York: Routledge, 2002) and John Leslie, *The End of the World* (New York: Routledge, 1996).

16. See J. T. Noonan, ed., *The Morality of Abortion: Legal and Historical Perspectives* (Cambridge, MA: Harvard University Press, 1970).

17. This argument could have been employed to continue supporting the use of torture and the institution of slavery. In the nineteenth century and even later there was no universal consensus that torture and slavery are utterly unacceptable and "intrinsically evil."

18. See B. Waters and R. Cole-Turner, eds., *God and the Embryo: Religious Voices on Stem Cells and Cloning* (Washington, DC: Georgetown University Press, 2003).

19. J. F. Langan summarizes these conditions: "Just-war doctrine," in R. P. McBrien, ed., *The HarperCollins Encyclopedia of Catholicism* (San Francisco: HarperSanFrancisco, 1995), 718–19. According to those who (wrongly) accept "preventive war," it could be justified to attack another nation, on the grounds that in the future it could become a threat, even though here and now it was not yet making any actual preparation to attack.

20. See further S. J. Pope, "The Convergence of Forgiveness and Justice: Lessons from El Salvador," *Theological Studies* 64 (2003), 812–35.

21. In taking moral stock of world history since 1965, a full-scale account should also include such positive items as the triumph of democracy over tyranny in some countries, some advance of women and their rights, improvements of health care in many countries, the persistent idealism and generosity of the young, the introduction of trials for war crimes, and a wider awareness of ecological dangers and human responsibility for the environment.

22. Geza Vermes sums this up: "In one respect more than any other [Jesus] differed from both his contemporaries and even his prophetic predecessors. The prophets spoke on behalf of the honest poor, and defended the widows and fatherless, those oppressed and exploited by the wicked, rich and powerful. Jesus went further. In addition to proclaiming these blessed, he actually took his stand among the pariahs of his world, those despised by the respectable. Sinners were his table-companions and

the ostracized tax-collectors and prostitutes his friends" (*Jesus the Jew* [London: SCM Press, 1994], 196).

23. See V. P. Furnish, *Go and Do Likewise: Jesus and Ethics* (New York: Continuum, 1999), and D. J. Harrington and J. Keenan, *Jesus and Virtue Ethics: Building Bridges Between New Testament Studies and Moral Theology* (Lanham, MD: Sheed & Ward, 2002).

24. See C. H. Cosgrove, *Appealing to Scripture in Moral Debate: Five Hermeneutical Rules* (Grand Rapids, MI: Eerdmans, 2002); R. B. Hays, *The Moral Vision of the New Testament: A Contemporary Introduction to New Testament Ethics* (San Francisco: HarperCollins, 1996); J. T. Bretzke, *A Morally Complex World: Engaging Contemporary Moral Theology* (Collegeville, MN: Michael Glazier, 2004), 79–108.

25. Let me provide an example taken from the *Criminal Statistics England and Wales 2002*, published by the government on December 29, 2003. In England and Wales 49,200 children between ten and seventeen committed crimes (that is, were sentenced for indictable offenses) in 2002—almost 30 percent more than the 39,000 committed in 1992. Over the same decade there had been more than a 50 percent increase in the number of girls involved in crime: from 4,200 in 1992 to 6,700 in 2002. The biggest increase came in child offenders aged ten and eleven; between 1992 and 2002 those found guilty of a crime rose by almost 150 percent. Beyond question, other factors are also involved in this very troubling trend. But for years crime researchers in Britain have been warning that family breakdown and homes without biological fathers generate lawlessness among youngsters. See also the literature quoted by M. J. McManus and his own findings: "The Marriage Debate: More than a Gay Issue," *America*, February 9, 2004, 16–18. McManus reports that a child of divorce is three times more likely than a child from an intact home to be expelled from school and twelve times as likely to be incarcerated.

26. See S. J. Pope, "The Magisterium and Same-Sex Marriage," *Theological Studies* 65 (2004), 530–65, and R. Sokolowski, "The Threat of Same-Sex Marriage," *America* (June 7–14, 2004), 12–14.

6. Relations with Others

1. General MacArthur's underclothes were sent to a laundry run by nuns, who not only washed them but also sewed tiny miraculous medals into the seams. They wanted the Virgin Mary to safeguard him as he rolled back the threat of a Japanese invasion.

2. The original verse ran: "I come from the City of Boston, The home of the bean and the cod; Where Lowells speak only to Cabots, And Cabots speak only to God" (John Collins Bossidy). When quoting these lines some people substitute "Lodges" for "Lowells." John Cabot arrived at Salem, Massachusetts, in 1700. The Cabots became famous for their wealth, talent, and philanthropy; through marriage with other prominent families, they helped to create the "Brahmins" or Boston aristocracy. A gifted Massachusetts family, the Lowells have included notable writers, a president of Harvard University, and an astronomer who predicted the existence of the planet Pluto. The Lodge family has so far produced one governor of Massachusetts and six U.S. senators, including Henry Cabot Lodge (1850–1924), who was a U.S. senator for over thirty years.

3. For the sake of the record, let me add that Rupert Murdoch, like me born in 1931, grew up a few miles away from my home in Frankston; his parents also belonged to Peninsula Golf Club. But I never met either him or his parents, then or later.

4. *The Theology of Secularity* (Notre Dame, IN: Fides Publishers, 1974).

5. For the London *Tablet* I contributed the obituaries of Frank (October 10, 1998) and Orietta (November 25, 2000).

6. D. Kendall and S. T. Davis, eds., *The Convergence of Theology* (Mahwah, NJ: Paulist Press, 2001). Earlier George had written the foreword to my *Experiencing Jesus* (London/Mahwah: SPCK/Paulist Press, 1994, and to my *Following the Way* (London/Mahwah: HarperCollins/Paulist Press, 1999); the latter was the archbishop of Canterbury's Lent Book for 2000.

7. See D. Martin, *Pentecostalism: The World Their Parish* (Oxford: Blackwell, 2002).

8. See my reviews of three of their books in the London *Tablet* for August 31, 1991; April 30, 1994; October 27, 2001.

9. For the reference and further details see J. Dupuis, *Toward a Christian Theology of Religious Pluralism* (Maryknoll, NY: Orbis, 1997), 228–33. See also E. Fisher, ed., *Catholic Jewish Relations: Documents from the Holy See* (London: Catholic Truth Society, 1999); and National Council of Synagogues and Delegates of the Bishops' Committee on Ecumenical and Inter-Religious Affairs, *Reflections on Covenant and Mission* (Washington, DC: Office of Communications, United States Conference of Catholic Bishops, 2002).

10. Aleksander Majur, *L'insegnamento di Giovanni Paolo II sulle altre religioni* (Rome: Gregorian University Press, 2004).

11. "A Summit Observed," in S. T. Davis, D. Kendall, and G. O'Collins, eds., *The Resurrection* (Oxford/New York: Oxford University Press, 1997), 3.

12. G. O'Collins, *Foundations of Theology* (Chicago: Loyola University Press, 1971), 47.

13. G. O'Collins, *Fundamental Theology* (Ramsey, NJ: Paulist Press, 1981), 114–29.

14. G. O'Collins, *Interpreting Jesus* (London/Ramsey, NJ: Geoffrey Chapman/Paulist Press, 1983), 202–8.

15. G. O'Collins, *Retrieving Fundamental Theology* (Mahwah, NJ: Paulist Press, 1993), 79–86.

16. G. O'Collins, *Christology: A Biblical, Historical, and Systematic Study of Jesus* (Oxford/New York: Oxford University Press, 1995), 296–305, 317.

17. See A. O'Boyle, *Toward a Contemporary Wisdom Christology* (Rome: Gregorian University Press, 2003), esp. 365–70.

18. See G. O'Collins, "Jacques Dupuis: His Person and Work," in D. Kendall and G. O'Collins, eds., *In Many and Diverse Ways* (Maryknoll, NY: Orbis, 2003), 18–29; id., "Christ and the Religions," *Gregorianum* 84 (2003), 347–62; id., "Jacques Dupuis's Contributions to Interreligious Dialogue," *Theological Studies* 64 (2003), 388–97.

19. See "Zâô," in G. Kittel, ed., *Theological Dictionary of the New Testament*, vol. 2 (Grand Rapids, MI: Eerdmans, 1964), 841, n. 66.

20. My best attempt at spelling out more fully reasons for holding Christ to be universal Revealer and what this means was in *Fundamental Theology*, 114–29.

21. "Vatican II Encourages Interreligious Dialogue," in W. Madges and M. J. Daley, *Vatican II: Forty Personal Stories* (Mystic, CT: Twenty-Third Publications, 2003), 176.

7. Theology for the Church and the World

1. It is a pity that Western Catholics, and in particular students of theology, are not encouraged more to experience at first hand the life and liturgy of their fellow Catholics in the Eastern Churches. Sadly they often know less about Eastern Catholics than they do about Christians not united with the bishop of Rome and about various non-Christian religions.

2. For the need of a philosophically alert mind in matters of terminology, see my "Jacques Dupuis's Contribution to Interreligious Dialogue," *Theological Studies* 64 (2003), 388–97, at 390–93.

3. In *L'uso di Fil 2,6–11 nella cristologia contemporanea* (Rome: Gregorian University Press, 1997), Nunzio Capizzi illustrates how major contemporary theologians writing in French, German, and Italian suffer from various limits and defects when appealing to the christological hymn of Philippians 2:6–11.

4. See G. O'Collins and D. Kendall, "Overcoming Christological Differences," *Heythrop Journal* 37 (1996), 382–90.

5. See the way the International Theological Commission, albeit cautiously, recognized in its 1997 "Christianity and the Religions" how the religions can be means that help their followers to salvation (nos. 84, 86).

6. See J. Dupuis, *Toward a Christian Theology of Religious Pluralism* (Maryknoll, NY: Orbis, 1997); id., *Christianity and the Religions: From Confrontation to Dialogue* (Maryknoll, NY: Orbis, 2002).

8. The Coming Church

1. In a document issued a few days earlier, the International Theological Commission maintained an old, but odd, distinction between the church (who is our all-holy mother) and her sinful sons and daughters. Where does this all-holy Mother Church exist? She seems to be an invisible, otherworldly entity. Hans Urs von Balthasar's dramatic image of the church as a "chaste prostitute (*casta meretrix*)" is closer to the truth; see his *Sponsa Verbi: Skizzen zur Theologie*, vol. 2 (Einsiedeln: Johannes Verlag, 1961), 203–305. Sanctified by the Holy Spirit, the earthly church remains sinful and constantly needs repentance on her pilgrimage to the final kingdom of God. As Vatican II expressed matters, the church is both "holy and always in need of purification" (*Lumen Gentium*, 8).

2. For anyone dedicated to the teaching of Vatican II, *Lumen Gentium* and *Gaudium et Spes* are central and vital. Hence one can only be astonished at the way Hans Urs von Balthasar ignored in the postconciliar years those two constitutions (and other documents of Vatican II). Between 1973 and 1983 he published in German the five volumes of his *Theodramatik*, which appeared in English as *Theo-Drama: Theological Dramatic Theory* (San Francisco: Ignatius Press, 1988–98). In their English version the five volumes run to nearly 2,700 pages. The two constitutions on the church from Vatican II make a fleeting appearance and only in volume 3: *The Dramatis*

Personae: The Person in Christ. Lumen Gentium turns up here on pp. 316–18 and in a passing reference on p. 417; on p. 444 there is reference to *Unitatis Redintegratio;* and that is all from the Council. In his five volumes von Balthasar dedicated many pages to the scriptures, the Fathers of the Church, medieval theologians, and modern authors, but he had no time for Vatican II. However one judges his massive work, one cannot describe it as coming from a theologian concerned to receive and live Vatican II.

3. New York/Oxford: Oxford University Press, 2002.

4. *De Arca Noe morali,* 2.8–9.

5. Gregory of Nyssa, *De beneficentia,* trans. S. R. Holman, *The Hungry Are Dying: Beggars and Bishops in Roman Cappadocia* (New York: Oxford University Press, 2001), 193–99, at 198.

6. See report in *Newsweek* for November 10, 2003.

7. The address by John Paul II appeared in various journals, including a special number of a review published by the Pontifical Council for the Laity commemorating *Gaudium et Spes: Laity Today* 39 (1996), 9–15, at 12.

8. See John Paul II, "The Ecological Crisis: A Common Responsibility" (message dated December 8, 1989, for the World Day of Peace, January 1, 1990), available in the *Osservatore Romano, Origins,* and other journals. In 1978 the pope had proclaimed St. Francis of Assisi the heavenly patron of those who promote ecology.

9. See T. C. Fox, *Pentecost in Asia* (Maryknoll, NY: Orbis, 2002), 25–26.

10. See G. O'Collins and M. Farrugia, *Catholicism: The Story of Catholic Christianity* (Oxford: Oxford University Press, 2003), 314–15.

11. See the interview with him in *Famiglia Cristiana,* December 14, 2003, 57.

12. See J. A. Coriden et al., eds., *The Code of Canon Law: A Text and Commentary* (Mahwah, NJ: Paulist Press, 1985), 6, 21, 312.

13. *Code of Canon Law Latin-English Edition* (Washington, DC: Canon Law Society of America, 1983), xxi.

14. See P. C. Phan, *The Asian Synod: Texts and Commentaries* (Maryknoll, NY: Orbis, 2002), 90.

15. This exhortation, by highlighting the "communion" of all the churches (for example, nos. 55–60), followed earlier teaching of John Paul II about the whole church being "the home and the school of communion" (*Novo Millennio Ineunte,* 43). Beyond question, "communion" is a very helpful organizing model for thinking about the whole church and living our Catholic (and Christian) lives together. In concluding the chapter on the church in *Catholicism: The Story of Catholic Christianity* (Oxford/New

York: Oxford University Press, 2003), Mario Farrugia and I drew matters together under the heading "the Church as Communion and Mission" (331–34). While not being an alternate model of the Church, "subsidiarity" expresses, however, what a healthily operating communion between the Bishop of Rome and the bishops of particular churches entails in practice. This is precisely the point made in the preface to the 1983 Code of Canon Law.

16. See P. Jenkins, *The Next Christendom* (Oxford/New York: Oxford University Press, 2002), 145–47. Some church officials, Jenkins observes, often frowned on and curbed the base communities in Latin America for being too biblically *and politically* inspired, with the result that many Catholics shifted to Pentecostalism. In his interview with the London *Tablet* for November 8, 2003, Cardinal Oscar Andres Rodriguez de Maradiaga insisted that Catholic base communities are still strong throughout Latin America. "But the difference is that while they used to have a markedly militant character before, now they are seen more as centres for civic education." The *Tablet* interviewer continued: "That shift, he says, is explained by political developments: in the 1970s and 1980s most Latin American countries were governed by dictatorships, which meant that the normal channels of expression—press and assembly—were closed off. Base communities became 'the only spaces in which to breathe and to develop political opposition.' But now that Latin American governments are civilian-democratic, the challenge for the popular movements in the Church is to bring an ethical sense into politics, to teach a sense of the common good."

17. In W. Madges and M. J. Daley, eds., *Vatican II: Forty Personal Stories* (Mystic, CT: Twenty-Third Publications, 2003), Sister Mary Luke Tobin recalls her experiences as an auditor, 197–200.

18. See J. D. Davidson, "Fewer and Fewer. Is the clergy shortage unique to the Catholic Church?" *America* (December 1, 2003), 10–13.

19. *La Documentation Catholique*, January 19, 2003, 58–107; an English version of the original French text was published as *From the Diakonia of Christ to the Diakonia of the Apostles* (London: Catholic Truth Society, 2003).

20. See her *Holy Saturday: An Argument for the Restoration of the Female Diaconate in the Catholic Church* (New York: Herder & Herder, 2000); and id., "Catholic Women Deacons," *America*, February 17, 2003, 9–11.

21. See H. Vorgrimler, in H. Vorgrimler, ed., *Commentary on the Documents of Vatican II*, vol. 1 (New York: Herder and Herder, 1967), 226–30.

22. K. Rahner, "The Spirituality of the Priest in the Light of his Office," *Theological Investigations* 19 (London: Darton, Longman & Todd, 1984), 117–38, at 127; this chapter was originally published in 1977.

23. *From the Diakonia of Christ to the Diakonia of the Apostles*, 100.

24. On the shortage and future of priests, see P. Steinfels, *A People Adrift* (New York: Simon & Schuster, 2003), 315–25.

25. *Theological Investigations* 19, 73–86, at 85; this chapter was originally published in 1977. In making this proposal, Rahner took back nothing of his high regard for the celibacy of diocesan priests; see his "The Celibacy of the Secular Priest Today: An Open Letter," in *Servants of the Lord* (New York: Herder & Herder, 1968), 149–72.

26. "Sein und Sendung des Priesters," *Geist und Leben* 51 (1978), 196–212, at 206.

27. See A. Hastings, *The Church in Africa, 1450–1950* (Oxford: Clarendon Press, 1996), 73–129; B. Sundkler and C. Steed, *A History of the Church in Africa* (Cambridge: Cambridge University Press, 2000), 49–62.

28. *The Tablet*, January 3, 2004, 31.

29. *Summa Theologiae*, I–II, 109, a. 1, ad 1um.

30. P. Jenkins, *The Next Christendom*, 32–33.

Appendixes

Appendix A: "The Synod of Bishops 1974"

1. [Dupuis came to the synod as secretary to Archbishop (later) Cardinal Lawrence Picachy of Calcutta. Dupuis could follow the synod proceedings even more closely by volunteering to become one of the team who provided the simultaneous translation during the general assemblies. G. O'C.]

2. The text of the synodal documents which were made public and a summary of some documents which have not been published are found in a special number of *Word and Worship*, January–February 1975. The same number also contains abundant information and comments by Fr D. S. Amalorpavadass, and the interventions made in the name of the CBCI by Archbishops Lawrence Picachy (first part), Angelo Fernandes (second part), and Cardinal Joseph Parecattil.

3 [Father Amalorpavadass was the younger brother of Archbishop (later Cardinal) Simon Lourdusamy. G. O'C.]

4. [Father Dupuis told me that he himself had prepared for Archbishop Fernandes this list of weak points. G. O'C.]

5. [Father Dupuis told me that he and Father Catalina Arevalo, a Filipino Jesuit working with the bishops from the Philippines, stayed up all night to help Father Amalorpavadass in preparing his draft for the conclusions. G. O'C.]

6. *Documentation Catholique*, December 1, 1974, 1011. The cardinals who joined Cardinal Marty in their appeal to the pope were Cardinals Suenens, Döpfner, and Poma.

7. Ibid., November 17, 1974, 956.

8. Ibid., January 5, 1975, 1–7, at 4; *The Tablet*, December 21–28, 1974, 1268–70, at 1269.

Appendix C: The Catholic Bishops' Conference of Japan

1. [In preparing for the 1998 Asian Synod, the General Secretariat of the Synod of Bishops prepared an outline of themes to be discussed at the synod (the *Lineamenta*) and sent it to the bishops for their comments and suggestions. G. O'C.]

2. [In the event, the postsynodal apostolic exhortation *Ecclesia in Asia* published by John Paul II in November 1999 contained two quotations from the pope's own address to the Sixth Plenary Session of the FABC in January 1995 (nos. 1 and 4), but no further quotation from or even reference to any of the FABC documents. G. O'C.]

SELECT BIBLIOGRAPHY

Alberigo, G., J. P. Jossua, and J. A. Komonchak, *The Reception of Vatican II.* Washington, DC: Catholic University of America Press, 1987.

Alberigo, G., and J. A. Komonchak, eds., *History of Vatican II.* Maryknoll, NY: Orbis Books, 1995–.

Bellitto, C. M., *Renewing Christianity: A History of Church Reform from Day One to Vatican II.* Mahwah, NJ: Paulist Press, 2001.

Bokenkotter, T., *A Concise History of the Catholic Church.* New York: Doubleday, 2004.

Cernera, A. J., ed., *Vatican II: The Continuing Agenda.* Fairfield, CT: Sacred Heart University Press, 1997.

Doré, J., and A. Melloni, *Volti di fine concilio: Studi di storia e teologia sulla conclusione del Vaticano II.* Bologna: Il Mulino, 2000.

Duffy, E., *Faith of Our Fathers: Reflections on Catholic Tradition.* London/New York: Continuum, 2004.

Fisichella, R., ed., *Il Concilio Vaticano II: Recezione e attualità alla luce del Giubileo.* Cinisello Balsamo: Edizioni San Paolo, 2000.

Gibson, D., *The Coming Catholic Church.* San Francisco: HarperSanFrancisco, 2003.

Himes, M. J., ed., *The Catholic Church in the 21st Century: Finding Hope for its Future in the Wisdom of its Past.* Liguori, MO: Liguori, 2004.

Hoge, D. R., et al., *Young Adult Catholics: Religion in a Culture of Choice.* Notre Dame, IN: University of Notre Dame Press, 2001.

Ivereigh, A., ed., *Unfinished Journey: The Church 40 Years after Vatican II.* London: Continuum, 2003.

Lamberigts, M., and L. Kenis, eds., *Vatican II and Its Legacy.* Leuven: Leuven University Press, 2002.

Latourelle, R., ed., *Vatican II: Assessment and Perspectives*, 3 vols. Mahwah, NJ: Paulist Press, 1988–89.

Lennan, R., *Risking the Church: The Challenges to Catholic Faith.* Oxford: Oxford University Press, 2004.

Lucker, R. A., and W. C. McDonough, eds., *Revelation and the Church: Vatican II in the Twenty-first Century.* Maryknoll, NY: Orbis Books, 2003.

Madges, W., and M. J. Daley, eds., *Vatican II: Forty Personal Stories.* Mystic, CT: Twenty-Third Publications, 2003.

Neusner, J., B. Chilton, and W. Graham, *Three Faiths, One God: The Formative Faith and Practice of Judaism, Christianity and Islam.* Boston: Brill, 2002.

Prendergast, M. R., and M. D. Ridge, eds., *Voices from the Council.* Portland, OR: Oregon Catholic Press, 2004.

Quinn, J. R., *The Reform of the Papacy.* New York: Crossroad, 1999.

Rosales, G. B., and C. G. Arevalo, eds., *For All the Peoples of Asia: Federation of Asian Bishops' Conferences: Documents from 1970 to 1991.* Maryknoll, NY: Orbis Books, 1992.

Rush, O., *Still Interpreting Vatican II: Some Hermeneutical Principles.* Mahwah, NJ: Paulist Press, 2005.

Steinfels, P., *A People Adrift: The Crisis of the Roman Catholic Church in America.* New York: Simon & Schuster, 2003.

Sullivan, M., *101 Questions & Answers on Vatican II.* Mahwah, NJ: Paulist Press, 2002.

INDEX OF NAMES